The Mayan Calendar

Solving the Greatest Mystery of Our Time:

The Mayan Calendar

by

Carl Johan Calleman

Garev – London (UK) – Coral Springs (US)
Bet-Huen Books – Laren (NL)

Printed in The Netherlands

ISBN: 0-9707558-0-5

Published by

GAREV Publishing International
8260 NW 49th Manor
Pine Grove – CORAL SPRINGS
Florida 33067 – USA
email: garevpub@aol.com
&
35 Winchester Street, 1st Floor
BASINGSTOKE – Hants RG21 7EE – UK
email: garevpub@aol.com

and

Bet-Huen Books
(an imprint of Petiet Publishing)
Hilversumseweg 12
1251 EX LAREN NH – The Netherlands
email: petiet@perigord.com

Table of Contents

Foreword

The Maya are mysterious. This is how this ancient culture has always been portrayed, and in the recent surge of interest a long row of documentaries has presented a picture of a people with practices and a view of the world that is very difficult for modern people to understand. One of the enigmas that have been highlighted is the advancement of their science and above all the calendar. The Maya have often been described as a people obsessed with time, and this obsession was encoded in their enigmatic calendar, in which the gods seem to be playing an often ominous role.

And yes, to a civilization such as our own that has institutionalized a sharp division line between religion and science—the priest has no authority to speak on matters of science and the university scientist has no authority to speak on matters of religion—a unified world view such as that of the Mayan sages can only appear as mysterious. But maybe it is really us, today, who live in a civilization that has lost most of its contact with the living cosmos and divine reality, that are the mysterious and enigmatic. And maybe it is for this reason that we cannot avoid the Maya altogether. It is a people that tends to return, probably until we learn what there is to learn from them, and intuitively many people sense that the solutions to many of the riddles of the human existence will originate from the Maya. Hence we have in the past few decades seen a rise in interest in the Mayan calendar.

It seems that there is something in the very word 'Maya' that tells us of its importance. Maya was the name of the mother of Buddha. It, Maia, was the name of the Roman goddess of spring from which the month of May has gained its name, and, with a small stretch, it was the name of the mother of Jesus, Maria. Almost as if the sound of the word Maya has some universal meaning implanted in the human consciousness, different cultures have given it the meaning of 'mother of light,' 'mother of spirit' or 'mother of knowledge.' Maybe not the knowledge itself, but the origin, a deeper female origin, of knowledge. And so I understand the search for the Maya as a search for the origin of knowledge, and I have come to understand this search for the origin as a means of retrieving a world view from which our lives may be understood as meaningful, a new world view which is unified and where no division line between science and spirituality exists.

Given that the ancient Maya lived in a universe of holy time it seems that the key to retrieving this world view lies in understanding, and in fact solving, the calendar in which their knowledge about holy time was encoded. What it means to solve the Mayan calendar, however, depends on one's perspective. Obviously, to the ancient Maya there was nothing to solve. To me, however, it seems that the meaning of the Mayan calendar needs to be translated so that it can be understood by other traditions than its own. To make such a translation is to solve the Mayan calendar, and this is the goal that I have set for my research.

Given this background, I am at one level surprised when I am asked the question of what created my interest in the Mayan calendar.'How can you not be interested in the Mayan calendar?' I think silently, and I have sometimes felt that the reason the person is asking is to somehow put a lid on the tremendous explanatory power of the Mayan calendar and the shake-up of anyone's world view that this results in. My verbal response to the question has, however, usually been to point out that the Mayan civilization, and ancient Mexican civilization generally, was very advanced and significant in the history of our planet. While London was only a village, Tikal and Teotihuacan each had some 100,000 inhabitants or more, meaning that it displays a great arrogance on the part of today's global culture to simply ignore the contributions these cultures may have made. There is really no reason for us who live today to find the only roots of our science in old Greece.

Yet most people seem dissatisfied by such an impersonal answer. They sense that there is something more to it. And yes, I have to admit, not every one of today's scientists has been going to the jungles of Guatemala in their search for the truth, and especially not those from remote Sweden. I also have to admit that significant contributions to the study of the Mayan calendar have often come from very unlikely sources—oddballs—from a standard academic perspective. In the history of Mayanism there are many examples of this: Ernst Förstemann, the librarian from Danzig who by his studies of the *Dresden Codex* provided the key insights into how the Mayan calendar was structured; Joseph Goodman, Mark Twain's newspaper boss, who discovered the correlation between the Long Count and the Gregorian calendar; Yuri Knorozov, the Leningrad ethnologist who cracked the Mayan script without ever having visited the land of the Maya; Frank Waters and José Argüelles, historians with esoteric leanings, who have outlined ways of interpreting the Mayan calendar that go far outside of the predominating materialist world view. Even the late Linda Schele, professor at the University of Texas, seems with her, as she would say herself, 'redneck' background to have viewed herself as an outsider in the world of academics.

And maybe this is the way it has to be. If the understanding of the Mayan calendar is something that implies not just a scientific breakthrough, not just another 'paradigm shift,' but a complete revision of our understanding of the world and what it means to be a human being, then we cannot expect those embarking on its study to walk the beaten path, and I suppose this has not been true for myself either. Events of a mystical nature probably have to guide everyone going into the study of the Maya.

The most extraordinary example in the history of Mayanism of such a mystical event is probably that guiding Knorozov to the translation of the Mayan glyphs, and it is worth recounting. During World War II Yuri Knorozov was a young student in Leningrad until he was drafted into the Red Army, where he was part of the units that seized Berlin and set an end to Hitler's rule in Germany. In the final assault on Berlin he saw the National Library in flames and so rushed in and at random grabbed a book to save it from the fire. The book turned out to be a facsimile of the only three surviving Mayan Codices that were known at the time, a book that was hardly available in any book store in Stalin's Russia. Back in Russia he was encouraged to take on breaking the Maya code, the Mayan script, and seven years later he published the solution in a Russian journal of linguistics. That it took an additional thirty years for this solution to be accepted in the West is a different matter. I can only imagine that he must have decided that grabbing this very book was a mystical event that was pointing out his mission in life.

So there seems to be an invisible universe providing guidance for the course of events, although most scientists will not readily talk about such matters. Nothing of such an extraordinary character has guided my own search for the mystery of the Maya, but then again there may not have been any need for this to get me going. I have been naturally attracted and free to travel. My first contact with Mexico was in 1971 when I crossed the border from California into the Sonoran Desert. I felt the urge to go further south to see the pyramids. The quality of our car in those freewheeling days, however, hardly encouraged such a trip and so we turned back to the US. But the attraction to Mexico stayed with me. Being raised in an intellectual European environment and quite familiar with its own history, the very fact that those pyramids existed in the New World posed an enigma to me.

And it is truly an enigma, although most people do not stop to think about it: If both continents have been inhabited by human beings for some thirty thousand years or so, how is it that they independently started to develop civilizations only in the most recent five thousand years and seem to have done so in parallel? At this first crossing of the border into Mexico I only went deep enough to ponder the enigma, and as I went back to Sweden and took up training as a graduate student in toxicology other things came to the forefront of my mind.

But something urged me to go back, and so I decided to learn some Spanish and stay with a Mexican family in November of 1979, following which a third-class train took me down to Merida, the Yucatan and Guatemala. And something happened to me there. I fell in love with the Mayan people, who with small signs seemed to tell me that I was somehow special there. They seemed to have seen something in me I did not see myself. So I went back to Sweden with a happy inner knowledge that I had a purpose in life, although I did not know yet what it was, and I clad my room in beautiful Mayan textiles to keep this sense of purpose alive.

But this second, much more extensive contact with Mexico also posed an enigma. As a biologist and medical scientist I was trained to think that life was an accident, but why then did I get this sense that life had a purpose given to me by something greater than myself? This seemed like a contradiction that demanded a resolution. Especially as I moved to take up work in Seattle in the beginning of 1986, experiences of remarkable synchronicities became the rule rather than the exception in this heyday of the American New Age movement. And the very fact that the relatively widespread celebration of the Harmonic Convergence had been based on Mayan calendrics—the days 1 Imix and 2 Ik in the Classical tzolkin count—made me realize that I was not alone in being inspired by the Maya.

Several spiritual pilgrimages to the land of the Maya then entrenched me deeper in their way of thinking. But it was only as I moved back to Sweden in 1994 that I started to work with their calendar full time and set as my goal to solve it, to somehow translate its meaning to modern people. And there was a reason that I went back to do this work. The geospiritual placement of Sweden was very favorable in the description of the Mayan calendar in terms that are understandable to modern people. And maybe, in this sense, there has also been a reason for me to have received a thorough scientific training. This has given me a deep appreciation for the scientific method and its insistence on accurate facts and logic. I am not implying that my interpretations cannot be questioned, only that this book is throughout based on facts and datings accepted by today's science. Thus, civilizations and worlds for whose existence there is no proof are, in contrast to in most current esoteric attempts of unifying science and spirituality, not part of the picture presented here.

Yet despite this empirical approach this book is not meant primarily for scientists, and so I have avoided making a large number of references or presenting long complicated arguments to back up my reasonings. Most facts can, however, be easily verified in a recent standard encyclopedia. A more thorough presentation, with references and detailed reasonings and descriptions of all the various creation cycles involved, has instead been given in an as yet unpublished manuscript of mine, *The Theory of Everything—The Evolution of Consciousness and the Existence of God Proved by the Time Science of the Maya,* which I hope one day will reach the public.

Since, unfortunately, Mayan calendrics are only rarely taught in modern schools I have to assume that the overwhelming majority of readers are as yet unfamiliar with it. For this reason, and not to unnecessarily burden the presentation with too much detail, I have placed discussions of the tzolkin and some hotly debated areas in the appendices. It is my hope that eventually most people will enter the rich treasure of Mayan calendrics, apply it to their own lives and use the Mayan calendar at least as a complement to our present, but the bulk of the book is intended to present an overall perspective on its meaning.

Finally, I would like to say that I have never seen it as my mission to speak the Mayan view of things or to bring the Mayan message to humanity. I feel the Maya are best equipped to do this themselves. For my own part I have in this book sought to extract what is universal in the Mayan calendar. So this is not a book by the Maya or a book claiming to see things as the Maya see them. I am alone responsible for these thoughts.

Nor is this a book about the Maya. I am not an anthropologist studying the Maya or their calendar from some purported outside position. It is a book partly inspired by the Maya, but also many other sources as well. I have seen it more as my task to convey to modern people what the Mayan calendar means to us and our own present civilization, because what we need to realize today, above all, is that the Mayan calendar is a universal calendar of potential value for all of humanity regardless of religion, race, gender or political ideas. The calendar may have been invented by the Maya, but the phenomena that it describes today occur mainly in other parts of the world, though most people do not know it. Hence comes its potential for unifying not only the religious traditions of the world but the various fragmented disciplines of modern science as well, and in the process unifying all of science with religion. Correctly understood, the Mayan calendar is thus a tool for unifying humanity and its various traditions of thought and making it realize that there is a purpose to our life on this earth as part of a larger plan. Above all, it is a tool for transcending borders and promoting a higher common perspective among all human beings. I hope you will agree and so want to participate in the exploration and dissemination of such a perspective.

Carl Johan Calleman,

Sundborn, Sweden, on the burner day 4 Ahau,
1.3.0 of the Galactic Underworld
(February 28, 2000)

The Mayan Calendar

CHAPTER 1
THE PYRAMID OF
KUKULCAN AT CHICHEN-ITZA

Of all the legends of pre-Columbian America, the legend of the Plumed Serpent, called by the Aztecs Quetzalcoatl and by the Maya Kukulcan, is one of the most important, and, it seems, one of the most difficult for a modern person to understand and relate to. We do not even know how to describe him—or it. Is the Feathered Serpent a myth, a cult, a religion, a legend, a person, a mental complex, a deity, a god, or what? All we can tell is that in some of the largest temple cities of ancient Mexico, for instance, Teotihuacan outside today's Mexico City and Chichen-Itza on the northern Yucatan peninsula, we find testimonies of the Plumed Serpent everywhere. In Chichen-Itza we find snakes lying in the grass, in the pictures on the walls and in a multitude of ways on its central pyramid, the Pyramid of Kukulcan. Also in Teotihuacan there is a beautiful and significant temple of Quetzalcoatl. Yet the ancients have written no guide for us explaining: 'The Plumed Serpent is . . .' In fact, his existence seems to have been so obvious to the peoples of ancient Mesoamerica that they saw no reason why anyone would need such an explanation.

Fig. 1 The Spring Equinox descent of the Plumed Serpent on the Pyramid of Kukulcan in Chichen-Itza (Photo Calleman).

The Pyramid of Kukulcan at Chichen-Itza

Fig. 2a Map of Mesoamerica, with today's borders.

Fig 2b Map of the Maya area.

But today it seems we do need one. Somehow the 'cult' of Quetzalcoatl defies our comprehension. Even the casual visitor cannot help but notice the advancement of the Mayan culture as evidenced through its architecture and art, or gathered from its advanced calendrical system, astronomy and mathematics. Why then was this advanced culture worshiping a snake, a snake that incidentally many times seems to laugh at us? It is also that the appearance of Quetzalcoatl is not like that of any of the other Mayan gods, which mostly come across as bizarre-looking, deformed humans. He seems to represent a more transcendental divinity than these do. There is something special about Quetzalcoatl.

At the Pyramid of Kukulcan at Chichen-Itza the spring equinox is a very special occasion. Every year at this time some sixty thousand pilgrims from many parts of the world visit Chichen-Itza. This is because on this particular day, and only to a lesser extent on the adjacent days, it is possible to watch the descent of Kukulcan along one of the staircases of the pyramid. What is revealed on this day is how seven triangles are projected on the staircase so as to create the appearance of the scales of a snake whose head is sculpted at the bottom of the staircase.

I had heard this phenomenon described to me several times, but before actually seeing it, it was difficult to understand how magnificent it truly is. Surely, if this had been in the Old World the Greeks would have counted it among the Seven Wonders of the World. The way the Pyramid of Kukulcan was positioned and built to produce this effect only at the equinoxes is truly astounding. If I were to make an attempt to build such a pyramid myself I would have no idea where to start. Even if I did it would seem an insurmountable task to plan its design mathematically so that seven triangles of light interspersed by six triangular shadows were projected on the staircase only at spring equinox. The whole building attests to a resonance with the Cosmos vastly superior to our own.

'What is the message of this projection?' we may wonder. The Pyramid of Kukulcan was the last major construction work performed by the ancient Maya, and therefore it possibly conveys some critical message. If they wanted to give a last triumphant expression of their culture this would have been the time to do it. Maybe then this was a message as much for a future that would understand it as it was for educating their contemporaries. They knew that their age in some sense would repeat itself, and they devised their calendar to describe this recurring pattern of time. Despite their great interest in following time and their meticulous recording of dates on the stele, the Maya are in fact essentially timeless. What they did for their present they did also for the future.

Chichen-Itza is what archaeologists call a silent city. This means that in contrast to the earlier southern Mayan sites that were suddenly deserted around AD 800, it does not have a lot of inscriptions telling of ceremonies performed by shaman kings at calendrical cycle shifts or the like. In Chichen-Itza, it is instead the architecture that speaks, and one must be open to hear the buildings talk. And the Pyramid of Kukulcan holds much education. A simple example is that when the number of steps in the four staircases (4 × 91) are added together and combined with the top level it gives the number of days in the year. A more important esoteric message is that the pyramid is built in a hierarchical fashion with nine terraces symbolic of the Nine Underworlds that the Maya believed constituted this creation. But let us return to Quetzalcoatl (in the following I will be using this more widespread Aztec name for the Plumed Serpent). Standard books on Mexican culture all repeat the same descriptions of Quetzalcoatl as if they had all been copying one another: The name Quetzalcoatl is derived from the beautiful Quetzal bird, the national symbol of Guatemala, and coatl, which means 'snake.' His name also means 'Precious Twin,' as he had a nemesis, a dark twin, Tezcatlipoca, who was worshiped by powerful priests in conflict with those who worshiped Quetzalcoatl. Quetzalcoatl was a deity that was transformed to the planet Venus and was worshiped all over Mesoamerica in ancient times. He was the wind god, and was considered one of the first creations of the Creator duality. He had contributed to the creation of the conscious universe and more specifically to the creation of culture, the arts, the sciences and the calendar.

Quetzalcoatl also sometimes took human form. Once he incarnated in the city of Tula, the capital of the Toltecs in northern Mexico, where he ruled as a god-king in the years AD 947-999 (some sources say a little bit later) under the name of Ce Acatl Tipiltzin, a high priest. Since this god-king attempted to have his people stop sacrificing humans he was driven away from his city by the worshipers of Tezcatlipoca. He then fled and embarked on a raft made of serpents at the Gulf Coast of Mexico and disappeared in the East. According to an alternative version he would go to the Yucatan peninsula and the city of Chichen-Itza, which he would invigorate spiritually and rule for a number of years. Before having left his native Tula he had, however, sworn to return on the day Ce Acatl in the year Ce Acatl in the Toltec-Aztec calendar and from this he received his name. In addition to these legends there are also those that talk about a light-skinned bearded man who was teaching all over Mesoamerica in the distant past. Legend has it that when this man returned he would plant a balanced cross in the soil.

As Hernan Cortes, the Spanish conqueror, landed in Mexico and raised a cross on Good Friday 1519 he landed close to the place from which Tipiltzin had departed, close to present day Veracruz. In the Aztec calendar this was in the year Ce Acatl (One Reed) and on the day Ce Acatl. Soon, the powerful Aztec Emperor Moctezuma II, who was able to raise an army of 100,000 men, heard about the arrival of the light-skinned, bearded newcomers. At least initially Moctezuma believed Hernan Cortes to be the returning Quetzalcoatl, and feared that his world would now come to an end. Yet, because the cross Cortes had raised in Veracruz was not balanced, some natives concluded that Cortes was not Quetzalcoatl, but an impostor.

In the following two years Cortes' army of 350 conquistadors and 16 horses and their native allies precipitated the downfall of the large Aztec Empire. In so doing, Cortes proceeded with much brutality and apparently was driven mostly by his lust for gold and acceptance by the royal crown of Spain, and today all parties seem to agree that Hernan Cortes was not Quetzalcoatl. Yet, one might wonder why the powerful ruler Moctezuma would become sleepless upon hearing about the arrival of this small band. Maybe somewhere he knew that his people acted in a way that it was not supposed to, partly in performing ritual sacrifices of human beings. Ce Acatl Tipiltzin, the god-king incarnation of Quetzalcoatl, had been opposed to such human sacrifices, and here we find a parallel to Jesus Christ, who preached an end to all kinds of sacrifices. This, and many other parallels between Jesus Christ and Quetzalcoatl, have led some to suggest that indeed Christ and Quetzalcoatl are identical in nature.

Although unknown in most of the world, these stories and their variations still play a very important role in the spiritual heritage of all Mexicans. In a way, to the Mexicans they provide a way of probing their mixed Indian and Spanish heritage and coming to terms with their roots. Yet today no one seems to know who Quetzalcoatl was, even though he appeared from the dawn of Mesoamerican civilization and among millions of people was a dominating focus of worship for at least a thousand years. In learning about these legends we should, however, be aware that the descriptions of Quetzalcoatl as a human being all have their origin in later Aztec/Mayan chronicles from the sixteenth century, sometimes written down by the Spanish. All accounts from Classical (about AD 200-900) and Post-Classical (AD 900-1200) times describe Quetzalcoatl as a divine principle and not as a human being. Everywhere in Teotihuacan and Chichen-Itza the temples bear witness to the presence of this principle, and the only symbol of worship in the Old World that could compare in importance to that of Quetzalcoatl in the New World is the Cross. And maybe, if Christ and Quetzalcoatl are the same, we can learn something about the return of Christ from the return of Quetzalcoatl. After all, the ancient Mesoamericans had a much more evolved sense of prophecy than most of us have today. The Maya especially had a very advanced calendar, which they used as a framework for their prophecies; this supposedly had been given to them by the Plumed Serpent. So when considering the return of Christ consciousness the Mayan calendar may be a good place to start.

CHAPTER 2
THE CALENDRICAL SYSTEM OF THE MAYA

CALENDARS AND WHAT THEY ARE USED FOR

An increasing number of people are attracted to the Mayan calendar. Many have a deeply felt intuitive sense that the Mayan calendar reflects a higher truth than the now dominating Gregorian calendar or any other calendar that is currently used in the world. I feel this recently increased interest in an age-old calendar that all but disappeared a thousand years ago signifies that we are now about to enter an era carrying a new consciousness of time, an era which, as we shall see, is itself predictable from the Mayan calendar. In this chapter I will thus briefly describe, with no ambition of being exhaustive, what I feel are the most important aspects of the Mayan calendar for people living today. In later chapters I will seek to convey why I think this is crucial to everyone's future.

The concept of the Mayan calendar is, however, not as unambiguous as it may first sound. The Maya used several different calendars, calendars that were used for different purposes and in different contexts. Certain individuals in charge of keeping track of the different days have maintained the continuity of these calendars. These 'day-keepers' have been working with maybe as many as twenty different calendars in parallel, calendars that in a multitude of ways were connected to one another. Adding to this diversity is the fact that over time the types of calendars have undergone change and some have varied among different cultures in the Mesoamerican region. It is thus more accurate to talk about the calendrical system of the Maya, a system where many choices are available when characterizing a certain day.

Determining which calendars to study depends on the purpose for which they are to be used. Some of the calendars used by the Maya may in fact have no advantages compared to the calendars that are most commonly used today. Others, including some that for a long time have not been used by the Maya themselves, may become indispensable tools for the future and serve to bring about a total shift in the way we look at the world. On a global scale these may contribute to a shift from the currently reigning materialist world view to a realization that the reality we live in is fundamentally spiritual in nature. On an individual level the use of a new calendar may make a person aware of her true purpose in life through the wider perspective of the world that this fosters. If we have been blinded to these matters it is partly because calendars condition our way of thinking in a most insidious way. A calendar does not appear to be a philosophical statement. It does not seem like something that actively maintains a certain world view, and yet this is exactly what it does. It is to a large extent because of calendars that we are deluded into materialist illusions. The pressure to use the same calendar as everybody else strengthens the grip of these illusions even more.

So let us then take a look at what calendars may be used for and how we can sort them out. The calendars that almost everyone uses today are founded on a view of time as primarily a physical phenomenon. This view of time has been supported by the very exact ways that currently exist for measuring physical time. While few people today may be able to describe what time is, we all seem to agree on how to measure a period of time, which is by counting the number of identical cyclical movements that it corresponds to. Examples of such movements (and units of time) are the earth's rotation around its axis (day), the earth's revolution around the sun (solar year), the revolution of the moon around the earth (month) or the mechanical cycles in watches (used for seconds).

The interest in physical cycles, and the solar year in particular, may seem natural since these determine the agricultural year. Hence, farmers have needed calendars based on the solar year to know when to plant the crops and to be able to plan their work in accordance with the shifting seasons. Thus, for thousands of years humanity has known the solar year to be about 365¼ days. In Europe, for instance, a calendar with a leap day every fourth year, the Julian calendar, was used until it became evident that this slipped in relation to the physical year. It slipped because of the discrepancy between the year of 365.25 days used in this calendar and the exact value of the astronomical year, 365.2422 days. To correct this, Pope Gregory XIII in 1582 decided to replace the Julian calendar with one that, through omitting leap days at certain century shifts, more exactly followed the astronomical year. This calendar has later come to bear his name. The introduction of the Gregorian calendar, which is dominant in the world today, has even further strengthened the idea that calendars are meant to facilitate a timekeeping that as exactly as possible adheres to the astronomical year.

The Maya, like all agricultural peoples, used a calendar to describe the agricultural, solar year, a cycle that they called the haab. This calendar consisted of eighteen 20-day periods called uinals, which were followed by a 'waiting period' of 5 days called the vayeb, during which the gods were said to rest ($18 \times 20 + 5 = 365$). The haab is thus different from calendars in most other parts of the world, which usually are based on months of approximately 30 days. In my own opinion, however, it is very questionable if the haab calendar, which, similarly to the Gregorian is based on the astronomical year, has anything to contribute to the world of today. Things do not become true just because they are Mayan.

Thus, despite the fact that today very few people, at least in the industrialized world, need a calendar to tell them when to sow or harvest, we are still stuck with calendars based on the physical year. In recent centuries, the original purpose and holy character of Anno Domini (in the Year of the Lord) in the Gregorian calendar has also largely been lost. Rather, this calendar has turned into a convention by means of which the wheels of industry may run smoothly by allowing people across the globe to coordinate their economic activities. Although it is still used for marking some religious festivals, the coordination of economic activities—deliveries, payments, production deadlines—has become the main purpose of the calendrical system we are now using. On an everyday basis it is used by people for knowing when to pay their bills, etc.

Maybe then something has been lost in the process of our accommodation to the physical calendars. The number of different calendars used by the ancient Maya, however, attests to a richness that is not limited to the physical, and it is in this that we may find a calendar for the future. Thus, I can think of at least three different types of calendars used by the ancient Maya. One type was astronomical (haab of 365 days, the Venus cycle of 584 days, the Mars cycle of 780 days and the moons alternating between 29 and 30 days), and another astrological (13 × 28 + 1 days). The third and most interesting type, however, is given by calendars such as the 360-day prophetic year called the *tun* and the 260-day sacred calendar called the *tzolkin*, which are not based on physical phenomena. Since today the thought that time is something based on physical movements is so ingrained in us, the calendars that boggle our minds the most are the very ones based on the tun and the tzolkin. In this book I will focus almost exclusively on the tun-based system, the system that among the Classical Maya played the predominant role. The other non-physical calendar, the tzolkin, which is not truly a time cycle, will be discussed only in Appendix I and a forthcoming book. I believe it is by the study and use of the tun-based calendrical system that we may develop an awareness of consciousness, a meta-consciousness, which will allow us to understand the factors underlying the evolution of consciousness. The tun is a unit by means of which we may return to the divine time governed by the frequencies of the invisible universe.

We should notice that there exists a very direct link between today's materialist philosophy and the linear/cyclical concept of time that underpins our own present calendar. For if we base our ways of measuring time on counting cyclical movements of physical objects we will soon come to embrace a linear concept of time. Five cycles of the moon, in other words, soon turns into the number 5 on a linear scale. Thus, because our concept of time is linear/cyclical, based on an illusion of an endless repetition of identical cycles, it cannot accommodate the phenomena of evolution or creation. Inherent in our linear view of time is the notion that time is just an endless repetition of cycles with no beginning and no end. With such a linear view of time humanity does not seem to be going anywhere special, and life then does not seem to have any purpose, with all the consequences such an attitude has had for the environment of our planet.

This linear/cyclical view of time encoded in our calendars thus perfectly matches the materialist notion that there is no God and that this universe does not evolve according to a divine plan of creation. It is in order to find the path to the spiritual processes of evolution of the universe that we need to replace the materialist linear/cyclical view of time with the Mayan tun-based periods of creation. The durations of these time periods are summarized in Table 1.

Summary of Time Cycles Linked to the Tun (360-day Year)
and Their Corresponding Durations in Physical Time

Kin			1	days
Uinal		=	20	days
Tun		=	360	days
Katun	20 tun	=	19.7	years
Baktun	20^2 tun	=	394	years
Piktun	20^3 tun	=	7900	years
Kalabtun	20^4 tun	=	158,000	years
Kinchiltun	20^5 tun	=	3.15 million	years
Alautun	20^6 tun	=	63.1 million	years
Hablatun	20^7 tun	=	1.26 billion	years

THE TUN AS THE KEY CALENDRICAL TIME PERIOD

The central unit in this table is the tun, which was divided into 18 uinals each of 20 days, or into 360 days, called by the Maya kin. In addition to these basic units there were units of time based on multiples of the tun, such as the katun, made up of 20 tuns, i.e., twenty 360-day 'years' corresponding to 19.7 solar years. Twenty such katuns would then in turn constitute a baktun, equaling $20 \times 20 = 20^2 = 400$ tuns, and so on, generating units of time that with every step have a duration twenty times longer than the previous. At first sight the longer periods of time generated in this way may appear incomprehensibly large. We may wonder why the Maya had names for time periods of about a billion years, when the average person today only thinks about time in terms of a few decades.

Despite the prominent role the tun-based system had among the Classical Maya it has been largely ignored in recent attempts to recreate their calendrical system. Partly this may be because of the fact that it does not correspond to a physical cycle, and partly it is because it has been lost also to the tradition of today's Maya, who, with the rest of us, have increasingly transferred to astronomical cycles.

The Maya, however, were not unique among the peoples of antiquity in following a 360-day year. So did, for instance, the Incas. In fact, in ancient calendars, it seems that the use of the 360-day year was the rule rather than the exception. The Egypt of the pharaohs, for instance, counted a 360-day year which was followed by 'the five days upon a year' when the gods were born. This rings the bell of the Maya and the Aztecs, who similarly thought that the gods disappeared during the

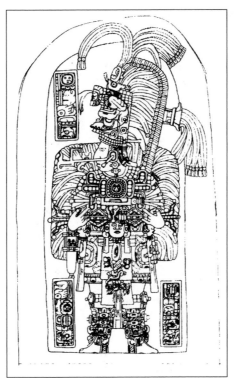

Fig. 3 The ruler Ah-Cacaw sets the tun and completes the katun (9.14.0.0.0 6 Ahau 13 Muan) at Tikal (Courtesy Schele and Freidel, *A Forest of Kings*).

5-day uayeb. Furthermore, the earliest sacred writings of the Hindus, the Vedas, give information about a calendar of 12 months each of 30 days, and the Chinese followed a 360-day divine year composed of 6 units, each of 60 days. At certain points this divine calendar would be supplemented with extra days to adjust the calendar to the agricultural years. The 360-day year is also known from ancient Scandinavian timekeeping and in a sense we see it reflected in the 360 degrees of the circle of Sumerian origin. A similar approach is used by astrologers who divide the yearly passage of the sun through the ecliptic into the 360 degrees of the circle. In the *Book of Revelation* (12:6 and 12:14) there is also a reference to the 360-day period being considered as a 'time.' What we may conclude from this is that the 360-day year was used independently in several cultures and especially in spiritual contexts as distinct from the agricultural year. The Tibetans may have made the most original attempt at coming to grips with the discrepancy between the 360-day and 365-day years, in that they also used a concept of a holy day, $365/360 \times 24 = 24.33$ hours, which was slightly longer than a physical day. Hence, the physical year would consist of 360 such adjusted days. This may not be recommendable, but it illustrates how people in strongly spiritual cultures have sought a resolution of the tension between the 360-day and the 365-day year, which we who live today have become almost entirely oblivious to. Yet, infants seem to seek the same solution.

Studies of babies under three months of age point to 24.33 hours as their average daily rhythm.

So maybe some significant truth was hidden behind the use of the 360-day year that the ancient cultures of humanity were aware of, since after all they were all aware that the astronomical year was longer than this. To find this hidden truth and the insights about the world that it was based on, we will seek to retrieve especially the calendar of the Classical Maya, which stands out on this planet in its advancement and accuracy. The particular consciousness that developed this calendrical system—the Western consciousness of what the Maya would call baktuns 8 and 9 (approximately the first 800 years AD)—is a part of the collective consciousness of humanity that for a long time has been lost. I believe that this very consciousness is the missing piece of the puzzle that will allow us to recreate a whole view of the world. What I suggest is that the tun-based calendars describe processes that explain why things evolve, and that this process of evolution is determined by a very strict time plan for the realization of God's purpose with this creation.

Today we know of at least three significant roles that the tun-based calendrical system played among the ancient Maya. The first is that the tun was considered as the prophetic year. Thus, it was on the day that the new tun—not the 365-day haab—began that the Mayan priests would gather, burn incense and cleanse their holy books with virgin water and read from them. These books were the *Books of Chilam Balam* (Jaguar Prophet), which contained calendrical information and recorded the histories of their various villages or towns. One of the priests would read from the books, deliver the prophecies and suggest remedies if dire times seemed to be approaching. This tells us a lot about how the Maya viewed the tun. It shows that they thought that the study of history could support their prophecies and it was for this very reason that each town kept records of it. It also tells us that prophecies were based on tuns or katuns, which were seen as parts of 'ages' of longer durations. In the *Books of Chilam Balam*, prophecies were consistently based on the tun and the katun, and never on the astronomical year.

Second, the katun shifts were the most significant times for ceremonies celebrated by the Classical Maya (about AD 200-900), when their divine shaman kings, so called ahauob, would perform rituals on the pyramids. At the tops of the pyramids these shaman kings would sacrifice their own blood and in a trance state, probably partly induced by psychedelic mushrooms, make contact with the Vision Serpent for guidance into the coming katun. Many altars, pyramids and buildings were dedicated at the beginnings of new katuns.

These rulers would also typically dedicate steles to celebrate the passage of a certain number of katuns since their births or the beginnings of their reigns. Hence, they would celebrate birthdays that were based on the number of 360-day years that had passed in their lives. This is obviously different from what we do today when we base our birthdays on the physical rather than the spiritual year. Birthdays, as all dates, would be described in the format 9.18.2.5.17 3 Caban 0 Pop, for instance, which was the day when the Copan ruler Yax-Pac celebrated the first thirty tuns of his life, his thirtieth spiritual birthday. This format means that 9 baktuns, 18 katuns, 2 tuns, 5 uinals and 17 kin had passed since the beginning of the Long Count, the long-term chronology used by the ancient Maya. This particular birthday coincided with the day 3 Caban in the tzolkin count and the day 0 Pop, the first day of the haab (which this year happened to fall on his spiritual birthday).

Because of such ceremonies a tremendously large part of the buildings and steles at the old Classical sites are dated, something which, incidentally, has made the job for archaeologists studying the Mayan culture relatively easy, at least where chronology is concerned. The ancient Maya would place much emphasis on when something happened or when a building was dedicated, to the extent that marking a specific date would often be a major reason for dedicating it. The Maya lived in a universe of holy time.

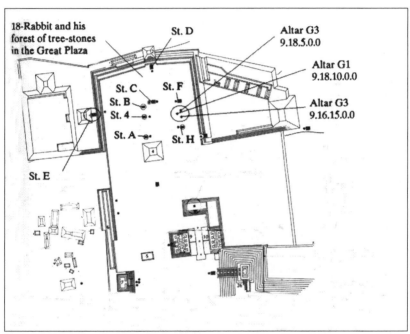

Fig. 4 Section of the archaeological area of Copan showing Vision Serpent Altars with their dates of dedication and statues of the ruler 18-Rabbit (Fig. 5) performing tun shift celebrations (Courtesy Schele and Freidel, *A Forest of Kings*).

The third role that the 360-day year had for the Maya was, as already hinted at, as the basis for their chronology, the Long Count, which they used for keeping track of the long-term passage of time. The Long Count, what the Maya would call an 'age,' consists of 13 baktuns = 13 × 400 tuns = 5200 tuns, and equals about 5125 solar years. This count took its beginning on August 11, 3114 BC and will thus come to an end after 5200 × 360 = 1,872,000 days, on December 21, 2012. The Mayan idea of an 'age' was thus different from, for instance, the Old World notion based on the precession of the earth (see Appendix V). An age was rather a divine creation cycle, ultimately based on the divine 360-day year, the tun, and I will refer to the creation cycle of 13 baktuns, periods of 400 tuns, as the Great Cycle.

Probably more than anything else in the Mayan calendrical system, the year 2012, the end of the age of 13 baktuns, fascinates modern people, since the very fact that a calendar comes to an end represents a decisive break with our current linear concept of time. The year 2012, sometimes exchanged with 2011 or 2013, has thus in the recent decade been mentioned in a number of New Age books as a year that signifies a time of fundamental shift in the spiritual evolution of this planet. What there is to know then is that this year finds its origin in the so-called Long Count, the chronology the Maya adhered to for about a thousand years, and the only way to find out if there is any basis in reality for suggestions that the year 2012 is a year of special importance is obviously to study the reality underlying the Long Count.

Fig. 5 This is one (Stele H) in the series of statues portraying the ruler 18-Rabbit; 9.14.0.0.0 (See Fig. 4). They were dedicated at the beginnings of five-tun-periods; 9.14.0. 0.0 (same date as celebrated in Tikal in Fig. 3), 9.14.10.0.0, 9.14.15.0.0, 9.15.0.0.0 and 9.15.5.0.0 (photo Calleman).

Fig. 6 One of the Vision Serpent Altars at Copan (see Fig. 4) (Photo Calleman).

To stimulate the effort to understand the Long Count, the durations of the 13 baktuns (13 periods of 394 solar years) of the Great Cycle have been summarized in Table 2. (For reasons that are explained in Appendix II the years have been slightly corrected in the table below.)

Table 2
(Corrected) Duration in Terms of Gregorian Years
of the Different Baktuns of the Great Cycle

Baktun no	Duration
0	3115-2721 BC
1	2721-2326 BC
2	2326-1932 BC
3	1932-1538 BC
4	1538-1144 BC
5	1144-749 BC
6	749-355 BC
7	355 BC-AD 40
8	AD 40-434
9	AD 434-829
10	AD 829-1223
11	AD 1223-1617
12	AD 1617-2011

In seeking to elucidate the meanings of these various baktuns we should be aware that in the Mayan view a special divine force, or deity, dominated each period of time. This deity would, after having entered office at its first day, the so-called seating day, be seen as ruling the period. It would thus be at the seating day of the new deity that the Mayan priests would convene to figure out, judging from their calendrical books and historical records of their villages, what their peoples had reasons to expect in the coming tun. This procedure is essentially the same as the one we will follow in this book, with the significant difference that today we have at our disposal the historical records of the entire planet, and not only those of a small Mayan town. Using the accumulated knowledge of historical research we will seek to understand what energies dominate each of these 13 time periods, these 13 baktuns of the Great Cycle, to elucidate the underlying basis of the chronology used by the Classical Maya. To begin with, it may be worth spending a few moments to ponder the possible historical significance of the various years and eras presented in Table 2.

BREAKTHROUGHS TO LIGHT

When seeing the sequence of baktuns in Table 2 there is usually one particular thing that people notice more than any other. This is that the beginning of baktun 8 saw the emergence of Christianity: Jesus Christ is thought to have been crucified in AD 33, while Paul, who in many ways became the founder of the Christian religion, was converted around the year 37. Then, in the year 49, at a meeting in Jerusalem, the Apostles made the decisive break with Judaism. At this meeting it was decided that anyone, including non-ethnic Jews who had not been circumcised and did not follow the Mosaic Law in all its detail, could become a member of the Christian community. As baktun 8 continued the number of followers of the Christian faith continued to grow, until, toward its end, the Christian church became the spiritual arm of the Roman Empire.

Why did all this happen, and, above all, why did Christianity emerge at this particular time? Jesus' message of the one God, love and compassion seems timeless, so why did this religion spread to the center of the Roman Empire immediately at the beginning of this baktun and why did it eventually lead the emperors to renounce their own divinity? It almost seems as if a new deity, which created a new 'energy' that dominated the minds of the people living at the time, ruled this baktun. If this is so, maybe then the Long Count of the Maya could help us understand why all of this took place, since the emergence of Christianity coincided so well with one of its baktun shifts (which incidentally was also the approximate time that the Long Count came into use). Certainly, if the Mayan baktuns reflect different 'energies' this would imply a significant change in our world view. This would mean that the baktuns of the Great Cycle in some sense describe the evolution of human spirituality and how new thoughts come into existence. One of the aspects of Jesus' teaching that distinguishes it from the Judaism from which it sprang was the emphasis placed on a future Kingdom of God, a Kingdom where human beings could attain an eternal life. In ancient Mesoamerican mythology Quetzalcoatl ruled baktun 8, and since this was a deity that brought light to human beings we may note a correspondence with the light of Christ. We thus embark on a theme that will run as a thread through this book: the reality the Mayan calendar describes is the same as that described in the Bible.

Another thing to note about the sequence of the 13 baktuns, pointed out already by Frank Waters in *Mexico Mystique*, is that its very beginning coincides with the emergence of the first higher human civilizations some five thousand years ago. Hence, the first use of writing goes back to the Sumerians, who around 3200-3000 BC (the dating of such plates of clay is not always easy) began using logograms for preserving information. Also, archaeologists usually agree that Pharaoh Menes, who unified Upper and Lower Egypt and founded its first dynasty, lived around 3100-3050 BC. Shortly afterwards the people of this nation were engaged in major construction work, and the oldest pyramid of Egypt, Djoser's Pyramid, has been dated using carbon[14] techniques to about 2975 BC. The beginning of the Great Cycle is also the approximate time of the first use of bronze. Taken together, much evidence seems to indicate that the first higher human civilizations, and certainly the first nations, emerged around the time of beginning of the Long Count.

It is then interesting to hear what the ancient Maya themselves had to say about the starting date of the Long Count. At the Temple of the Cross in Palenque—one of the most magical and beautiful of the Mayan temple cities—it is said that at the beginning of this creation the World Tree, the Wakah-Chan, was raised. It also says that at the beginning of the Long Count, 'the First Father, made appear with his Word' and then 'became the Heaven' as new light entered. This is fairly different from how most people view things today. Yet, it seems to imply that the first higher human civilizations emerging on this planet might have been the results of the beginning of a new divine creation. This would mean that it was not an accident that Egypt and Sumer appeared at the particular time they did. Rather, their appearance would be the result of the beginning of a new age, of one of the 'worlds' of the Maya. If this is so, the Mayan Great Cycle would really be a chronology of the whole planet, affecting East and West alike, and not be of relevance only to Mesoamerica. It would also mean that our civilizational advances ultimately are manifestations of the World Tree and divine LIGHT and that the Mayan Great Cycle is the chronology of the emergence of this LIGHT.

If the first of these 13 baktuns began with a new Heaven, it seems logical, as indeed I suggest, that also each one of the following baktuns represents a new Heaven through which LIGHT can pass. This would among other things mean that the emergence of Christianity at the beginning of baktun 8 would be the result of one of these Thirteen Heavens that were raised by the First Father. The existence of Thirteen Heavens in divine creation would then also explain the holiness of the number 13, expressed for instance in the number of disciples of Jesus (12 + 1 = 13) and in many other ways by different spiritual traditions from across the world.

THE TWINS OF THE BEGINNING AND THE END

But where is the creation of the Thirteen Heavens all going? To answer this we will begin by comparing events and phenomena that first turned up at the beginnings of the first and of the last of these Thirteen Heavens, in the years 3115 BC and AD 1617, respectively. In the Mayan view these two Heavens would be considered as the twins of the beginning and the end. Thus we can see in Table 3 that if the First Heaven started with the emergence of the first higher human civilizations—writing, nations with rulers considered as divine and large construction works—then the beginning of the Thirteenth Heaven saw the emergence of more advanced expressions of these very same phenomena. (Note a possible source of confusion here, in that we will count the baktuns in the traditional way starting with zero, while the count of the Heavens will start with one.)

To exemplify, stimulated by the new LIGHT at the beginning of the First Heaven of the Great Cycle, the human beings would learn to inscribe the first signs in tablets of clay. At the beginning of the Thirteenth Heaven the use of writing, which had by now undergone significant development, instead underwent a great change in the way it would be distributed. Daily newspapers and regular mail services, for instance, first appeared at this time, and following the beginning of baktun 12 writing could be used for disseminating information on a much wider scale than previously. I am thus suggesting that the Thirteenth Heaven represented the highest expression of an evolution that had begun with the First Heaven and progressed through the influence of the various Heavens in between. The pairs of twins in the table would then represent the beginnings and the ends of several such progressions through the world age of nations, the Great Cycle.

Table 3
Comparison of Phenomena Emerging during
the First and Thirteenth Heavens of the Great Cycle

First Heaven (3115 BC)	Thirteenth Heaven (AD 1617)
First writing (Sumerian logograms)	First daily newspaper (Amsterdam, 1618) First national archives (Sweden, 1618) First national mail service (Denmark, 1624)
First nation (First Dynasty of Egypt)	Modern nation (sovereignty principle, 1648)
First numbers (Menes' labyrinth)	Logarithm tables (Briggs, 1617), Slide rule (1632), Calculation machine (Pascal, 1642)

First astronomy (Sumer)	Scientific revolution (Kepler, 1619; Galileo, 1632; Descartes, 1637)
First belief in Creator God (An)	Protestantism established (1648)
First buildings of worship (Djoser's Pyramid)	St Peter's Basilica (Rome, 1626)

The beginning of the Thirteenth Heaven also saw the beginning of the scientific revolution, when a heliocentric world view fought its way through the resistance of the Catholic church. As José Argüelles pointed out in his *Mayan Factor*, it was in the year 1619, at the very beginning of baktun 12, that Johannes Kepler published his epoch-making work, *De Harmonice Mundi*, with the formula describing the orbital movements of the planets. Kepler's work was groundbreaking in that it was the first time higher mathematics was used in formulating a law of nature. Simultaneously, Galileo discovered the moons of Jupiter using the telescope he had just invented and started to apply the experimental method to mechanical problems. At this time a new ideal emerged as to how humans should acquire knowledge about nature, an ideal whose most influential exponent was the brilliant Frenchman René Descartes. According to this ideal human beings may gain knowledge about the world that surrounds us by being objective, experimenting and using instruments and formulating mathematical laws to describe our findings. Descartes also suggested the reductionist ideal of understanding a problem by splitting it up into its smallest components and then putting the pieces together again in the right way.

Today most people see this way of thinking as self-evident since it has formed the basis for the technological development of the modern world. Much of our educational system has also been designed to teach students about laws of nature and their mathematical formulations. Nonetheless, at the time of Kepler and Galileo the notion of a mathematical law of nature was a complete novelty.

Hence, the beginning of baktun 12 saw the launching of an entirely new mentality, which was expressed in many different ways although the scientific revolution may have been the most evident. It thus seems that our perception of the world around us, and the way we think, is influenced, if not determined, by the particular Heaven that rules. The Thirteen Heavens would then reflect a progression through different mentalities as described by the Mayan chronology. Yet, even if this chronology provides an accurate temporal framework for understanding the history of our planet, we also need a spatial framework, the four directions and their center, to be able to follow its course, the evolution of the divine plan.

CHAPTER 3
THE YIN/YANG OF
HUMAN HISTORY

*We may know more about the universe
than our ancestors did, and yet it seems
they knew something more essential about it than we do.*
Vaclav Havel

THE FOUR DIRECTIONS

When the Spanish first came to the land of the Maya in 1517 they found great painted crosses in the centers of worship of the natives, and, on the island of Cozumel off the Yucatan peninsula, for instance, a pyramid had a three-meter-high cross of lime in its courtyard. They learned that these crosses were representations of the World Tree, and that for this reason they had been painted green, as they still are today. The World Tree (Figure 7), the Wakah-Chan in Mayan language, is what divides the world according to the four directions, and, as we shall see later, the Great Pacal also conceived of this as having a galactic dimension. Since the Spanish conquest this World Tree has been merged with the cross of the Catholics in the beliefs of the Maya, although the cross still retains much of its ancient meaning as the center of the Cosmos. It is because the World Tree establishes the four directions of the world that the number 4 has become one of the holy numbers of the Maya.

The view of the world as having four directions, and thus four corners, is a common trait of the cosmologies of all Native American peoples. In these, there was also a center of the world, by the Maya called Yaxkin, to which all the directions were related. At first sight, this view may not appear any different from the standard European view, but the meaning given to these directions is clearly different from what is common today. In the Native American view, and in this the Maya were no exception, the four directions embody spiritual qualities that influence human life differently depending on the particular time cycle reigning. While in the typical European view the four directions are merely seen as a passive coordinate system applied to the earth with no inherent spiritual meaning, the spiritual forces embodied by the four directions are the very essence of the Native American view.

The reason the Maya use the World Tree as a symbol for the Cross creating the four corners of the world is that they see this Cross as being alive. In their own region the beautiful ceiba tree, whose sap is used for making the incense called copal, is seen as a manifestation of the World Tree, the living cross. This Tree was also believed to have been the birthplace of the first human being. As I will argue later, this may be the plain truth.

In Classical times, the World Tree was seen as a portal that penetrated into the Otherworld, the beyond, and it not only lived, but also, as all trees, generated life in the form of fruit. In the ancient Mayan belief the World Tree existed before

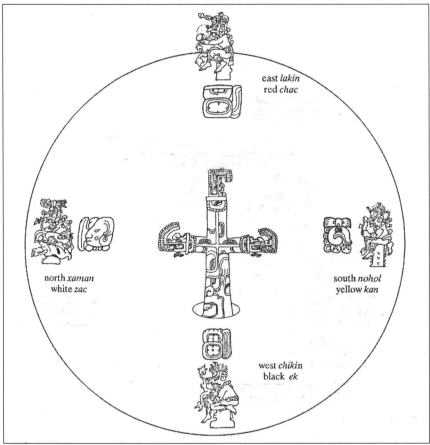

Fig. 7 The Mayan view of the world with the World Tree at the center of the four directions. Note that the Maya would place the Eastern direction at the top (Courtesy Schele and Freidel, *A Forest of Kings*).

anything else did, even before the physical universe as we know it had been created. It was a deity that existed before anything else. As Creation approached it became pregnant with life and from its branches came not only all the physical emanations of this Creation, but also light and segments of time. Mayan rituals are still today centered on nurturing the World Tree in the invisible universe and giving it life through ceremonies reenacting Creation and the four directions of the world.

The Aztec Creation myth is centered on the same theme. In the Aztec variety the omnipotent Creator god, Ometeotl, created the four different Tezcatlipocas, each represented by one of four colors and four directions. The White Tezcatlipoca of the Western direction was another name for Quetzalcoatl, whose nemesis was the Black Tezcatlipoca. The cross creating the four directions was the source of the

The Mayan Calendar

dualities that were generated along its arms and these arms were also the sources of life. We may well understand that as the Spanish landed in the New World with the Christian cross, which to them had a very different meaning, this became the cause of much confusion.

Organizing the world according to four directions and their different spiritual qualities may seem inherently sound to many of us, given that we have strong notions about mental and spiritual differences between East and West. Yet, if we are to take this view seriously, and assume that the World Tree is real, this poses the problem of where its center is actually located. In ancient times the center was obviously always identified with the geographic location of the particular group, tribe, people or city-state who conducted a ceremony of the four directions or tried to understand how the spiritual winds were blowing during different years. This would imply that there are many different centers of the world. Such a view would, however, be contradicted by the almost universal feeling that there is a fundamental difference in mentality between people of the East and people of the West. While the East has typically been dominated by collective structures and has a meditative streak, the West is individualist, extroverted and action-oriented.

So where would be the line separating East from West and what is its relationship to the planetary Medicine Wheel? To identify this in a more profound sense, we will need to use the Mayan Great Cycle to identify in what directions the spiritual winds have been blowing as the Heavens have changed, that is to say, at its baktun shifts. We also need a hypothesis—a model of the earth that organizes human cultures according to the four geographic directions. This model that I am suggesting adheres to the so-called Hermetic principle of the esoteric traditions—'As above, so below'—and is based on the existence of a number of parallels between the 'global brain' of the planet we inhabit and the human brain according to below:

Global Brain	*Human Brain*
Western Hemisphere	Left brain half
Eastern Hemisphere	Right brain half
Germany	Hypothalamus
Italy	Hypophysis
Nordic countries	Epiphysis
Central Africa	Cerebellum
Hawaiian Islands	Eyes

THE GLOBAL BRAIN

According to this model the rational, action-oriented Western Hemisphere parallels the left, 'male' brain half with its analytical thinking and center for speech, calculation and sequential logic. The meditative Eastern Hemisphere, on the other hand, parallels the right, intuitive, wholeness-oriented, 'female' brain half, which is also the center for our spatial and artistic abilities. Also, in the same way that people use their left hemispheres during the normal operation of their brains and that this brain half is responsible for their external interactions, the present world looks mostly to the West, and especially to the United States, for leadership. And while most people in the Eastern Hemisphere live their lives in a more historical context, North Americans typically live their lives in the context of the present with a more operational attitude toward life.

In this global brain structure, divided approximately along a midline through the 12th longitude East, what is currently Germany-Italy hypothetically corresponds to the hypothalamus-hypophysis complex, the central regulatory center of the mammalian brain. In today's world Italy and Germany may not always be thought of as being in such central positions, but during the Renaissance and the Reformation they certainly were. Through the Roman and German-Roman empires, as well as the Papacy, they have dominated at least Europe's history for some fifteen hundred years. Further north along the same midline the Nordic countries, and especially Sweden, hypothetically represent the pineal gland or epiphysis. This is a small organ in the mammalian brain, which integrates the amount of light for the purpose of regulating the time of birth of the offspring. Central Africa, the origin of mankind, would in this model correspond to the primal cerebellum, the oldest part of the brain, with its critical role in balance, motion and emotionality. On the opposite side of the world from this, the Hawaiian Islands, with the international telescope city on the rim of the volcano Mauna Kea and the giant telescopes of Maui, would correspond to the eyes through which this planetary brain looks out into the cosmos.

With this framework the different mentalities in different areas of the world can be seen as the results of a process of creation that serves to generate different fields in the planetary context rather than as products of random historical development. Later we will find that this model of the earth as a lateralized global brain, with a Western and an Eastern Hemisphere, can provide a spatial framework for the solution of such seemingly diverse problems as the disappearance of the Maya and the disappearance of the dinosaurs. Moreover, if this model is true, if there is a basis in reality for the parallels between the human and the global brain, a remarkable consequence is that human beings have been created in the image of the earth, a notion with profound implications not only for theology, but also for the theory of biological evolution and who human beings are.

HISTORY OF HEMISPHERIC SEPARATIONS

To verify the model above we will track historical events occurring at the baktun shifts of the Great Cycle in relation to the hypothetical midline through the 12th longitude. As we already pointed out, the first higher human civilizations with writing, monarchy, large-scale constructions and a religion with a Creator god emerged in the area called the Fertile Crescent stretching from Egypt through Israel and Syria to Mesopotamia. It was not until about the beginning of baktun 6, the Seventh of the Thirteen Heavens of the Great Cycle which was raised in 749 BC, that a higher civilization developed in a location on the 12th longitude East. This was as, in the latter half of the eighth century BC, the Etruscans in northern Italy (Figure 8) developed a system of writing. At about the same time the first stable settlements on the Palatine were also established, something that was reflected in the year of the mythical founding of Rome, 753 BC.

After this establishment of a historic culture at the hypothetical midline at the beginning of baktun 6, it becomes possible to follow historical events in relation to this line at baktun shifts. Thus, the next baktun, baktun 7, began with the Persian King Artaxerxes III Ochus moving west to reconquer Egypt and Asia Minor and subjugating the Athenians (Figure 9). A historic wind from the East toward the planetary midline thus initiated this baktun.

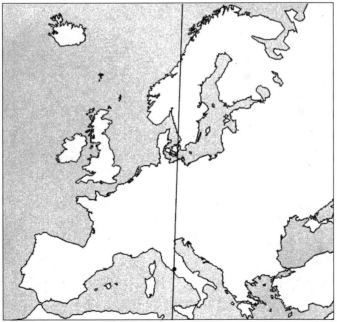

Fig. 8 Europe during the beginning katun (749-729 BC) of baktun 6: The emergence of Etruria as a historical culture and the mythical founding of Rome (753 BC).

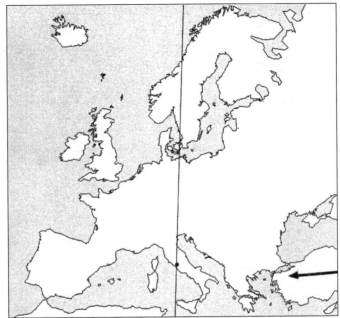

Fig. 9 Europe during the beginning katun (355-335 BC) of baktun 7: Military campaigns of King Artaxerxes II of Persia.

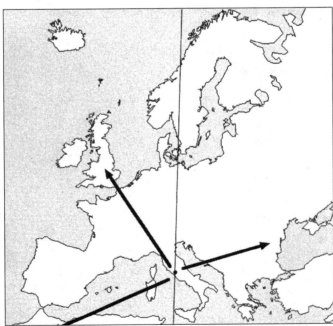

Fig. 10 Europe during the beginning katun (AD 40-60) of baktun 8: Expansion of the Roman Empire to include present day England and Wales, Morocco, Algeria and Bulgaria.

At the following shift, at the beginning of baktun 8 in AD 40 (Figure 10), a forward policy came to dominate in the newly established Roman Empire, which in the following twenty-year period was expanded to include today's England and Wales, Morocco and Algeria and Bulgaria. This expansion from the midline began at the same time as Paul went out on his missionary journeys to Asia Minor and Greece to spread the Christian faith. We may also note that a baktun of 400 tuns is 144,000 days long, a number well known from the *Book of Revelation*, which was written in the beginning of baktun 8.

Fig. 11 Europe during the beginning katun (AD 434-454) of baktun 9: The invasion of the Huns under Attila and the collapse of the west Roman Empire.

After this, in AD 434, we arrive at the beginning of baktun 9 (Figure 11). In this very year Attila became the ruler of the Huns and thus the most powerful ruler of his day. At the beginning of baktun 9 he attacked central Europe from the east. This attack pushed the Germanic tribes to sack Rome and led to the effective collapse of the Western Roman Empire. Hence, the Western Roman Empire collapsed exactly as baktun 9 began, and, as we shall see again later with the Maya themselves, the Thirteen Heavens have a lot to do with the rise and fall of different civilizations. The period that in Europe followed upon the onslaught by the Huns has later come to be called the Dark Ages, since during the following few hundred years no higher center of civilization existed there and Europe was traversed by marauding Germanic tribes. In the time cosmology of both the Aztecs and the Maya, the Tenth Heaven, which ruled baktun 9, was presided over by the god of darkness, something that highlights its destructive character.

Europe did not come alive again until at the beginning of the ninth century AD. Then, at the Treaty of Verdun in the year 843, a few years into baktun 10, the first European proto-nations, and notably Germany, emerged from the division of the empire of Charlemagne. This awakening incidentally happened simultaneously with the collapse of the Classical Mayan sites in Chiapas and Guatemala. This collapse was partly a result of the front line of human history moving markedly north, both in Europe and in Mesoamerica, at the beginning of baktun 10.

The move north was also evidenced in the sudden vitalization of a previously remote part of the world, Scandinavia, which is more directly relevant in our tracking of movements to and from the hypothetical midline. Thus, the beginning of baktun 10 saw the beginning of the journeys of the Vikings. Suddenly the peoples living in Scandinavia, after having been settled for several thousand years, went out on bold travels that would eventually lead them all the way to Greenland and America. As part of this outpouring, the ancestors of today's Norwegians and Danes would, at the beginning of baktun 10, raid the British Isles to the point where England was in fact conquered by the Danish King Knud. In the other direction, Swedish Vikings were making their way into the Russian river system and reached Bysans in the year 839, ten years into the new baktun. Those that lived in western Sweden went on raids toward the west, whereas those living east of the hypothetical midline went east (Figure 12).

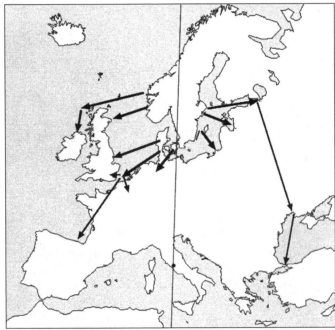

Fig. 12 Europe during the beginning katun (AD 829-849) of baktun 10: The raids of the Vikings towards the West and the East. Birth of Germany, the nucleus of the German-Roman Empire, and other European proto-nations at the Treaty of Verdun (AD 843).

Traditional historical science has never been able to produce a satisfactory explanation of why the Vikings went out on these raids. Having the Mayan chronology in hand sheds new light on the problem, however, as the raids of the Vikings took their beginning right at a baktun shift. Thus, at the beginning of baktun 10 the winds of history seem to have driven people away from this planetary midline.

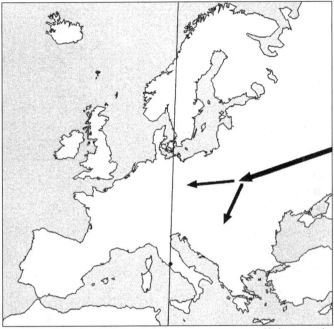

Fig. 13 Europe during the beginning katun (AD 1223-1243) of baktun 11: The Mongol Storm.

A movement that is probably even more difficult to understand from a traditional historical perspective is that which came to dominate the next baktun shift, namely the Mongol storm. At the beginning of baktun 11, the Mongols—who not so many years earlier had been a small people herding sheep in the Gobi Desert—arrived in eastern Europe after having conquered all of China and Asia in between. They did not make a halt in their expansion until they arrived at the planetary midline (Figure 13). Although the reason they halted there might have seemed like an accident (the Great Khan in Mongolia had died and one of his heirs who led the storm toward Europe wanted to return to Karakorum to see to his interests at the funeral), it seems that this 'accident' was somehow part of a larger plan manifesting within the framework of the cosmology of the four directions.

Be that as it may, baktun 11 began with a violent movement from the East toward the midline, and it should be pointed out how it is exactly at baktun shifts that these movements from the East hit Europe. Thus, it was in the same year as baktun 9 began that Attila became the ruler of the Huns, and it was in the year 1223, as baktun 11 began, that the Mongol storm reached the same area of eastern Europe.

Here we may pause to consider two things. First, that we are using a chronology, that of the Great Cycle, which is based on the tun, the divine year. Had we instead been using a calendar based on the physical year, then this would not have described with such exactness the times when these migrations from the East have hit Europe. The winds of history thus follow a tun-based chronology. Second, we should take note of the massive character of these violent movements. The empire created by Genghis Khan and his heirs around the beginning of baktun 11 was to set its mark on Russia and Asia for several centuries. Genghis Khan was recently elected by the *New York Times* (1995) as the Man of the Millennium, presumably not because of good behavior, but because of the impact the empire he created had on history. The Mongol storm created a unified field of the Eurasian continent which allowed it to be crossed by a variety of phenomena from East Asia to Europe, such as gunpowder, the compass, book printing and the plague. As the baktun progressed things were also beginning to move in the opposite direction. The point to see here is that the movements coinciding with these baktun shifts are no minor events dug up just to prove a theory. The Mongol storm created the largest empire in human history and the movements set about at the beginning of other baktun shifts had similarly significant impacts.

Finally then, in this rapid progression through the latter baktun shifts of the Great Cycle, we arrive at the beginning of baktun 12 (Figure 14). In central Europe this baktun shift was marked by the beginning in 1618 of the Thirty Years' War,

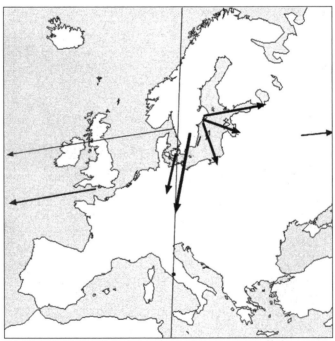

Fig. 14 Europe during the beginning katun (AD 1617-1637) of baktun 12: Expansion of Sweden and the participation of the Nordic countries in the Thirty Year's War. The beginning of the colonization of North America by the English Pilgrims and expansion of Russia through Siberia to the Pacific Ocean.

which raged between Catholics and Protestants. As part of this scenario, Sweden in the north turned into a major European power. In the year 1617 its King Gustavus Adolphus seized the Baltic coast of Russia, followed by present-day Latvia and parts of Prussia from Poland. A small expansion in the westward direction was also evident in the founding of a colony in North America in 1638. Thus, baktun 12 also began with movements from the midline. Sweden, of which Finland was at the time also a part, came to play the decisive role in asserting the Protestant creed due to its intervention in the second half of the Thirty Years' War. The result of its alliance with France and the Dutch struggle of independence from the Spanish crown was the de facto collapse of the German-Roman Empire.

Concurrently with this Swedish expansion directly from the midline, the British and Dutch colonizations of North America, which would later provide the foundation for the United States, began. Simultaneously, the Sioux, Arapaho and Cheyenne peoples moved west into the Great Plains and displaced the peoples that had previously been living there. An expansion eastward from Europe also started at the beginning of baktun 12, as the Russians, after having ousted the Mongols about a century earlier, founded several cities in Siberia and reached the Pacific Ocean in 1639. The latter two examples especially show that at great distances from Europe movements took place at this time that emanated from the midline.

Summarizing the various movements from and toward the planetary midline at the baktun shifts of the Great Cycle reveals a fairly clear pattern, presented in Table 4. There we can see that movements from the planetary midline toward the East and West initiate baktuns with even numbers whereas movements from the East toward the midline initiate baktuns with odd numbers. The Mayan notion that different time cycles, and the various corresponding Heavens, have different characteristics—expressed as if different deities ruled them—now begins to make sense. Judging from the pattern of violent migrations presented in Table 4, it thus seems as the seven baktuns with even numbers are ruled by divine forces that are somehow different from those that rule the six baktuns with odd numbers.

Table 4
Violent Migratory Movements from and toward the Planetary Midline
at the Beginnings of the Later Baktuns of the Great Cycle

Baktun 6	Settling of Rome	
Baktun 7		<--- Persians
Baktun 8	<--- Roman Empire --->	
Baktun 9		<--- Huns
Baktun 10	<--- Vikings --->	
Baktun 11		<---- Mongols
Baktun 12	<---Sweden--->	

In addition to these movements to and from the midline in the western and eastern directions, history seems with every new even-numbered baktun to move north, at least from what we can see in the Northern Hemisphere. Thus, it moves from a southern location in Egypt, Sumer and Crete at the beginning of the Great Cycle to Greece and Rome during baktuns 6 and 8 and to Germany during baktun 10. Typically, Denmark becomes a great power during baktun 10, whereas Sweden, even further to the north, becomes one at the beginning of baktun 12. This movement north of the center of gravitation of history is paralleled in other parts of the world. In the Americas it moved from Chiapas and Guatemala during baktuns 8 and 9 to Yucatan during baktun 10, to the Aztecs in central Mexico during baktun 11 and to North America during baktun 12.

Although it has not been detailed here the history of nations such as England and the Netherlands that are located clearly west of the midline is very clearly affected by this wave-like pattern, with their attentions alternating between East and West at baktun shifts.

THE INVISIBLE CROSS

How is this pattern of directional movements at the baktun shifts of the Great Cycle to be explained? It can be explained if we postulate that a Cross of invisible boundaries is introduced in the creation field, i.e. the Heaven of the earth, as each new baktun with an even number starts. This Cross of creation field boundaries introduces a creative tension along the lines where it is introduced, and this creative tension results in, among other things, migratory movements of peoples away from these lines. Thus, at the beginning of even-numbered baktuns there is movement north from the equator as well as from the planetary midline in both the eastern and the western directions. In contrast, as the Cross disappears at the beginning of odd-numbered baktuns, movements will be directed toward the planetary midline.

Judging from the migratory movements we have been tracking through this progression of Heavens, the arms of this Cross, which dominate the even-numbered baktuns, seem to go through the 12th longitude East and the equator. The arm that divides the planet into a Western and an Eastern Hemisphere goes through Rome and Copenhagen, whereas the equator separates the Northern and Southern Hemispheres. If we accept that the creation field of this planet fundamentally is organized in this way we must conclude that the center of the Cross is located in central Africa, in what is currently Gabon. And, as we shall see, if we accept this view the history of mankind becomes much easier to understand.

Each of the 13 baktuns thus seems to correspond to a specific creation field, what we have previously identified with a Heaven in the Mayan cosmology. The earth may thus be seen as anchoring a consciousness field, or matrix for creation, where the effects of these Heavens, including pulsating movements back and forth, are manifested. The creation fields of baktuns with even numbers are characterized by a marked difference in mentality between East and West. In contrast, the Heavens of the baktuns with odd numbers favor East-West contacts and result in a more unified consciousness without distinctive lines separating that of the West from that of the East. The two basic types of Heavens, or creation fields, corresponding to even- and odd-numbered baktuns, respectively, are shown in Figures 15a and b.

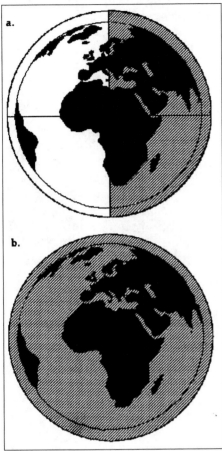

Fig. 15

(a) The global creation field with its boundaries and Yin/Yang-duality during the even-numbered baktuns of the Great Cycle.

(b) The global creation field during the odd-numbered baktuns of the Great Cycle.

If this pattern is so obvious, somebody may then object, why has it not been discovered earlier? The answer is that nobody has previously studied European history with the Mayan calendar as a template, and in the absence of this map of time a pattern cannot easily be discovered. The Gregorian calendar, based on the physical year, that we are still using, predisposes us to a materialist thinking that blinds us to the true nature of Creation and its inherent rhythm of evolution. In fact, its use keeps us from understanding the true nature of God. Another reason that this pattern has not been noticed before is that it develops according to a rhythm that is slow in comparison to a human life span. A person living forty years or so would only very vaguely experience waves of history with a periodicity of 394 years. Yet, at the intensive changes around baktun shifts several of the actors in this drama of history have seen themselves as acting on behalf of the will of God. Perhaps the strength of the winds of history have created in them a sense of a divine origin of these winds and made them see themselves as servants of these.

The history of humanity as it has developed through the Thirteen Heavens of the Great Cycle may then truly be described as a wave pattern, and this is meant in a literal sense. A wave-like movement results from the introductions of the Cross at the beginning of even-numbered baktuns. These create wave-like alternations between dualistic and unitary Heavens in a progression that starts with duality, passes through unity and in a few rounds recreates duality at a higher level. The result of these shifts in the creation field of the earth is the cosmic drama which appears to be enacted by the forces of the West and the East, male and female, yang and yin or LIGHT and DARKNESS (Figure 15). Such a notion of a drama involving the male and the female forces of the Cosmos, recognizing both separation and unity between the two, is shared by many ancient philosophies, although that of the Chinese may have become the best known. The adventures of the Mayan Hero Twins, Hunahpu and Xbalanque of the *Popol-Vuh*, are, however, metaphors for the same thing. The fundamental truth that the consciousness field of the earth has the basic structure in Figure 15a seems to have been known by all ancient peoples. This is evident, for example, from the Sun Wheel (Figure 16), sometimes called the Cross of Vuotan, the father god of the Germanic peoples.

Fig. 16 Bronze Age Sun Wheels from tomb in Kivik, Skåne, Sweden (Bob G. Lind, *Ales stenar*).

It now makes sense that Quetzalcoatl and Tezcatlipoca similarly are symbols of the yang and yin that dominate the polarized field of the even-numbered baktuns in Figure 15a. Not surprisingly then, in the cosmology of the Aztecs, Quetzalcoatl—the White Tezcatlipoca—was associated with the West. This deity was known to have disappeared in the East toward the end of baktun 10, and because a unitary field with no LIGHT in the Western Hemisphere ruled during baktun 11 he remained hidden. Maybe we are narrowing in on the enigma of Quetzalcoatl.

The use of the Mayan chronology puts almost everything in a different perspective. No longer does the yin/yang cosmology appear as merely an abstract philosophical principle. Instead, in light of the exact determinations of the time periods which condition the pulsating drama described by the baktuns of the Great Cycle it becomes clear that the yin/yang cosmology has a real foundation. This foundation is provided by a wave pattern, which is a very useful tool for understanding the evolution of human history. Using the Mayan Great Cycle we can now in fact study how yin and yang manifest themselves in the physical world. All that is needed to understand the wave-like process of history and the ensuing play of yin and yang is to accept the existence of a Holy Cross serving as an all-encompassing wave generator operating according to a rhythm provided by the Great Cycle. After all, all wave-like movements and vibrations need a wave generator.

Fig. 17 a & b
Christian Crosses:

a - *Above left:*
Early Celtic Cross;

b - *Right:*
Golgatha Cross. From the Church of Falun
(photos Calleman).

Is this Cross then the same as the World Tree that played such an important role in Mayan myth? Well, the Classical Maya are not here for us to ask. Yet we do know that according to their Creation myths the World Tree had been raised at the beginning of baktun 0, the first of the even-numbered baktuns. Since we have indeed found that it is during these even-numbered baktuns that this invisible Cross dominates the creation field of the earth (Figure 15a), it does make perfect sense that this Cross is identical to the World Tree (Figure 7). At the beginning of the Great Cycle, history began as the First Father raised the World Tree at its first even-numbered baktun. It is difficult to see that something other than this Cross would generate such a strong spiritual experience of the four directions of the world emanating from the World Tree.

We may now ponder the symbol of the cross. In general, the cross has come to be seen as a Christian symbol reminding us of the crucifixion of Jesus, and in the minds of billions of people this is what it symbolizes (Figure 17b). Yet, the cross has been used as the Sun Wheel symbol by almost all cultures of this planet since about the time of the beginning of the Great Cycle. And not even in the Christian religion is the cross such an unambiguous symbol of the Golgotha cross as it would at first sight seem. In Christian myth the idea of the cross as a symbol of the World Tree is actually present too. It is said, for instance, that the cross upon which Jesus was crucified was made out of the first tree, the Tree of Life of the Garden of Eden, which was the Jewish equivalent of the World Tree.

Therefore, the crucifix has sometimes been adorned by leaves to symbolize that this cross comes from the Tree of Life, and, especially in early medieval times, Christian crosses were often balanced (Figure 17a) and more reminiscent of the age-

Fig. 18 Saint Menas to the left and Jesus to the right with a cross in his glory. Coptic icon (Louvre, Paris).

old Sun Wheel than the Golgotha cross. Sometimes such a balanced cross, which looks more like the creation field boundaries in Figure 15a, is even part of the glory of Christ (Figure 18).

Thus, in certain ways the Mayan and the Christian myths seem to be pointing in the same direction. Considering that the crucifixion of Jesus occurred at approximately the same time (Figure 10) that a new Cross of consciousness boundaries was raised, it seems likely that the reality underlying the Mayan and Christian Crosses and World Trees is the same, namely, the invisible Cross ruling the even-numbered baktuns. In the New Testament there is in fact also an indication that Jesus, as he speaks to an audience about the need to choose sides— '. . . and those who do not take their cross and follow me. . .' (*Matthew 10:34*) —was aware of the existence of such a Cross introducing dualities.

Given what we have discovered regarding the existence of a True Cross ruling the Heavens, we may wonder to what extent Christianity has derived its power from this Cross, considering that the creative tension it induces affects everyone on the planet. To what extent could it have been an advantage for the Catholic church to have its center located in Rome exactly under this Cross, and to what extent have its interests been confounded with the power of the True Cross? Similarly, we may wonder how the Lutheran and Calvinist churches, which also originated from the arm of the True Cross, have benefitted from this. These are important questions to ask, and regardless of the answers that we give to them it will probably serve everyone to be aware of the existence of a True Cross, the Creator duality that shapes the human consciousness.

This study of the Cross represents the beginning of a more tangible study of how divine archetypes influence human consciousness. On the level of consciousness the

Cross of Vuotan is thus real, and is not an arbitrarily designed symbol. As mentioned, the Sun Wheel, used also by Native Americans as the Medicine Wheel and by astrologers to symbolize planet earth, became widespread as a symbol about five thousand years ago. The reason the Cross ever since has been expressed in symbols and myths is that human beings then gained an intuitive awareness of its existence in the beyond as the First Father raised the World Tree at the beginning of the Great Cycle. There may be innumerable other archetypes with a real existence in the Heavens, yet the Cross is probably the most important of all archetypes since it creates our sense of orientation in the world and has become especially powerfully felt. Through our resonance with it, it has become imprinted on the consciousness of human beings in a pulse-like way during the even-numbered Heavens. Without the Cross life would totally lack structure.

The ancients expressed their insights through myths, such as that of the World Tree, while we who live today mostly describe the world through science, or at least think we do. Myths are, however, not inherently less true than our current science. Myths and science, in this case historical science, are views of the same reality seen through different filters, different frames of consciousness, corresponding, as we shall see later, to distinctly different Underworlds. Today, ancient myths may actually serve as guidance for us into the future, because those myths that are true will correspond to a deeper and more spiritual frame of consciousness, where the whole universe is seen as alive and divinely inspired. Most of this mythological frame of consciousness and its symbolism was created by the Thirteen Heavens of the Great Cycle.

On the other hand, I feel it should be said that if we do not have backup in empirical fact, i.e., modern science, for our interpretations of myths our conclusions might end up anywhere (and, incidentally, in today's New Age literature they often do!). The amount of facts generated by our current science is vastly more extensive and exact than those possessed by our predecessors. We simply know more than they did, and only if we can find backup for ancient myths in the empirical facts of modern science can they truly serve as guidance for our future. Yet the knowledge base of modern science has become so fragmented that in the absence of ancient myth it is almost impossible to make use of it for the creation of a world view that is truly whole. Only if we can unify the two perspectives, that of science and that of myth, into a coherent view, which at the same time is true and magical, will we be ready for the future and the next, even more expanded, frame of consciousness.

CHAPTER 4
THE HERMETIC PRINCIPLE:
AS ABOVE, SO BELOW

The idea that what goes on on earth is a reflection of what goes on in the Heavens, at higher hierarchical levels of the universe, is an age-old principle—'As above, so below'—that is usually associated with the Hermetic tradition. This way of thinking dominated all ancient civilizations, but it has also been revived in the modern idea that we are living in a holographic universe where every component of the universe reflects, and in some sense includes, the universe as a whole. That what happens in our individual lives ('Below') is a reflection of what happens 'Above' has also become a common everyday philosophy of the last decade of the twentieth century. Although we may rationalize this correspondence differently, many now feel guided or directed by forces Above which make certain things Below 'meant to happen' and others 'not meant to happen.' Influenced by Western astrology, many have in recent decades interpreted the course of events on earth as if it in some sense was caused by the planets or the stars and have taken the celestial bodies to mean the Above or the Heavens. The Thirteen Heavens that are described here are, however, not caused by the planets or anything else that is physical. Planetary movements can only explain cyclical, repeating phenomena, but not evolution. Thus, they cannot explain the irreversible climbing to higher frames of consciousness that is the hallmark of the divine process of creation.

What then might the invisible Cross Above, with a powerful presence in every other Heaven of the Great Cycle, serve to explain Below? How does it make certain things 'meant to happen' and others not? How does the Cross influence the thinking of individual human beings? To exemplify these matters we will look especially at the Thirteenth Heaven of the Great Cycle, the one that came to rule at the beginning of baktun 12, the baktun we are still living in. The events that marked the beginning of this baktun—the Thirty Years' War, the scientific revolution and the birth of the modern nation-state—set the stage for the whole era to come. We will thus look at these phenomena in some more detail and see how they are related to one another and above all how they are related to the dominance of the Cross of this particular Heaven.

To begin with we may notice that it was simultaneously with the Swedish expansion from the midline, and its intervention in the Thirty Years' War (1618-1648), that with Kepler and Galileo the scientific revolution began—also at the midline. What is the connection? We may recall that in the Mayan view of the World Tree it was its branches that bore fruit. And indeed it was along one of these branches, the planetary midline, that the scientific revolution began, in Prague and Florence, as the Thirteenth Heaven of the Great Cycle was raised. Both phenomena, the expansion from the midline and the new ways of thinking, were effects of the Cross being raised at the beginning of baktun 12. Yet these effects manifested at two different levels: the military expansion from the midline on the level of the planetary creation field and the scientific revolution at the level of the human individual in resonance with this field. It seems logical that this new dualistic creation field would in some ways lead individuals in resonance with it to experience a separation between the two hemispheres of their brains, thus resulting in new ways of thinking.

THE SCIENTIFIC REVOLUTION

Thus, people—and especially those living in the Western Hemisphere—would begin to use their left brain halves—with their faculties of mathematical computation, sequential logic and verbal expression—in a new way at this baktun shift. The first fruits of this would ripen at the midline. But the new way of analytical thinking would later move west, through the France of Descartes (who, as an aside, invented the coordinate system of mathematics at the same time as the planet became dominated by the coordinate system of the Cross) to the England of Isaac Newton, where the effects of the new duality were very markedly seen. As the baktun drew to a close, the focal point of the scientific thinking generated by the yin/yang duality of the Thirteenth Heaven eventually moved all the way west to the United States.

The Cross introduced during the even-numbered baktuns of the Great Cycle creates a duality where more divine LIGHT falls on the Western Hemisphere (Figure 15a), and for this reason breakthroughs in science have taken place almost exclusively in this hemisphere. The LIGHT falling on the Western Hemisphere favored capacities—mathematics and analytical thinking—of the left brain half in resonance with this hemisphere. Since it is along the vertical arm of this that the duality between LIGHT and DARKNESS, or between Quetzalcoatl and Tezcatlipoca, gives rise to a tension seeking creative resolution, such breakthroughs were initially expressed through individuals located in a favorable position for being in resonance with the branches of the Cross. It is no wonder then that among the Aztecs, Quetzalcoatl, the Western principle of LIGHT of the Creator duality, was seen as having given rise to culture.

The LIGHT/DARKNESS duality that these early pioneers of science came to resonate with made them aware of new distinctions between the material and the spiritual aspects of reality and this in fact became the key to their success. Prior to the beginning of baktun 12, and especially toward the end of the sixteenth century, astrology had in Europe been the dominating focus of the study of celestial movements. The interest was in the spiritual qualities that the planets might possess and in the predictions of earthly events that could be made from their positions. In fact, to treat the planets as physical objects whose orbits could be described by exact mathematical laws would not really be consistent with this earlier view of the planets as spiritual entities, or even intervening deities, affecting the lives of human beings.

As the Heaven of baktun 12 began to dominate, a sharp mental distinction was introduced between the physical and the spiritual in people in resonance with this Heaven and its duality between LIGHT and DARKNESS. As a result of this, the early pioneers of science were able to distinguish the material aspects of reality from the spiritual, and hence they were able to formulate the mathematical laws that describe the planetary orbits and most importantly the law of gravitation, which crowned this development. What the early pioneers did was to look upon the planets with a new distinction between the spiritual and the material, a distinction that would prove crucial for the later development of science and technology and man's control of the material world. By regarding the planets exclusively as material objects with the measurable property of mass, and disregarding any possible spiritual influences on their part, the mathematical laws governing their behavior became evident. Despite all the loose, and mostly non-empirical, discussions of a 'new physics' during the twentieth century, Newton's laws are still applied in all practical applications of mechanics. The airplanes we sit in and the space probes we launch are still built in accordance with the science that was developed as a result of the distinction between spirit and matter that emerged at the beginning of baktun 12.

In a way what I am doing here is reasserting the existence of Newton's absolute space and time. Though maybe not in exactly the way he thought of it, our studies seem to imply the existence of an invisible spiritual reality manifested most evidently in the Cross, defining four directions which provided the coordinates of an absolute space. The idea that there exists an absolute space and an absolute time independent of matter has, however, now largely been lost, largely because of Albert Einstein's theory of relativity and the materialist bias of many other of today's physicists. But in the Mayan view, the only thing that really exists—in the sense of having an eternal reality—is the World Tree, and the visible physical manifestations of this are only secondary. In this we may find support, from an unexpected direction, for Newton's idea of an absolute space.

We may also find support for Newton's concept of an absolute time. Newton's absolute time is the time of the invisible universe, time which exists independently of any physical movements, and what we are studying here is indeed the time of the invisible universe. The time of the invisible universe is described by the tun-based system of the Maya, segments of time hanging on the branches of the World Tree, as they saw it. The tun-based calendars describe the alternations between different Heavens in the invisible universe. True absolute time is the time of the invisible universe, generated by the vibrations of the True Cross, and the purpose of a true calendar is thus to describe the vibrations of this Cross and the periodic alternations between Heavens that it causes. All calendars reflecting the periodicity of the physical objects in the visible universe are only secondary in nature, and as we shall see later they are imperfect reflections of the vibrations of the Cross. Thus, at closer thought it may be realized that calendars based on astronomical cycles are only approximations of those based on the invisible Cross.

It would, however, be a mistake to think of the early pioneers of the scientific revolution as materialists. They were aware of a divine reality, such as that of an absolute space and time, beyond the material manifestations of Creation, and sought to express this in their theories. What was behind their endeavors was a desire to show that there is a divine plan behind the human existence, and it was to provide evidence of such a plan that they sought to establish mathematical laws to describe the physical movements. The ambition of Kepler in his *De Harmonice Mundi* was to demonstrate the underlying harmonies in the celestial movements, and that of Newton when he mathematically described a clockwork model of the universe was to prove the existence of God.

Rather than as materialists, the scientists of the beginning of baktun 12 may be qualified as dualists. The philosophy developed by Descartes, for instance, has often been referred to as dualistic, since it made a clear distinction between the body and the soul, the spiritual and the physical. From our current perspective, we can now see that this philosophy had its origin in the new duality generated as the True Cross raised the Thirteenth Heaven of the Great Cycle. Only later, in the mid eighteenth century and onwards, did this dualism develop into the notion that the human soul and God do not exist. To this idea we will return in Chapter 9.

Of course, I should also add that the equatorial arm of the Cross has had an effect on the mentality of human beings in resonance with it. As with every even-numbered baktun, when the leading edge of civilization has shifted north to the Northern Hemisphere, a corresponding shift in mentality has taken place all over the planet. This has led from the more primal, earthly, emotional levels of experience linked to the cerebellum to the more intellectual level associated with the cortex and the front lobes of the brain. This change in mentality may also be tracked through the baktuns of the Great Cycle.

THE FALL OF DIVINE RULERS

The distinction between the physical and the spiritual that humans became more clearly aware of at the beginning of baktun 12 also had very immediate effects on politics and religion. It is in this perspective we may see the outcome of the Thirty Years' War, which marked the survival of the Protestant faith, the collapse of the German-Roman Empire and the emergence of the modern nation-state. Although Luther and Calvin had formulated the Protestant creed already a hundred years earlier, it was only after the Thirty Years' War that its survival was guaranteed. Yet the outcome of the Thirty Years' War should not be seen so much as a defeat for the Catholic church as it was for the German-Roman Empire, the guarantor of the political power of the Papacy.

The Holy Roman Empire had, at the initiative of the Pope, been instituted about two baktuns earlier. Through the mediation of the Pope, the power of its ruler had thus been seen as legitimized by God. The collapse of this empire in fact meant the completion of a process—the separation of the spiritual power of the rulers from the world—that had begun already at the beginning of the Great Cycle. Hence, if we track this separation from the beginning of baktun 0 and forward, we find that early rulers such as the pharaohs would be recognized by their subjects, and presumably also by themselves, as man-gods whose worldly power purportedly was based on a divine origin. Gradually, however, the rulers of the early civilizations of the Great Cycle became recognized as human beings. The powerful Persian kings ruling around the very midpoint of the Great Cycle (baktun 6) would, for instance, unlike the pharaohs, not present themselves as gods, but as the representatives of these on earth. Later, although the Roman emperors in baktun 8 still sought to develop a cult around themselves as divine, this cult generated conflicts with the Jews in the eastern provinces of the empire, and in the western provinces it is questionable how many ever believed in it. Toward the end of baktun 8 the emperors had to acknowledge Christianity as the spiritual arm of the empire in the hope of obtaining some otherworldly legitimacy. The price they had to pay was to give up their own claims to divinity. So when the German-Roman emperors became the most important rulers in Europe in baktun 10, the process of secularization of imperial rule had come to a point where these presented no claims to being gods themselves. Instead, they based their legitimacy on the spiritual endorsement of the Papacy, proclaimed as the earthly representative of Jesus Christ. Finally then, at the beginning of baktun 12 the power of these emperors was broken and no longer could rulers claim to be legitimized by the divine. The monarchs that emerged as the modern nation-state came into existence during the first decades of baktun 12 ruled 'by the Grace of God.' Thus they were then considered as purely human.

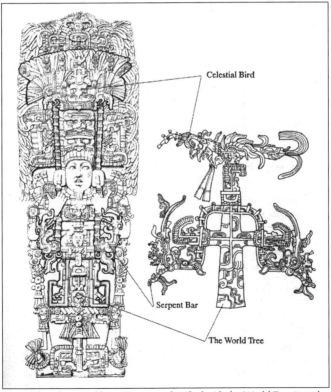

Fig. 19 The ruler 18-Rabbit at Copan as identified with the World Tree (see also Fig. 5) (Courtesy Schele and Freidel, *A Forest of Kings*).

What was behind this long process? What I would like to suggest is the workings of the True Cross, which pulse by pulse with every even-numbered baktun created a distinction between the physical nature of human beings and the spiritual nature of the divine. The increasingly strong presence of the Cross tended to locate, in the minds of people, the source of divine power in the otherworldly, invisible realm rather than among their rulers. The collapse of the Holy Roman Empire, marking the completion of the whole process, thus ultimately came about as a result of the new distinction between spiritual and material generated in the minds of people in resonance with the new Cross that was raised at the beginning of baktun 12. Under the Heaven of this baktun, the worldly power of the rulers could no longer be based on a presumed spiritual legitimacy. By resonance with the duality of the Cross people at large began to be able to see this. Hence, the reason the institution of the Holy Roman Empire lost its power at this last baktun shift was that the new distinction between the material and the spiritual then came to dominate the minds of people. This is a parallel phenomenon to the scientific revolution which, however, is only expressed in another way.

This process in the Heavens, creating a corresponding distinction between the material and the spiritual in the human mind, to no small degree also affected the power of the Mayan rulers, the ahauob, who were portrayed as divine personifications of the Cosmos. The institution of divine kingship arose among the Maya during baktun 8 and was thus contemporary with the Roman Empire, whose rulers also sought, although with some difficulty, to present themselves as divine. The rule of the ahauob, however, lasted until the beginning of baktun 10. Then, as the Cross at this baktun shift was again introduced on a planetary scale, the Classical Mayan culture collapsed. Of course, it may be possible to find superficial materialist explanations for this collapse such as warfare, epidemics or invasions and, indeed, such scenarios may very well have been among the immediate causes of the cultural demise. But if we recognize the divine plan generating Heavens that humans are in resonance with as the primary factor behind the evolution of human consciousness, then these immediate causes are somewhat beside the point, only serving to bring about, in one way or another, what was meant to happen anyway. If consciousness is primary to matter, then whatever happened on the physical level is only secondary. At a more basic spiritual level the reason the southern Mayan cities collapsed was that the Cross at the beginning of baktun 10 introduced a distinction between physical and spiritual which no longer allowed the shaman kings to portray themselves as divine. For rulers who were identifying themselves with the World Tree (see Figure 19), the rise of the True World Tree, with a new distinction between the spiritual and the physical, could only have catastrophic consequences. They were standing right at the cross hairs of the new dualistic vision of their subjects. Their false claims of divinity would directly clash with the new vision that was gained by their subjects at this particular time. If the divine personifications of the Cosmos, the ahauob, which had been the unifying centers of the Classical Mayan city-states, lost their spiritual power, then the collapse of their culture only becomes a logical consequence. Adding to these problems was the fact that the arm of the Cross going through the equator then pushed history north across the globe, leading to the collapse of many tropical civilizations.

The Mayan culture that emerged on the northern Yucatan peninsula in Chichen-Itza and other places at the beginning of baktun 10 apparently had a very different political system as compared to the earlier southern sites. There it is very difficult to find stone lintels depicting rulers, let alone divine rulers, and it seems that the rulers of this later Mayan culture wisely chose a much less visible role in the lives of their cities. Archaeologists suggest that the many sculptures and temples dedicated to the Supreme Plumed Serpent, Kukulcan, in Chichen-Itza signify that it was now the political power of the state itself, rather than that of its rulers, that was legitimized by the cult of the Plumed Serpent. In the consciousness of the new distinctions generated by the Cross during baktun 10 such a system of rule would stand a better chance of surviving than that of the ahauob. This would be a parallel to how in Europe the German-Roman emperors emerging at the beginning of baktun 10, in contrast to their Roman predecessors of baktun 8, could no longer present themselves as divine and had to subordinate themselves to the institutions of Christianity.

THE BIRTH OF THE MODERN NATION-STATE

The Westphalian Peace Treaty, which concluded the Thirty Years' War, had some very significant facets, making it more than just another treaty. First of all, it recognized the sovereignty principle according to which all European nations were recognized as sovereign, and this is by many seen as the birth of the modern nation-state. Above all, this sovereignty meant that the signatory powers recognized the right of all nations to decide without outside interference what Christian creed they would belong to. Thus all nations in the European context were now in principle recognized as equals, and this had been negotiated by the world's first international conference. The very existence of an international conference was a sign that the modern nation had then been born since the existence of international relations presupposes the existence of mature nations that would engage in such. Another contemporary aspect of this was the work of the Dutch thinker Hugo Grotius on international relations. The whole notion of international relations presupposes the existence of mature nations.

In the years leading up to this treaty several nations, especially in northern and northwestern Europe, which represented the edge of the development at the time, had already introduced significant changes in government. This meant that a national continuity was established, a continuity that would prevail irrespective of the dynasty that happened to rule these nations at any given time. A fundamental shift thus took place in which the monarch came to be regarded as belonging to the nation rather than the other way around, reflecting the completion of the fall of divine rulers.

We may take national archives as an example of this. Sweden's national archives, instituted in 1618, are generally recognized as the world's first. Yet, as we know, even in the ancient days of Sumer, Assyria and Babylon the rulers would have archives to keep records of most dealings of the state and the court, such as taxes, soldiers, agreements and treaties. These archives were, however, the private possessions of the rulers and their dynasties, and they would typically be destroyed as these rulers and the capitals they had built fell. The national archives of baktun 12, however, served not the continuity of a ruling dynasty, but that of a nation, and they would thus remain in existence even as dynasties and forms of government would undergo significant change.

Ultimately all of these changes were conditioned by the raising of the True Cross at the beginning of baktun 12, since, in the new duality this created, much of the previous power of the monarchs would be seen as usurpations of divine power. England and the Netherlands, located in the West, and maybe especially influenced by the new Light, at least temporarily established a republican rule. It was, however, only later, in the next Underworld, the Planetary Underworld, that the republican road would be that taken by the majority of the nations of the world. The purpose of the Great Cycle was different. It was to develop the nation as the frame of human consciousness, that is, as the largest whole that human beings would see themselves as belonging to. Following its establishment at the beginning of baktun 12, the nation-state has then, largely due to the expanding effects of the True Cross, been spread across the world. With the independence of Namibia in 1990 all peoples of the world, with only a few tiny exceptions, have become organized in sovereign nations.

The modern nation was thus created by the Thirteenth Heaven of the Great Cycle, which was the most advanced result of a development that had began under its First Heaven, as Pharaoh Menes founded the very first nation about five thousand years earlier. As a result of this process the role of the rulers has markedly changed, and one of the long-term developments of this creation is that it is going in the direction of no human having power over another human being. But for this, it seems we still have some way to go.

One more thing should be considered here regarding the effects of the creation field boundary that was introduced between East and West at the beginning of baktun 12. Because of the LIGHT/DARKNESS duality it entailed, the vertical arm of the Cross created a marked difference between the cultures of the West and the East, a difference that contrasted with the unified field during baktun 11. This East/West distinction generated its most extreme expressions during the Cold War in the latter part of the twentieth century, when regular contacts even between neighboring countries on both sides of the Iron Curtain (essentially coinciding with the vertical arm of the Cross) were shut down. Since our present baktun had been initiated by the introduction of an invisible boundary between East and West (Figures 14 and 15a), it is not very surprising that, as we began to approach the close of the baktun, the Cold War has now come to an end. Thus, the Berlin Wall, a physical manifestation of this midline, fell, and at this point in time (2000), the world again constitutes a unified whole without insurmountable lines of division.

CHAPTER 5
HISTORY OF THE HOLY CROSS:
THE EVOLUTION OF THE HUMAN RELIGIONS

The great religions of humanity have been greatly influenced by the existence of the Holy Cross, to the point where one might say that this is the most important factor that has determined the particular forms they have taken. The human perception of the divine is seen through the filter of a creation field that is organized by the Cross, and so the theologies and religions of humanity have been profoundly influenced by regional differences in resonance with the Cross. Where we live in relation to the arms of the Cross, in other words, influences how we perceive the divine reality. In addition to this, all kinds of particular and individual human interests, as well as power and greed, have mixed in with the formulation of the historical religions. These religions have, for instance, played a very important role, as we have already seen, in giving power to worldly rulers during the Great Cycle, and in this worldly considerations have certainly played an important part. Already in this we may see that other factors than the pure quest for the truth have shaped religions, but the particular LIGHT/DARKNESS duality generated by the Cross has also made it more difficult to see the truth in some places than in others.

THE CHALDEAN-JEWISH-CHRISTIAN TRADITION

Our study of the influence of the Thirteen Heavens on the evolution of the human religions will begin with the tradition that has attracted the largest number of professed adherents. This is the Chaldean-Jewish-Christian tradition, which during the course of baktun 12 has come to be entirely dominant in the Western Hemisphere. In Table 5 this is described as the tradition of the Center, although this tradition originated somewhat east of there.

Table 5
The Evolution of the Human Religions during
the Even-numbered Baktuns of the Great Cycle

West		Center		East
baktun 0 (3115 BC)		Sumer's Anu		
baktun 2 (2326 BC)		Abraham's move to Cana (2300)		

baktun 4 (1538 BC)		Moses (1480)		Traditional (Shang)
baktun 6 (749 BC) Zapotec Tzolkin (550)		Isaiah (748) Deutero-Isaiah (550) Pythagoras (550)		Confucius (551) Zoroaster (550) Lao-Tsu (600) Buddha (552) Reincarnation in India
baktun 8 (AD 40) Quetzalcoatl Teotihuacan		Jesus/Paul (33/37) Christianity, Talmudic Judaism		Buddhism in China (60)
	baktun 9		Islam (632)	
baktun 10 (AD 829) Second Quetzalcoatl in Chichen-Itza		Expansion of Christianity to northern, eastern Europe Crusades, Papacy		
	baktun 11		Second wave of Islam	
baktun 12 (AD 1617)		Expansion of Christianity (Pilgrims 1620)		

In tracking this we will concentrate on the even-numbered baktuns, whose beginnings are most markedly influenced by the raising of the True Cross. As far as we know, the notion of an omnipotent Creator God first emerged in baktun 0 of the Great Cycle. Already at this early time the Sumerians seem to have worshiped an omnipotent God of Heaven who went by the name of An, or Anu. In ancient Sumer this Creator God, however, had to share his place with a number of gods such as harvest gods, house gods, city gods and many others that were seen as animating the material aspects of existence.

Fig. 20 Mayan cross including a balanced cross of flowers (Courtesy Freidel, Schele and Parker, *Maya Cosmos*).

As we may read from the Biblical patriarchs living in baktun 2, who brought the belief in this Creator God from Chaldea to Cana, it seems that the extended pantheon of the Sumerians had then lost much of its previous role. Yet this belief was not stronger than that even two baktuns later, many would worship the Golden Calf on the way back from the desert. It was thus only with Moses in baktun 4, and the Ten Commandments that he brought to the Jews as a message from God, that a consistent monotheistic creed emerged on this planet. The first of these Ten Commandments is 'Thou shalt have no other Gods before me' *(Exodus 20:3)*. Although this expressed a purely monotheistic creed it was limited in that it seemed to apply only to the Jewish people. God was seen as the God of the Jews, and at the time it was hardly a concern of the Jews whether other people would believe in Him or not. 'Thou' in the First Commandment refers to the Jews, who were seen as a people chosen by God. Also in Egypt, in a short interlude during this baktun 4, Pharaoh Achnaton would introduce the notion of one God, which was to be expressed in the worship of Aton, the sun disc.

The idea of God being exclusively the God of the Jews did not begin to change until the beginning of baktun 6, as the great Jewish prophets—Isaiah, Amos and Hosea—began to teach. In the first year of this, the seventh of the 13 baktuns, the prophet Isaiah was called (748 BC) to his mission. Isaiah, who in the Jewish tradition is considered the foremost of the prophets next to Moses, and plays a crucial role in the Christian tradition as well, taught that God was using invading peoples, such as the Egyptians and Assyrians, to punish the Jews for their ungodly ways. This would then mean that the God of the Jews was seen as ruling other peoples also and hence also the course of history of the world. In the second part of the *Book of Isaiah*, believed to have been written by another prophet usually referred to as deutero-Isaiah (the second Isaiah), who lived around 550 BC at the very midpoint of baktun 6 of the whole Great Cycle of the Maya, this change in thinking was brought to its full consequences. Deutero-Isaiah taught that, although the Jews were special in the eyes of God, He is nevertheless the God of all human beings. Deutero-Isaiah also suggested that the Jews had a mission to spread the word of God to other peoples. At the time, however, this call was not much heeded and Judaism never became a proselytizing religion.

Although some may not yet have grasped it, I see this insight—that there is but one God who is the God of all humanity—as the most fundamental insight of the Great Cycle, the very core of the particular consciousness it carries. Although the Chaldean-Jewish-Christian tradition would undergo change as the Great Cycle progressed through its later baktuns, this would remain its most fundamental truth.

And we should note that this universalistic creed in God was first expressed at the midpoint of baktun 6, which in fact is the midpoint of the entire Great Cycle.

What happened at the beginning of baktun 8 has already been briefly discussed. Christianity split off from Judaism and started to spread across the world. There are some distinct differences between the Christian and the Jewish faiths that contributed to this split. The Christians emphasized forgiveness as compared to the ancient idea of 'an eye for an eye . . .', practiced not only by the Jews, but also everywhere else in earlier days. Jesus Christ also taught that at the end of time there would be a Kingdom of God where people would have eternal life, and this Kingdom was where the human soul was meant to go. Probably the idea that life on earth has a purpose and that history is going somewhere had not previously been stated as clearly as it came to be in the New Testament.

Other than this, the nature of the faith became universalistic, not only in theory, but also in practice. The Christians broke with the idea that in order to embrace this new faith you needed to be an ethnic Jew and, as a sign of this, be circumcised and follow the Mosaic Law in all of its details. Jesus said: 'Go ye therefore, and teach all nations . . .' *(Matthew 28:19)*. Christianity thus became not only a universalistic but also a proselytizing religion, which aspired to be embraced by the whole world. As a step toward this a parish had already formed in Rome, on the planetary midline, in the 40s. Highly symbolic of this shift of the geographic center of the monotheistic tradition is the destruction by Roman soldiers of the Temple of Jerusalem in AD 70. After this, the menorah, the seven-armed candelabra symbolic of God's Creation in seven DAYS and six NIGHTS, was carried to Rome in triumph. Not only had Christianity already from the very start of baktun 8 implanted itself under the vertical arm of the Cross, the holy center of the old Judaic faith was also destroyed and the symbol of the divine process of Creation taken from Israel to Rome. There, the institution of the Papacy would emerge, and throughout baktun 8 the following of the Christian faith, and the political power of its church, would only continue to increase. Toward the end of the baktun Christianity became the state religion of the Roman Empire, and in its latter half the Bible would be canonized in its present form and kept as a testimony to future generations.

During the Dark Ages of baktun 9 the leading role of the Papacy would, however, come to be challenged both by the Irish and Byzantine churches and above all by Islam. As this baktun came to a close, though, the central role of the Papacy was reasserted through its initiative to reinstate the Holy Roman Empire. During the course of baktun 10, many peoples in northern and eastern Europe were also converted to the Christian faith, and the European kings as well as the German-Roman emperors gained their legitimacy through the crowns given to them by the Pope. Toward the end of baktun 10 the Papacy reached the zenith of its worldly power by even humiliating the emperor, and as areas that during the previous baktun had been lost to Islam were regained in the Crusades and the Reconquista of Spain.

Finally, at the beginning of baktun 12, as already mentioned, the Thirty Years' War would lead to the political establishment of the Protestant creed, a creed that through the pilgrims of this time also began to spread to North America. Baktun 12 was thus the time when the conversion to the Christian faith of all of the

Americas came to be completed, and when Christianity, through colonialism and missionary activities, spread also to other parts of the world, notably Africa, Siberia and Oceania.

But what is the difference between the Catholic and the Protestant creeds? One is obviously in the relationship to the Papacy. While the Catholics consider the Pope as the representative of Jesus Christ on earth and have declared him to be infallible, to most Protestants he has appeared more human than that. At a more profound level, however, there seems to be a difference in the relationship to God and His Creation. Much blood would run in the religious wars regarding the nature of the blood of Christ, and there seems to be a significant difference in nuance in how the Holy Communion is viewed. Among Catholics the wine used in the Holy Communion was through its consecration regarded as truly the blood of Jesus Christ, whereas Protestants saw the wine as merely symbolic of the blood of Jesus. Moreover, among the Protestants the worship of saints and their relics came to an end. Among the Calvinists, possibly the most ardent Protestants, most of the decorations were even removed from the churches.

It thus seems as if the Catholics worship and hold as holy the physical manifestations of God's Creation to a higher degree than the Protestants, who emphasize God's transcendent nature, His existence in the beyond, at the expense of holy relics, etc. This difference between Protestants and Catholics is then understandable from the new distinction between the material and the spiritual that I previously pointed out was a result of the beginning of baktun 12.

THE ROLE OF THE HOLY CROSS

It can thus fairly clearly be seen that it is especially during the even-numbered baktuns 8, 10 and 12 of the Great Cycle that Christianity has expanded its range of believers and institutional power. What this means is that it has expanded during those baktuns that, according to our analysis of migratory movements in Chapter 3, correspond to the Heavens that are dominated by the True Cross. And, not surprisingly, in the later baktuns of the Great Cycle the Papacy in Rome, Calvin in Geneva and Luther in Worms, all residing under the midline, have formulated the most influential doctrines of the Christian faith. Because of the creative tension induced by the Cross these doctrines first originated along one of its arms, but as they have spread from there they may have been modified in the process. Thus, it is not the Christian church that has spread the Cross; it is the Cross that has spread the Christian church.

It may be appropriate here to point out that the meaning of the symbol of the cross has changed over the history of Christendom. In the earliest days of Christianity, during baktun 8, the Golgotha cross seems to have been almost completely absent as a symbol in the catacombs of Rome. The oldest known pictorial representation of the Golgotha epic is from the Basilica of Santa Sabina (AD 420-430) in Rome. It is thus from the beginning of baktun 9, a baktun when the World Tree was absent, which the Maya considered to be ruled by the God of Death. Before this, that is, during baktun 8, it seems that the Christians tended to

Fig. 21 Thorvaldsen's Statue of Christ.
(Vår Frues Kirke, Copenhagen)

place the emphasis on the resurrection of Jesus. Throughout baktuns 9 and 10, however, the Maltese Cross, or other balanced variants, remained very common, and it was only in later medieval times that the picture of the suffering Christ on the cross became widespread. This happened during another baktun, baktun 11, when the Holy Cross did not rule the Heaven. It was also during this baktun that Hernan Cortes raised an unbalanced cross, on Good Friday 1519, upon his arrival in the land of the Aztecs. In conclusion, it is during the odd-numbered baktuns, when the True Cross does not exert its spiritual power, that most of the focus has been on the cross at Golgotha.

To summarize the evolution of the Chaldean-Jewish-Christian tradition throughout the Great Cycle, it seems that it reflects at least three clear tendencies. First, it includes a progression from polytheistic to monotheistic systems of belief. While in ancient Sumer, at the beginning of the cycle, the Creator God had to share his place with many other deities, progressively with every even-numbered baktun their role would diminish. While the Jews at the time of Moses became the first to embrace a monotheistic creed, it was later, through Christianity and Islam, that monotheism spread around the world.

The second tendency of the Great Cycle is to develop in human beings a belief in a God who is universal—the God of all human beings—starting with each people having its own gods, and its own particular ways of worshiping them, and progressing to religions seeking to include all mankind regardless of nationality. Third, there exists a tendency toward an increasingly transcendent view of God. At the beginning of the cycle people would worship all kinds of gods animating physical phenomena—city gods, harvest gods, house gods, etc.—while toward the end of the cycle the transcendent nature of God, His existence above all the physical manifestations of Creation, is increasingly realized. Hence, the progression through the Thirteen Heavens increasingly generates monotheism, universalism and transcendence in the beliefs of the human beings.

All of these, monotheism, universalism and transcendence, are related and are consequences of the same thing, namely the increasing dominance of the True Cross as we progress through the even-numbered baktuns of the Great Cycle. Due to the progressively increasing power of the True Cross, people, at least on a subconscious level, have come to believe in one unified power in the beyond dominating all of Creation. What we have previously discussed as the fall of divine rulers, the human usurpers of divinity, is really nothing but a reciprocal of these tendencies.

Fig. 22 Pharaoh Djoser's step pyramid in Saqqara, Egypt (~3000 BC), which is one of the world's oldest major construction works (baktun 0). Although today only six distinct terraces remain, the pyramid is believed originally to have been built in Seven stories (Courtesy of the Egyptian Tourist Board).

This progression through the baktuns of the Great Cycle can be likened to climbing up and down a seven-storied pyramid (Figures 22 and 23). In a way it is in the beginning of the Great Cycle that the hard work, the climb, is made, because it is then that the truth has to be worked out and make its way through the old thinking. The process of formulating the truth will then be essentially complete as we reach the overview gained at the highest level of the seven-storied pyramid. It is thus at the baktun 6 level that we see some direct visible effects of the Cross, and the most profound truth of the whole cycle is realized. As we step down the pyramid the Cross will serve to spread the most fundamental truth that was realized at the top. Relatively speaking, the act of spreading this truth, with the spiritual winds generated by the Cross at our backs, is more of a downhill climb.

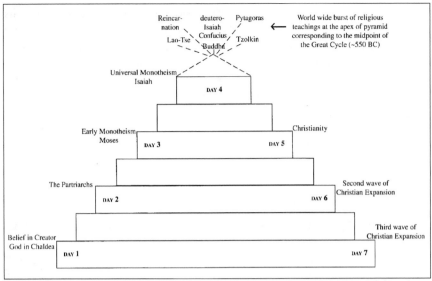

Fig. 23 The ascent and descent of the Seven-storied pyramid of Creation as expressed through the Chaldean-Jewish-Christian tradition of religiosity.

THE SEVEN DAYS
AND SIX NIGHTS OF GOD'S CREATION

Why then is it especially at the beginning of even-numbered baktuns that prophets have been inspired to step forth with significant new teachings regarding the nature of God and the purpose of Creation? Why is it at the beginning of even-numbered baktuns that the most important steps have been taken in the evolution of the Chaldean-Jewish-Christian tradition? This synchronicity between the messages of prophets and the beginning of the even-numbered baktuns is especially evident with Moses, Isaiah and Jesus/Paul at the beginnings of baktuns 4, 6 and 8, respectively.

Part of the explanation for this is in the appearance of the True Cross during these very baktuns, but we shall also notice that in the Mayan creation story it was only as the World Tree was raised by the First Father that the LIGHT would enter. Thus, there are seven even-numbered baktuns when divine LIGHT, shining especially at the Western Hemisphere (Figure 15a), allows prophets and their followers to see the divine reality for their inner visions and six intermediate periods of DARKNESS when the True Cross is absent.

The conclusion then comes naturally: The seven even-numbered baktuns and the six odd-numbered baktuns of the Maya are none other than the seven DAYS and six NIGHTS, respectively, of God's Creation as it is described in the Book of Genesis and symbolically represented by the seven candle lights of the Jewish menorah. This may well be the most significant message of this book, and can be formulated as a very simple equation:

$$\text{Seven DAYS} + \text{Six NIGHTS} = \text{Thirteen Heavens}$$

This equation is then the 'solution' to the Mayan calendar, providing the key to its demystification and allowing its mathematical language to be understood by other traditions or lines of human thought. As in future chapters we will study different Underworlds—not only that generated by the Great Cycle—we will find that the same pattern of seven DAYS and six NIGHTS will recur in all of these. It will thus provide the key to the understanding of each one of the Underworlds. This is, however, far more extensively presented in *The Theory of Everything*. The equation above is also a special case of the divine filtration pattern of LIGHT provided by the tzolkin, the sacred 260-day calendar of ancient Mesoamerica (see Appendix I), which is a temporal microcosm of Creation consisting of seven uinals of LIGHT with six intermediate uinals of DARKNESS.

In a way, the equation above should not come as a surprise. If, after all, we inhabitants of the New World and Old World alike are all part of the same Creation, and if God and His Creation is universal, then commonalities must exist between the ways in which Creation was understood on the two different continental blocks of the planet regardless of for how long these had developed separately. If we are all ruled by the same Heaven, part of the same Creation, children of the same God, then Creation stories in different parts of the world must deal with the same reality. The above equation thus provides the crucial bridge between the Mayan calendar and a few billion people—Jews, Christians and Muslims—that revere holy scriptures stating that God created the world in seven DAYS and six NIGHTS. The identification of the True Cross alone may provide a bridge from the Maya to Christianity, but the identification of the seven DAYS of God's Creation will expand this bridge also to Judaism and Islam. The creation stories all describe the same thing: the One Reality.

This equation, as simple as it is, also provides a bridge to empirical science, since the existence of the Thirteen Heavens ruling the 13 baktuns can be empirically verified. The Mayan calendar, as we have now started to see, provides empirical evidence that we are living in a Creation governed by a divine plan designed by an omnipotent intelligence, God. Thus, we have, maybe for the first time, a proof of the existence of God, which is not based on feelings or abstract philosophical reasoning, but on empirical evidence provided by the factual basis of modern historical research and science.

What is unique in the cosmology of the Maya is thus not the idea that we are living in a divine creation, or even a divine process of creation progressing through alternating periods of LIGHT and DARKNESS. At least on a subconscious level the adherents of the major monotheistic religions were aware of this too, and in ancient times this knowledge was probably shared by the many other traditions that considered the number 7 as holy. What is special about the contribution of the Maya is that they have very exactly calibrated the seven DAYS and six NIGHTS of the divine process of Creation with physically based time, that is, the passage of solar years, which here throughout has been expressed by years in the Gregorian calendar.

The insight that we are living in a Creation that progresses and develops according to a special rhythm has very significant consequences for the way we look at life, and at our own roles in this Creation. Among other things it means that the evolution of our consciousness is not under our own control to the extent that many seem to believe, or would like to believe. If the design plan of God controls the evolution of consciousness by processes that are invisible and beyond the reach of our physical manipulations, then maybe, after all, the future of our lives is in God's hands only. This is something that the ancients seem to have known, but for the past two hundred years or so has been largely denied by humanity.

Fig. 24 The Seven-armed Jewish Menorah – Symbol of divine creation.

In the *Book of Genesis* the idea that the world was created in seven DAYS and six NIGHTS is of course portrayed as something that had happened in the past, whereas here we present Creation as something that we are in the midst of, as an ongoing process. Thus, the interpretation made here may not be the one a fundamentalist would make. Instead, it is one that conforms to empirical evidence combined with a somewhat modified understanding of the ancient scriptures. If we are to assimilate the wisdom of the ancient peoples (seven DAYS and six NIGHTS is a good example), it thus seems that this has to be done from an insight that their wisdom came from a different consciousness than ours, and that this consciousness had particular limitations, but also strengths. Their consciousness was in a very real sense different from ours since, compared to the one ruling now, a different Heaven shaped it.

The consciousness of time, for instance, was very different among the ancients. Moses, who is credited with having written the *Book of Genesis*, is believed to have lived sometime early in baktun 4, under the Fifth Heaven of the Great Cycle. The consciousness that was generated by this particular Heaven did not include a strong sense of the direction of time. No long-term calendars had yet been invented and no perspective of an eternal life or a millennium of peace at the end of history had been proposed. This was yet to come, during later even-numbered baktuns of the same cycle. Thus it seems that although people at the time, and Moses in particular, intuitively became aware that there was such a thing as a divine creation process of seven DAYS alternating with six NIGHTS, they had not yet gained a kind of long-term perspective of the passage of time that would allow them to realize that this was an ongoing process.

The Mayan calendar, properly used, is thus above all a tool to help us come in phase with the divine process of Creation and find our true purpose in life. We may in fact ask if it would be possible to realize one's own purpose in life without recognizing that we are living in a Creation that has a purpose created by God. Could we as single individuals have a purpose that is unrelated to the purpose of God's plan? While we may not yet be able to formulate God's purpose with Creation with any certainty we can still develop tools, calendars, that are in phase with the rhythm of divine Creation and seek to harmonize our own lives with these rhythms of the larger whole. This does not mean that for this purpose we may use any calendar, just because it happens to be called 'Mayan.' If it is to serve us and not lead us further astray from the purpose of God's Creation it needs to be a True Calendar, a calendar that correctly describes the vibrations of the World Tree. In my own opinion this True Calendar is provided by the tun-based system of the Maya.

It seems that with the use of such a tun-based calendar we see patterns that remain hidden if we use the Gregorian calendar. The reality of the cosmic plan only becomes visible to those using the Mayan calendar. Hence, *today the choice between world views is presented as a choice between calendars.* Those choosing to believe in a divine creation, a cosmic plan that has both meaning and purpose, will choose the Mayan calendar so that its patterns become evident. Those who, on the other hand, choose to believe in a materialist world view and in a universe that has come into existence by accident, will obviously stay with the Gregorian calender or some other calendar that is based on physical time.

Why were the Maya unique in their endeavor to calibrate the rhythm of divine Creation? A general answer is that they embodied the Western consciousness of their time. Thus, compared to their contemporaries in Europe or the Far East they sought an understanding of Creation that was more analytical and mathematical. This analytic side was expressed in a cosmology that distinguished between the roles of different deities, rather than that of a single God, and in their exact calendars, which mathematically describe the rhythm of divine Creation.

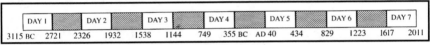

Fig. 25 The DAYS and the NIGHTS of the Great (National) Cycle.

Maybe the Maya were not as unique in their calendrical ambitions as it would initially seem. The date of the beginning of the Jewish calendar, 3761 BC, was meant to describe the beginning of Creation, which was thus not all that different from the beginning of the Long Count in 3114 BC. More surprisingly, maybe, the oldest known long-term calendars of this planet are the Assyrian era of Nabunassar, starting in the year 747 BC, and those of Rome aiming back at the year 753 BC and of the Greeks to the first mythical Olympic games in the year 776 BC. The beginnings of all three of these semi-mythical calendars seem to have targeted, at least subconsciously, the beginning of baktun 6. If this interpretation is true, it would mean that for more than a thousand years Europe used a calendar, the Roman, whose beginning was set at the beginning of a new DAY, baktun 6. Maybe also the beginning of the Gregorian calendar in the year AD 1 can be seen as a rough approximation of the beginning of baktun 8, and that of the Muslim calendar in AD 622 as an approximation of the midpoint of baktun 9. So the Long Count may have parallels in other chronologies, but these were not equally accurate. Moreover, these Old World chronologies seem to have missed the idea of alternating time periods with different qualities.

If the Assyrian and Roman calendars were estimates of the beginning of the LIGHT of baktun 6, and there was a six-year difference between these, we may wonder if the Mayan Long Count, which places this beginning about two years earlier than the Assyrian, is exact or had some small error. In light of the previous discussion, the whole question of the true calibration of the Great Cycle with the Gregorian calendar has actually come in an entirely new perspective compared to previously. Traditionally, this discussion has focused on determining what day in the Gregorian calendar that the Creation date of the Long Count, 0.0.0.0.0 4 Ahau 8 Cumku, corresponded to. Most researchers today would give this as August 11, 3114 BC, a conclusion which I also accept. But the formulation of the correlation problem now becomes different. If the Great Cycle describes the divine process of Creation with its seven DAYS and six NIGHTS, the important question is if the Long Count is an exact calibration of these divine time periods. (Note that a distinction has been introduced here between the Great Cycle of seven DAYS and six NIGHTS and the Long Count, the chronology that was actually used by the Maya.) For reasons I will discuss in Appendix II it seems that there is indeed an error of 420 days in this correlation, something that creates a discrepancy that may not have been very important to the Maya, but is absolutely crucial for us who live at the present time.

RELIGIONS OF THE EAST

As we can see in Table 6, the exact midpoint of the Great Cycle around 550 BC was also in the Eastern Hemisphere a point in time marked by innovative religious thought. At about this time the philosophies of Buddhism, Confucianism, Zoroastrianism and Taoism as well as the Hindu thoughts of reincarnation were first developed. In fact, the dates of birth for both Confucius and Buddha are given exactly at the midpoint of the Great Cycle, 551 and 552 BC, respectively. (Although these dates may be mythical they indicate at least a subconscious awareness of their followers of the time when the whole process of the Great Cycle and its baktun 6 was cresting.)

In the role played by a supreme Creator God there is, however, a very noticeable difference between these cosmologies of the East and those of the Center that we described earlier. The role of a supreme Creator God is clearly much more strongly emphasized in the Center as compared to in the East, where belief in Him has never been widespread, at least not in the sense of a personal God. Although some thinkers, such as Mahatma Gandhi, have suggested that the cores of all major religions are monotheistic, in the Eastern religions this is something that has to be extracted and is not immediately evident from these teachings. Even if Brahman is viewed as a supreme Creator God he is certainly not the only God in the pantheon of the Hindus, and in the Buddhist tradition a Creator God is not acknowledged at all. Buddhists in fact do not see the world as having been created at a certain point in time, but instead look upon the universe as endless cycles of creation and destruction with no beginning or end. In ancient China the Cosmos was, along a similar line of thought, believed to have been created by itself rather than by a Creator God.

All of this becomes understandable if we recognize that the consciousness of humanity during the Great Cycle has developed as a resonance phenomenon with the vibrations and pulsations of the True Cross, whose vertical arm goes through the 12th longitude East. In Europe and the Mediterranean the consciousness of people would then be most directly affected by the baktun-based pulsations of the Cross creating a duality between LIGHT and DARKNESS. The sharpest effects of a wave generator are evident in its proximity. This, in turn, meant that people there developed a belief in a personal Creator as a source of these pulses. In the East, in contrast, among Hindus, Buddhists, Confucians and Taoists, the Cosmos did not come to be perceived in this way. Partly, this was because during the Great Cycle the adherents of these religions and their prophets were living on the SHADOW side of the planet, and partly it was because they were living at such a great distance from the vertical arm of this Cross. It seems that the further East we go in ancient times, the less of a belief there was in a Creator God, and in the Chinese philosophy yin and yang seem to have been regarded more as forces of nature than as aspects of the divine. The absence there of a perception of a First Cause of the human existence was also evident in the absence of a long-term calendar since, as we have seen, these reflect some notion of an ongoing Creation. In China, the years would instead be counted from the beginning of each of their imperial dynasties, and thus ultimately be dependent on worldly matters.

Islam, finally, seems to play an intermediate role between the Center and the East in this context. Its symbols are the crescent moon and the evening star, symbols of the NIGHT. And, indeed, it was founded as the Qur'an was completed in AD 632, at the exact midpoint of the NIGHT of baktun 9. Thus, its role may be seen as one of bringing LIGHT into the DARKNESS. Because it was formulated and shaped by a NIGHT, Islam has also mostly spread during the NIGHTS when the Cross was absent in the Heaven. It has also mostly expanded toward the East, which during the Great Cycle was the SHADOW part of the planet (Figure 15a). Thus, prior to baktun 12, as the Russians began their expansion of Christianity into Siberia, Islam represented the only significant monotheistic religion in the Eastern Hemisphere.

Although Islam is a monotheistic religion its message has become somewhat different from that of Christianity, since it was formulated east of the midline and during a NIGHT. While Islam has reflected an Eastern mentality in its emphasis on collective expressions of worship, such as prayers and pilgrimages, the more Western Christianity has emphasized individual expressions. Since Christianity was conceived during a DAY, which generally is a time when human creativity flourishes, its emphasis has been on the individual crafting his own destiny, while that of Islam, conceived during a NIGHT, has been on submission to the will of God.

From this discussion of the emergence of the human religions, it thus seems as if these have been conditioned partly by factors of which humanity hitherto has been unaware. These factors are the Heavens that provide the frameworks for the human consciousness throughout the course of the Great Cycle of the Maya, and these Heavens are none other than the seven DAYS and six NIGHTS of the Jewish-Christian-Muslim creation story. What this means is that the emergence of the human religions, and their respective views of the origin of the Cosmos, ultimately is a reflection, more or less distorted, of the divine process of Creation itself. A central factor influencing the evolution of the historical religions is the True Cross, reigning over the planet during the even-numbered baktuns, the DAYS. Because the various religions have originated in different locations in relation to this Cross, and the separation between LIGHT and DARKNESS that this affects, and because they have originated during different baktuns, they have developed differently in different times and places.

In my own view, there is indeed only one truth, the truth about God and His/Her Creation. Because of our human shortcomings and limited perspectives, and a resonance with the True Cross that is only partial, however, it is only to a limited degree that we can see this truth, and the degree to which we can see it varies between peoples and individuals. Yet, the process of divine Creation moves us in a direction where we are all coming closer to the truth.

Thus, some of these religions may be truer than others. Yet each one of them may have a unique value and give a unique contribution to the truth that we in the present time of cross-fertilization may need to assimilate or at least consider. What seems common to them all, however, is that in one way or another they reflect our human shortcomings, our limited views of the One Reality, and our inability to grasp this in its fullness. Only the divine reality is real, eternal, and the material world is but an illusion. Yet, because the divine reality may be more difficult to see than the material, we tend to understand the divine in the image of ourselves, the human beings, and thus, the major religions have very much emphasized the role of its founders and prophets. True, there have been many great prophets in the history of mankind. We should honor them for what they have done. But this should not lead us to deny that the appearances of these prophets, and the messages that they have brought to us, have always been brought against the background of the divine process of Creation, the cosmic plan designed by God, which is the ultimate source of our existence.

CHAPTER 6

THE NINE UNDERWORLDS

THE BASIC FREQUENCIES OF CREATION

We have now looked at the Great Cycle in some detail. Yet today we know that the world did not begin only five thousand years ago with the emergence of the written language, the first pyramids and the first nations centered on pharaohs. The Great Cycle did not begin in a vacuum. It had the considerable previous evolution of the universe to stand on, and today's science has shown beyond a doubt that the world is much older than the Great Cycle. It tells us that the universe came into existence some fifteen billion years ago as matter was first created from light in the Big Bang, and that since then our galaxy, solar system, the earth and its biological organisms have all come into existence, apparently out of an evolutionary process.

Interestingly, the Maya also were aware that the world was much older than fifty-one hundred years. Thus, on one stele discovered at the ancient site of Coba on the Yucatan peninsula (Figure 26) the Creation date of the Long Count is placed in the context of several creation cycles of 13×20^n (13 times 20 multiplied n times with itself) tuns. What this means is that Creation may be regarded as a composite of several creations, each being built on top of another in a hierarchical structure. The idea of several world ages, replacing each other and ending in catastrophes, is typical of Mesoamerican thought, and we may still see this in the ceremonies of today's Maya, where monkeys from a 'previous creation' may be enacted. The Nine Underworlds, which are such different 'creations,' may be identified as each being generated by a cycle twenty times shorter than the one it was built on. Indeed, one of these Underworlds, the Third Underworld, did carry the particular frame of consciousness of the monkeys, which is a level of consciousness in between that of the other animals and that of the human beings. This Underworld began 13×20^5 tuns (41 million years) ago and developed the frame of consciousness of monkeys. Thus, the first monkeys appeared on this planet some forty million years ago and have pulse by pulse evolved into human-like anthropoids.

Counting Nine Underworlds, the first of these, which is made up of 13 hablatuns, started 16.4 billion years ago, very close to the estimated time for the Big Bang, the beginning of Creation. The creation of this First Underworld provided the material foundation for the rest of Creation: matter, galaxies, solar systems and cells. Since the higher cells emerged at the beginning of its seventh DAY and represent the highest level of consciousness of this particular Underworld, I have referred to this as the Cellular Underworld in the pyramid of Figure 27. The starting dates and some concomitant events typical of the aspects of consciousness that these cycles develop have been summarized in Table 6.

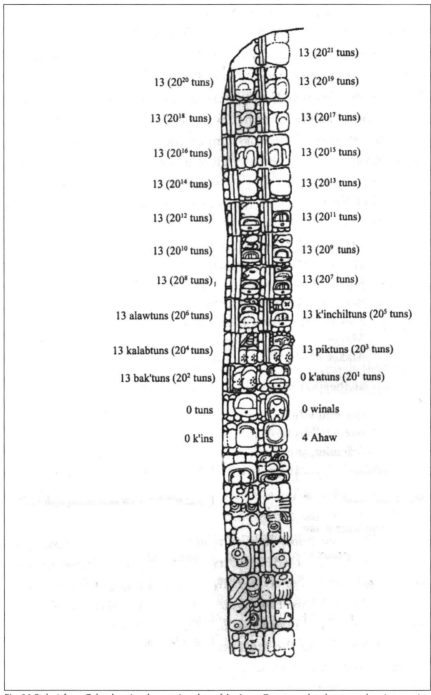

13 $(20^{21}$ tuns)

13 $(20^{20}$ tuns)   13 $(20^{19}$ tuns)

13 $(20^{18}$ tuns)   13 $(20^{17}$ tuns)

13 $(20^{16}$ tuns)   13 $(20^{15}$ tuns)

13 $(20^{14}$ tuns)   13 $(20^{13}$ tuns)

13 $(20^{12}$ tuns)   13 $(20^{11}$ tuns)

13 $(20^{10}$ tuns)   13 $(20^{9}$ tuns)

13 $(20^{8}$ tuns),   13 $(20^{7}$ tuns)

13 alawtuns $(20^{6}$ tuns)   13 k'inchiltuns $(20^{5}$ tuns)

13 kalabtuns $(20^{4}$ tuns)   13 piktuns $(20^{3}$ tuns)

13 bak'tuns $(20^{2}$ tuns)   0 k'atuns $(20^{1}$ tuns)

0 tuns   0 winals

0 k'ins   4 Ahaw

Fig. 26 Stele 1 from Coba showing the creation date of the Long Count as related to several major creation cycles of Thirteen Heavens in the tun-based system (Courtesy Freidel, Schele and Parker, *Maya Cosmos*).

Table 6

Table 6
Starting Dates for the Nine Major Creation Cycles

Cycle	Duration of cycle (modern dating)	Initiating phenomena
Universal	13 x 20 kin = 0.72 yrs	(?)
Galactic	13×20^0 tun = 12.8 yrs	(?)
Planetary	13×20^1 tun = 256 yrs	Industrialism (1769)
National	13×20^2 tun = 5,125 yrs	Written language (3100 BC)
Regional	13×20^3 tun = 102,000 yrs	Spoken language (100,000 yrs)
Tribal	13×20^4 tun = 2 million yrs	First humans (2 million yrs)
Familial	13×20^5 tun = 41 million yrs	First monkeys (40 million yrs)
Mammalian	13×20^6 tun = 820 million yrs	First animals (850 million yrs)
Cellular	13×20^7 tun = 16.4 billion yrs	Matter, 'Big Bang' (14-16 billion yrs)

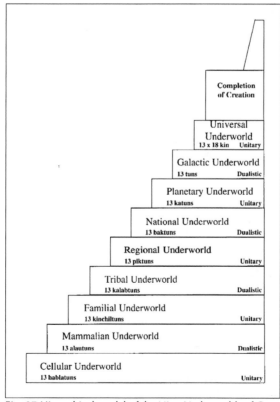

Fig. 27 Hierarchical model of the Nine Underworlds of Creation symbolized by a pyramid built in Nine levels. The Unitary and Dualist nature of the respective Underworlds have been indicated

The fact that the First Underworld goes back all the way to the Big Bang has far-reaching consequences. First, we here have a definite proof that the tun-based calendrical system of the Maya is not based on astronomical movements or biological cycles. It can in fact be used to describe the process of creation from a time when no solar systems, or even galaxies, existed. Thus, the tun-based calendrical system describes divine creation processes that are primary to all of their material manifestations. The processes that the tun-based system describe go back to a time when God began this Creation with His Word, that is, the vibrations of the World Tree.

Second, the First Underworld covers the time all the way back to the Big Bang. Thus, everything that we know to exist—all of Creation—is a result of the creation of these Nine Underworlds, each being created by Thirteen Heavens (if we liken a Heaven to a slide picture, then an Underworld is its projection by divine LIGHT on the screen). What this means is that all of Creation, the evolution of all things that exist, can be described by nine progressions of Thirteen Heavens. The Great Cycle, the only one of these progressions that we have hitherto discussed, thus creates only one of the Underworlds, the Sixth, the one that created a national frame of consciousness. Among the Maya the deity ruling over this particular creation was referred to as the Six-Sky-Lord.

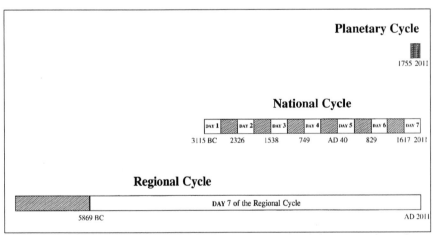

Fig. 28 The temporal relationships between the Regional, National and Planetary Cycles as shown to scale. The Seventh DAY of the Regional Cycle (bottom row) provides the foundation for the entire National Cycle (middle row), whose Seventh DAY in turn provides the foundations for the entire Planetary Cycle (top row).

As we climb the nine-storied pyramid to the higher Underworlds, the length of the time periods that these progressions through Thirteen Heavens dominate will, however, decrease. The duration of the rule of each Underworld will be twenty times shorter than the one it builds on (Figure 28), going from hablatuns in the Cellular Underworld, via alautuns, etc., to uaxaclahunkins in the highest Underworld, the Universal. If again we regard the Cross as the primary wave generator of Creation, we may realize that the vibration frequency of this Cross

The Mayan Calendar

increases with every higher Underworld. It increases from the lowest frequency of 1/hablatun to the highest of 1/uaxaclahunkin—increasing some twenty-five billion times in the process. This increase in the basic tones of Creation (there surely are a number of overtones, too) affects the type of phenomena that are generated by the various creation cycles. In this Creation the basic matter was created in the Cellular Underworld, and as it has proceeded to higher Underworlds, mental and spiritual dimensions of existence have increasingly come into play. This especially became the case as human beings were created as co-creators, a process that began in the Fifth Underworld. Thus, the invisible Cross may be seen as an instrument programmed to generate a symphony, where tones of higher and higher frequencies come into play in a preset pattern. (A better metaphor than a symphony may be a caller starting by calling in the drums, and then calling in one instrument after another to add to those that are already playing.)

THE BIRTH OF THE HUMAN BEING

The Fourth of these Underworlds, the Human, began with the emergence of the first human beings, who according to fairly unanimous anthropological research first appeared in central Africa about two million years ago. We have previously identified the center of the Cross, or the World Tree, as the point where the 12th longitude East meets the equator in central Africa, in what is currently Gabon. It is noteworthy then that somewhat east of there the oldest remains of members of the human species, *Homo habilis*, have been found. In this context human being is defined according to the standard anthropological definition as an animal that is able to make tools, and *Homo habilis* apparently was the first species on this planet to accomplish this.

These facts provide for very interesting parallels to Mayan and Christian myth. According to one Mayan myth the first human being was born out of a tree. This is indeed exactly what we have found to be true; the first human beings were born where the Cross between the branches and the trunk of the World Tree is formed, in central Africa. Likewise, in Biblical (and, incidentally, also Nordic) myth, human beings were born out of the Tree of Life as Adam and Eve were thrown into the world after having tasted its fruit. According to Christian myth, the Tree of the Garden of Eden would later be used to make the cross of Jesus, again identifying the World Tree and the Cross with the birthplace of human beings, since through his crucifixion Jesus was supposed to give new life. In the physical world, the Cross of this Tree corresponds to Central Africa, not far from where the first human beings are known to have originated.

Creation then brings about the evolution through Nine Underworlds, going from levels where consciousness, or the Universal Mind, is manifested in physical ways, from the matter of which everything is built up, to more and more ethereal or spiritual levels. To accomplish this the human beings in the five highest Underworlds continue to transform the already created matter and thus become co-creators with God. In this regard, in that of human beings becoming co-creators, it is the Fifth Underworld, created by the Regional Cycle, which started about 102,000 years ago, that represents the most important turning point. It is with the Fifth, and midmost, of the Nine Underworlds that human beings become truly creative and start producing a diversified spoken language, sophisticated tools and art, and with every Underworld built on this human beings become increasingly important as co-creators.

Earlier I suggested that what was formulated during the Seventh Heaven of the Great Cycle, the midpoint of the Thirteen Heavens, was the most fundamental truth of that cycle. With a similar line of reasoning I would then also suggest that it is in the Fifth Underworld, which is the midmost of the Nine Underworlds, that the most fundamental aspect of Creation, of all of Creation, comes into existence. This most fundamental part of Creation is the human being, a creative being with a free will. Thus, what this Creation seems to be all about is the human being, who has a special place and responsibility for its evolution. This is also in line with what is expressed by several religious traditions. From the perspective of Creation the speaking *Homo sapiens* of the Regional Underworld thus represents a turning point. Many Mayan pyramids were in fact built in five levels to symbolize that the Fifth Underworld is the midpoint of the Nine (going up and down a five-storied pyramid is thus also like passing through all the Underworlds). The same is also true for the many pagodas in China and much of the Far East, where the number 5 is the holiest of numbers.

Table 7

The Highest Expressions at the Beginnings
of Day 7 of the Major Cycles

Cycle	Beginning of seventh day	Highest expression
Universal	AD 2011	?
Galactic	AD 2011	?
Planetary	AD 1992	Computer networks (1992)
National	AD 1617	Modern nation (1648)
Regional	8000 YA	Agriculture (8000 YA)
Tribal	160,000 YA	*Homo sapiens* (150,000 YA)
Familial	3.2 MYA	*Australopithecus afr.* (3.0 MYA)
Mammalian	63.4 MYA	Placental mammals (65 MYA)
Cellular	1.26 BYA	Eukaryotic cells (1.5 BYA)

(YA = years ago, MYA = millions of years ago, BYA = billions of years ago)

In Table 7 a summary of phenomena emerging at the seventh DAY of each of the Underworlds is presented. If these are combined with the phenomena in Table 6, twin pairs comparable to those of the beginning and the end of the Great Cycle in Table 3 are the result. Each of the Underworlds creates different types of phenomena corresponding to the specific frame of consciousness it generates, and, although these processes are spread out over very different lengths of time, there is in all of them a common pattern in the rhythm of evolution. The phenomena in Table 6 were all generated as the god of procreation ruled and those in Table 7 as the Creator duality ruled (Appendix I). Thus, there are common traits in what emerged during the First (Table 6) and Thirteenth (Table 7) Heavens of all the Underworlds, and the same is true for all the various Heavens. Each DAY and NIGHT in the different Underworlds tends to manifest phenomena that emerge at the same point in the progression from seed to fruit. To take an example, in all the Underworlds DAY 5 represents a major breakthrough to LIGHT, but, depending on the Underworld, the LIGHT has manifested either in the creation of the sun, humans learning to control fire or as the emergence of Christ consciousness (Table 8).

Table 8
Major Breakthroughs to LIGHT *and Seeing during the Fifth* DAY
(Dominated by the God of Fire) of the Different Creation Cycles

Cycle	Beginning	Aspect of LIGHT
Galactic	Nov. 23, 2006	?
Planetary	AD 1913	Dual nature of light, general theory of relativity (1915)
National	AD 40	Universal Christian religion (AD 49)
Regional	40,000 YA	Esthetics (Art) (40,000 YA)
Human	800,000 YA	Fire (800,000 YA)
Anthropoid	16.0 MYA	Color vision (?)
Mammalian	315 MYA	Transition to land (300 MYA)
Cellular	6.25 BYA	Solar system disc (5.0-6.0 BYA)

(YA = years ago, MYA = millions of years ago, BYA = billions of years ago)

In *The Theory of Everything* the Nine Underworlds, each created in seven DAYS and six alternating NIGHTS, are discussed in detail and compared, and there it becomes evident that they share a common pattern. Regardless of the particular Underworld, the same DAYS or NIGHTS share specific traits and energies. As an example, the fifth DAY compared in Table 8 was according to the Aztecs ruled by the god of Light, a description which seems to fit several of the phenomena in the table. Such comparisons provide the basis for understanding the tzolkin, a filtration pattern for divine LIGHT of 13 × 20 units shared by all the Underworlds.

The Creation of the universe is thus organized in a hierarchical way, so that each new Underworld is built on the foundation of the previous. The emergence of higher cells at the beginning of the seventh DAY of the Cellular Underworld, for example, set the stage for the evolution of the multicellular biological organisms during the Thirteen Heavens of the Mammalian Underworld. This, in turn, led to the emergence of the higher mammals at the seventh DAY of this Underworld. The highest expression of the Second Underworld, the higher mammals, then set the stage for what was created during the Third, and so on. The temporal relationships between the different Underworlds are exemplified in Figure 28, and they are thus shown on a somewhat different scale compared to the pyramid in Figure 27. An Underworld is created in a time twenty times shorter than the one it was built on.

Thus, the Great Cycle, creating the Sixth and National Underworld, to which we have until now given all of our attention, is just one among several creation cycles, and it was built on the foundation of five lower Underworlds. As of this writing (2000), as I will discuss in more detail later, we have come to the seventh DAY of the creation of the Seventh Underworld, the Planetary, which in turn stands on the National Underworld. There are thus now only two more Underworlds to go—the Galactic and the Universal—and what will happen as a result of these will be the object of the last chapters of the book. The nine-storied Mayan pyramids are seeking to tell us that reality is created in a hierarchical way and that each Underworld stands on the foundation of another. In this hierarchical structure, the different frames of consciousness, Regional, National and Planetary, do not replace each other. Nor do they follow one upon another in an endless sequence like the current linear/cyclical thinking might lead us to believe. Instead they add to each other (Figures 27 and 29) so that the creation of all the Underworlds will be completed at the same time, October 28, 2011.

THE PLANETARY ROUND OF LIGHT

What may be the most fruitful way of looking at the ascent of a nine-storied pyramid of Creation is, however, as a passage through different dualities of LIGHT. This is what is shown in Figure 29, where these dualities are shown from the perspective of both the North Pole and the back side of the planet. Each of these dualities will create a very different vision for the people who are in resonance with the global creation field and literally make them see things in different LIGHTS. In short, what this means is that all the different Underworlds are not determined by the same duality of LIGHT, something which in the long run would create an enormous imbalance between people living in different areas of the planet. Instead, looked upon from the North Pole, the line that separates the LIGHT from the DARKNESS rotates 90° with each new Underworld that is being created. This means that the distribution discussed during the Great Cycle with the LIGHT focused on the Western Hemisphere (Figure 15a) was particular to that Underworld. When it comes to the different distributions of LIGHT in the Planetary Round, the same is true for them as for the different Underworlds generally; they do not replace each other, they add to one another, enveloping each other, as it were. Only as, in the year 2011, our eyes will be in resonance with the front side of the planet will a perfect balance be recreated. Until then we will have problems adapting to the cosmic imbalance.

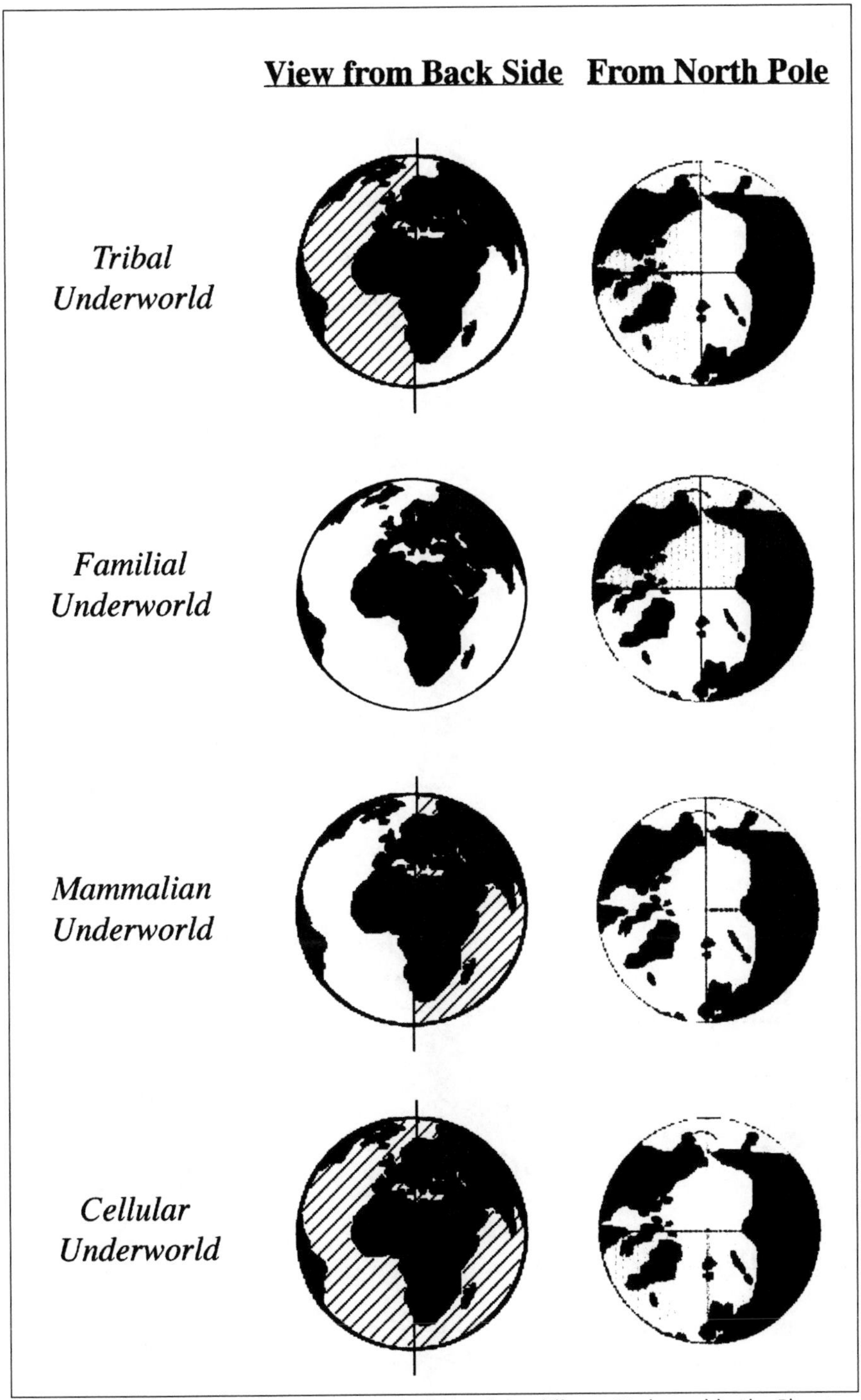

Fig. 29 (also see next page) The Yin/Yang dualities of the different Underworlds (the Planetary Round of LIGHT) viewed from the Back Side of the earth and from the North Pole.

View from Back Side   From North Pole

Universal Underworld

Galactic Underworld

Planetary Underworld

National Underworld

Regional Underworld

Thus, as consciousness climbs from the First to the Ninth Underworld of the pyramid it is also shaped by the Round of LIGHT that gives each of these Underworlds their specific characters. This means that a soul—a 'consciousness package'—as it climbs the staircase of the pyramid, simultaneously participates in a circular movement because of the Planetary Round of LIGHT. The result is a spiral movement, which is a metaphor that has commonly been used to describe the evolution of the soul. Because of the widening frames of consciousness a vortex is formed from this spiral ascension—the vortex of life.

Looking at the ascent of the pyramid from the perspective of modern knowledge we may identify a sequence of different frames of consciousness, each being associated with a particular Underworld. Since these frames expand from the Cellular to the Universal, the purpose of Creation seems to be with every Underworld to widen and elevate the frame of human consciousness.

To exemplify this, we may recognize that during the Great Cycle the frame of human consciousness was the nation. Thus, in the particular consciousness developed by the National Underworld, the greatest whole that people would identify with was their own nation, and throughout this creation cycle people would almost invariably be willing to risk their lives by participating in wars fought on behalf of the nations they identified with. Why? Because in the Underworld in which they lived the nation provided the highest greater whole that they would identify with, the very frame of their consciousness. To fight for king and country was then seen as a noble activity serving the highest good people knew of: the nation.

In the Planetary Underworld ruling today, however, much of this has changed, and as we have now reached its seventh DAY, the highest good is rather represented by the planet, as expressed in widespread environmental concerns and a generally accepted ideal of peace. True, wars are still being fought today, but the ideal of going to war for one's country is rarely expressed. In this way, the national frame of consciousness has been transcended by the planetary, and the progression to higher frames, or dimensions, of consciousness represents the chief direction in which the universe is evolving.

The National Underworld had in turn also been built on lower, more limited, frames of human consciousness such as families, tribes and regional cultures. In this way, the purpose of Creation may be seen as expanding the frame of consciousness to ever-widening levels, until at the highest level we will be able to see things from the highest perspective possible, that of the universe, the perspective from which all things were created. The truth will then be revealed to us, and to assimilate this truth is what the next eleven years will be all about. Our frame of consciousness is about to be raised to a perspective where we will recognize the truth about God's Creation. At that point, we will realize that we are not separate from Him/Her, something that our current planetary frame of consciousness does not fully allow us to do. This process, which will lead to expanded frames of consciousness, will be the result of the divine process of Creation described by the calendrical system of the Maya. This ultimately then is the calendar of the evolution of consciousness. Since the new frames of consciousness developed with every new Underworld do not replace, but add to, the previous ones, we are in this step-by-step process evolving into beings with a multidimensional consciousness.

ASCENSION THROUGH THE
NINE UNDERWORLDS OF CREATION

Fig. 30 The Pyramid of the Jaguar in Tikal - the tallest pyramid in the Americas (Photo Calleman).

Thus, what we can see and how we see it ultimately depends on the highest Underworld we live in, the one that provides the frame of our consciousness and the predominant filters for our vision. Things do not look the same in the National Underworld as they do in the Planetary. Things do look different if you have a pair of glasses where one eye is transparent and the other dim, compared to if both are dim (Figure 29). Things also look different if you have a fish-eye lens compared to the narrow focus of a telescope. Such differences produce even stronger effects if we are not aware that they exist, which is more or less true for all of us, when it comes to the Planetary Round of LIGHT. That we see things differently now than the ancients did is thus not just a matter of conventions in the human community having changed. The difference is real, and things do look different. There are

The Mayan Calendar

some things that the ancients could see that we do not see and there are some things that we can see that they did not, and this cannot be changed with merely an intentional change in attitude on our own part. The reason that so many people are now taking an interest in the ancients—not only the Maya but several other cultures as well—is that our consciousness, as it is entering the Galactic Underworld, is changing. This is essentially because the cycle now beginning, similarly to that of the ancients, has a dualistic frame of consciousness, in which the divine reality will again be more easily visible. Thus, at this particular time there may be something important for us to retrieve in the ancient sources, something that only now, because of our changing consciousness, is becoming understandable to us.

On an individual level we are shaped by all of these levels, or dimensions, of consciousness, all of these dualities of LIGHT generated by lower Underworlds. Some parts of us, some levels of our consciousness, are more dualistic than others. Dualistic levels of consciousness usually carry an aggressive assertive energy, whereas unitary levels of consciousness are more inclusive and softer. Thus, the animal in you, the tribe in you, your nation and galaxy represent dualistic levels of consciousness, whereas your cells, family, region, planet and universe are unitary (Figure 27). In our lives as individuals we tend to switch between these levels depending on the occasion as the focus shifts from the more basic to the higher levels of consciousness. In this upward spiral movement we experience what the Hindus would call Kundalini energy.

These dimensions of consciousness build on and are prerequisites for one another and none of them can be jumped over. We, or at least humanity looked upon as a whole, cannot attain a planetary frame of consciousness unless we already have a reasonably strong national frame. These frames are probably best visualized if we imagine them as layered outside of one another in wider and wider spheres enveloping us to produce a multidimensional consciousness. What this concentric organization means is that, for instance, when we go from a national to a planetary frame of consciousness we do not suddenly lose all links to the nation and our national identity. What happens is that our national identity is relegated to a lesser role within the context of a predominating planetary frame of consciousness.

As the evolution of consciousness progresses through these alternating dimensions of unity and duality it proceeds from unity in the First Underworld until unity finally is recreated at the very highest level of existence, the Universal, expressed in a unity with God and the divine cosmic consciousness. From this we may realize why the ahauob, the Mayan shaman kings, would climb all the way to the top of the nine-storied pyramids to perform their ceremonies. By doing so they sought through trance states to ascend to the universal level of consciousness and, at least symbolically, to return to unity with the Cosmos. The progression through the Thirteen Heavens in any of these individual Underworlds is subordinated to this ascension through the Nine Underworlds and the ensuing spiral cosmic drama of LIGHT and DARKNESS. Although some Underworlds, such as the National, generate duality, the large-scale picture of the Nine Underworlds is thus going from unity to unity. This may bring us to the realization that duality is just an illusory aspect of particular Underworlds and is not meant to prevail. The dualities between male and female, East and West, LIGHT and DARKNESS are only temporary. And yet, as illusory as they are, the dualities are nonetheless necessary aspects of the divine process of Creation. Without duality there would be no Creation.

A BRIDGE TO THE EAST

In the Nine Underworlds covering all of creation and going back all the way to the Big Bang we have now identified the basis in reality of the holiness of the number 9 among the Maya. To them, judging from the importance of the nine-storied pyramids they built, this was the holiest number of all. The number 9 represented the highest level of consciousness, its cosmic, or universal, level at the top of the pyramid.

The number 9 was revered as holy in many other ancient cultures as well. In ancient Nordic myth the Cosmos consisted of nine worlds. In Islam, Ramadan, the month of fasting, is the ninth month of the year, and the Jews not only have the important Hanukkah ceremony with a nine-armed candelabra, but there were also nine doors to the holiest part of the Temple in Jerusalem. Nonetheless, in the Judeo-Christian Creation myth there is no indication that there would be several creations of seven DAYS and six NIGHTS. This obviously is a very fateful omission, with wide-ranging consequences, and maybe it is for this reason that several groups of Christians to this day maintain that the world is no more than five thousand years old, in stark contrast to the massive empirical evidence generated by today's science.

In the Far East a multitude of pagodas and other buildings attest to the holiness of the numbers 5 and 9. Both Hinduism and Buddhism also hold the number 108 as a very holy number. In the tradition of Tibetan Buddhism it is said that he who circumambulates the holy Mt. Kailas in Tibet 108 times will reach nirvana. In the Hindu tradition many sages will take the number 108 as one of their names and there are 108 Upanishads in the Vedic scriptures. It is there said that creation is the result of the 108 transformations of Shiva. We may understand the holiness also of this number if we consider that there are Nine Underworlds, each of which is being created by Thirteen Heavens. Since the wave-like movement through the Thirteen Heavens is generated by twelve transformations between DAYS and NIGHTS, all of creation is then generated by $9 \times 12 = 108$ transformations. These are the transformations of Shiva, the creator and the destroyer. The 108 circumambulations of Mt. Kailas leading to nirvana may then be seen as a way of symbolically enacting the passage through all of Creation (corresponding to attaining enlightenment toward the end of 2011).

In this way, the Mayan cosmology of Thirteen Heavens and Nine Underworlds may build bridges in all directions that serve to produce a coherent picture. The perspective derived from the cosmology of the Maya, with its calendrical system as a critical part, may serve to create common ground, which is not only abstract, but tangible, for all of humanity: Christians, Jews, Muslims, Hindus, Buddhists, New Agers, scientific secularists (which includes a large portion of today's China) and, not the least, today's Maya. The message is: the different religions of humanity, as well as our science, all seek to describe the same reality, the One Reality, but have, because of the diversified evolution of consciousness resulting from the dualities of the Planetary Round of LIGHT, come to see this through different glasses.

Why is it among the Maya that we can find the keys to building bridges between the religions of the world and to modern science? Again, a great part of the explanation to this lies in the fact that theirs was a Western consciousness, the Western consciousness of baktuns 8 and 9. While in ancient times all peoples had a fundamentally spiritual world view and were very much preoccupied with understanding Creation, the Maya with their Western consciousness gave a pronounced role to numbers and analytical thinking for their understanding of the Cosmos. They may thus have been especially well equipped to express the spiritual aspects of the ancient religiosity in terms that are understandable and verifiable to us who live today—if only we are willing to look in other directions than we have become used to.

Some people ask how the Maya knew all the things that they did. It is really for the same reason that we who live today may know the very same things. True, we have instruments that allow us to make more accurate measurements and a vastly more extensive base of knowledge. But what ultimately guides us, and guided the ancient Maya, to put all these facts together in a coherent way is our intuition and resonance with the Cosmos, the One Reality common to all humanity. What above all made the Maya different from people living today is that they were intensely preoccupied with understanding Creation. This was what their entire lives revolved around, whereas today it is the focus of only a minority. Only as we progress through the Galactic Underworld is this minority likely to significantly increase.

Can we then say with certainty that these Nine Underworlds are identical to the ones of the ancient Mesoamerican cosmology? After all, as the reader may have noticed, there is a multitude of 13×20^n cycles, far more than nine, in the stele shown from Coba. Well, we will never really know, although the idea that the universe is organized in this way speaks to us very strongly everywhere in the Mayan region. Its most significant pyramids, The Pyramid of the Jaguar in Tikal, The Temple of the Inscriptions in Palenque and the Pyramid of Kukulcan in Chichen-Itza, are all built in nine levels. Also, the Great Cycle was considered as ruled by the Six-Sky-Lord and was thus the sixth out of the nine levels. If this fundamental organization of the Cosmos then fits with the factual basis of modern science there is every reason to adopt the view presented here. If the temporal cosmology of the ancient Maya may serve to create a complete unified science without violating the results generated by thousands of scientists who have spent millions of days of hard left-brain analytical work to establish the facts of science, then we have strong reason to take this seriously. And I feel that if we were now to throw the factual basis of this science out, which many today seem to be willing to do, we would truly throw out the baby with the bath water. Maybe we would then deprive ourselves of the fruit that has been the most important purpose of this science, the goal set already by its early pioneers: to establish the existence of God and help us understand Creation.

THE SHOOTING OF SEVEN-MACAW
AND THE FALL OF ADAM AND EVE

The Planetary Round of LIGHT, which really is a resonance phenomenon with a Galactic Round of LIGHT, will prove to be the most useful for understanding our situation today. In this section we will see what insights this added perspective might provide on the ancient Mayan Creation myths. As we may see in Figure 29, when the Great Cycle began, and the First Father raised the World Tree with its duality of LIGHT and DARKNESS, it did so against the background of the unitary creation field provided by the seventh DAY of the Regional Cycle. Thus, the creation field of the Regional Underworld was not characterized by a hemispheric duality between LIGHT and DARKNESS. Instead, this was an era of LIGHT in the sense that the visions of the human beings were then in resonance with the LIGHT falling on the Pacific front side of the planet.

Fig. 31 One-Ahau, the Hero Twin of *Popol-Vuh*, shoots Seven-Macaw as the bird lands in the World Tree (Courtesy of Freidel, Schele and Parker, *Maya Cosmos*).

The *Popol-Vuh*, sometimes called the Bible of the Maya, may have something to say about this change of creation fields as the National Underworld began to be created on top of the Regional. The *Popol-Vuh* tells above all about the adventures of the Hero Twins Hunahpu and Xbalanque and their role in the Creation of the world. Hunahpu, which is the name of the first-born twin, is derived from Hun Ahau, which translates into 'the One Lord' or 'the One Light.' Hunahpu thus represents the light and male principle of the Cosmos (in the National Underworld that created this Mayan myth, male and light went together). Xbalanque, on the other hand, comes from the prefix 'X' (meaning 'she of') and 'Balam' (meaning 'jaguar'), and represents a nocturnal animal in its female aspect. Thus, the two Hero Twins are here simply interpreted as personifications of the yang and yin of the Cosmos. What yin and yang mean precisely are the DARK and the LIGHT sides of the planetary creation field as it manifested in the National Underworld.

After describing a few earlier creations, which failed to successfully create human beings, the *Popol-Vuh* introduces the story of Seven-Macaw, a bird with a shining beauty that made the world look dark. The Hero Twins thought that Seven-Macaw inappropriately magnified himself, since he thought of himself as being the sun and the moon, and was vainglorious and boastful. Since the Hero Twins feared that the attitude of Seven-Macaw would inspire vanity in the creatures of the world, and that he would inhibit the new creation, they decided to shoot the bird down to show him his real place. Hunahpu used his blowgun to shoot the bird down from his favorite tree so that he fell and broke his jaw. The Twins then took help from their grandparents against the angered bird and persuaded Seven-Macaw to let them remove the shining metal from his eyes, upon which the bird died.

We may wonder what this myth is all about, especially since it is very commonly depicted in Classical Mayan pieces of art. Of course, it may be a good lesson for someone not to present himself as the sun, but in the context in which it is presented—before the beginning of the present creation of the Great Cycle and the National Underworld by the First Father—another thing comes to mind. Seven-Macaw may simply be the allegorical representation of the Heaven ruling the seventh DAY of the Regional Underworld. As we can see from the Planetary Round of LIGHT (Figure 29), this Heaven looked all bright to the human beings, whose vision was then entirely dominated by LIGHT. It is easy to see that this particular Heaven, or any of its manifestations, could have become vainglorious, as no shades would be seen. What adds to this interpretation is that the shooting of Seven-Macaw is described as an event in the sky and that this event was necessary for the First Father to begin this creation. It is also part of the picture that Hunahpu and Xbalanque are the sons of the First Father. Thus, Seven-Macaw is shot down from the sky so that the new creation started by the First Father, and involving the LIGHT/DARK polarity of Hunahpu/Xbalanque, could take its place. While the rule of Seven-Macaw during the seventh DAY of the Regional Underworld may have appeared as a paradise, Creation went on with the building of the new National Underworld, with the difficult and not so vainglorious life of duality. God had other, greater things in mind for the human race.

The innocent Regional Underworld that was ruled by Seven-Macaw in many ways seems to have been fairly idyllic. It was the era of early agricultural societies before the war-like expansion of the patriarchal nations had begun. This era, a non-dualistic era where God's LIGHT would always shine visibly to the human beings, most likely is also what the Garden of Eden refers to. But in this Creation there is more to come, and for this reason life in paradise needed to come to an end. As the Cross was raised the duality of LIGHT and DARKNESS, a prerequisite for human creativity, was introduced. (Eating of the fruit of the World Tree in the Garden of Eden then meant that humans started to enjoy the fruits of creativity of the True Cross.) The innocent life of the Regional Cycle, the first paradise of humanity, was then forever gone.

There is more to note in the Biblical myth that indicates that it describes the same thing as the shooting of Seven-Macaw: In the Garden of Eden it is the serpent that lures 'the woman' into eating of the fruit of the Tree of Life, who then entices Adam to do the same. The serpent does so by saying that if the two eat of the fruit they will be able to see the difference between good and evil as through the eyes of God. And later, as a result of having eaten of the fruit the two became aware of being naked, which is to say that they became aware of the difference between man and woman. This seems to be immediately understandable from the Planetary Round of LIGHT; as the creativity of the World Tree started to bear fruit, as a result of the yin/yang duality introduced (the snake is a common symbol of duality), people at the beginning of the Great Cycle indeed became aware of the difference between man and woman and between good and evil. As a result of their resonance with the dualistic LIGHT/DARKNESS creation field of the planet they then became able to make these new distinctions. That the introduction of duality at the beginning of the Great Cycle indeed is what the Fall of Adam and Eve describes seems all the more likely given that it dates to about the same time when, according to the Maya, Seven-Macaw was defeated. In the Jewish tradition this Fall has been set at 3761 BC, which, all things considered, is fairly close to May 26, 3149 BC, when, according to the inscriptions of Palenque, Seven-Macaw was defeated to prepare for the new creation with the duality of Hunahpu and Xbalanque.

In the Jewish-Christian myth the expulsion of Adam and Eve from the Garden of Eden is, however, portrayed as an act of God to punish them for their sinful act of eating from the forbidden fruit. This supposedly was the reason that all women were later to give birth in pain and resulted in an 'original sin' that all mankind has inherited. In the perspective we are developing here such an interpretation seems almost ridiculous and seems to serve nothing but to instill fear in people. Rather than some original sin, or an inherent evil in woman, it seems that the step out of the Garden of Eden was a step very much intended by the divine plan. In view of the step-wise creation of the Nine Underworlds, and the Planetary Round of LIGHT which determines the pattern of duality-unity of these Underworlds, eating of the

Fig. 32 Adam and Eve in Paradise with the snake and the fruit of the Tree of Life (Lucas Cranach the elder – Bayerische Staatsgemälde Sammlungen, Munich).

The Mayan Calendar

fruit seems to have been a necessary step in the evolution of the universe, exactly as planned by God. This step may not have been convenient to take, and human beings may not have liked to take it, but it was not taken because we did something wrong or because God wanted to punish us. Rather, God had some higher plans for us.

From the perspective of theology this is an important discovery. Countless generations of human beings, and in particular women, have been told that they are in this world because they did something wrong, or in fact, that by their very nature they are wrong, since an original sin cannot be corrected. Many verses in the Bible tend to demean women. Many have thought it wrong to seek knowledge (because Adam and Eve ate from the fruit of the Tree of Knowledge and supposedly were punished for it) and many have thought that human beings, just by being here, just by being human, have done something wrong, something sinful.

We can now see that such thoughts, still today maintained by some Jewish-Christian traditions, by themselves are products of the very patriarchal frame of consciousness generated by the National Underworld, a frame that was dominating in the Heaven when these traditions were conceived. From a new understanding of Creation based on the cosmology of the Maya we may realize that the step taken as Adam and Eve ate from the fruit of the Tree of Knowledge, as duality was generated in the world, in fact was exactly what, according to the divine plan, was meant to happen. God hardly resented the first humans for following His/Her plan. One more thing in the Biblical myth should be noted here. It is said there that death was a result of the eating of the fruit, i.e., the new dualistic awareness brought about by the erected World Tree of the Great Cycle, but it also says that if Adam had eaten more of the fruit he might have become immortal. Maybe then it is by eating more of the fruit that we will eventually attain a frame of consciousness that will bring immortality. This will happen as we reach the Universal Underworld, which judging from the Planetary Round of LIGHT looks like a second paradise.

CHAPTER 7

THE GALACTIC WORLD TREE
AND THE STAR OF BETHLEHEM

Seek Him that maketh the Pleiades and Orion
Amos 5:8

THE MAMMALIAN UNDERWORLD

The first four Underworlds of Creation are essentially Underworlds where the astronomical, geological and biological foundation is laid for the later mental and spiritual evolution of mankind. To study these Underworlds reaching billions of years into the past we can hardly consult the ancient peoples of the planet, such as the Maya or the Jews, who had only vague notions about when and how different minerals, plants and animals had been created. Thus, the descriptions of the order in which the animals and plants were created, both in the *Book of Genesis* and the *Books of Chilam Balam*, seem to have been considerably scrambled. In these old scriptures one often gets the impression that the animals were created out of nothing to their ready form. The detailed studies of modern biology have, however, shown beyond a doubt that today's species are the result of an evolution, which, starting with single cells, has led to the human beings of today. They have also successfully dated the emergence of many species.

Regarding biological evolution I will limit the discussion to the Second of the Underworlds, what is here called the Mammalian Underworld, whose creation began 13 alautuns, or 13 × 63.1 million years = 820.3 million years before the present. The progression through these 13 alautuns, Thirteen Heavens alternating between seven DAYS and six NIGHTS, is what has propelled the biological evolution of animals and plants. This Second Underworld starts with the very first multicellular organisms, appearing on this planet as its first alautun begins, and is completed by the emergence of the higher mammals at the beginning of alautun 12.

As a first observation in Table 9, describing the emergence of significant new classes of animals, we may note that very significant steps were taken in the evolution of the brains of these close to the beginnings of the even-numbered alautuns, the DAYS, of the Mammalian Cycle. While it has not been included in the table, it can also be shown that several mass extinctions, such as that of the dinosaurs sixty-five million years ago, took place very close to alautun shifts. This would then be a parallel to how several major human civilizations would collapse close to the baktun shifts of the National Cycle.

Table 9
The Development of Classes of Multicellular Animals
during the Even-numbered Alautuns (DAYS)
of the Mammalian Cycle (MYA = millions of years ago)

Alautun	DAY	Beginning MYA	Classes of organisms (modern estimate)
0	1	820.3 MYA	First clusters of cells (850 MYA)
2	2	694.1 MYA	First symmetrical soft-tissue animals, Ediacaran Hills fauna (680)
4	3	567.9 MYA	Cambrian explosion: Trilobites, ammonites, molluscs (570)
6	4	441.7 MYA	Fishes (440)
8	5	315.5 MYA	Reptiles (300)
10	6	189.3 MYA	Mammals (190)
12	7	63.1 MYA	Placental mammals (65)

The emergence of these various classes of animals throughout the Mammalian Cycle will not be discussed in detail here. Suffice it to say that the emergence of the first multicellular organisms at the beginning of the cycle represented a true revolution in the organization of life compared to the single cells generated by the First Underworld. We may here compare the subordination of cells to the higher organization of multicellular organisms with how, at the beginning of the National Underworld, local cultures came to be subordinated to nations. An example of this was when Pharaoh Menes unified the smaller prehistoric kingdoms in Upper and Lower Egypt into one nation. Thus, as a new Underworld begins a higher, more complex organization of life always emerges in response to the new, wider frame of consciousness.

In the close parallels between the emergence of important new classes of animal species and the alautun shifts of the Mammalian Cycle we can now find evidence that biological evolution is not a random process. It does not happen by accident, but according to a plan for the evolution of consciousness. Thus, it is not primarily driven by mutations in DNA, as the Darwinist philosophy dominating current academic biological thought would like to have it. The plants, animals and human beings are intentional results (intentional in the design plan of God) of creation cycles of Thirteen Heavens which step by step have led to the emergence of classes of animals with brains increasingly better equipped to receive information from the Cosmos.

The role of DNA has, incidentally, been vastly exaggerated in today's biological science. The information content of DNA is much too small (about four billion base pairs) to determine the size, shape and organization of our organs and body (our brains alone are made up of some 100 billion cells organized in a complex arrangement). The emphasis on DNA in today's academic research goes back to the still dominating reductionist view in which essentially fruitless attempts are made to explain the whole in terms of its parts rather than the other way around. In the holistic view that is presented here, biological organisms are created according to the Hermetic principle and thus DNA is seen as a microcosm of more complex biological structures rather than as a determinant of their evolution.

The reason that the rather simple and telling pattern in Table 9 has not previously been discovered is only partly that the Mayan calendar has not been used as a template in the study of biological evolution. (Incidentally, if its datings seem too good to be true, the reader is wholeheartedly referred to a recent standard textbook of evolutionary biology.) The other and more profound reasons are philosophical: In the view of today's academic science, to be a creationist, that is, to question Darwinism, is absolutely taboo. Many radical thoughts in many areas of science may be proposed, but not this, that human beings could have been created by God. The reason for this taboo is that if Darwinism does not hold, the most important pillar upon which today's materialist philosophy of science is built would collapse. Such a collapse would affect all branches of academic science. In recent decades several proposals have been advanced to create a more spiritually oriented world view, often based on the so-called new physics, but the effects of such discussions on academic science have been only minor. This is because the critical pillar of today's science is not physics, but biology, and unless a viable alternative to Darwinism is presented, it is hardly possible to rationally argue that there is a spiritual purpose to human life. As a consequence, anyone seriously aspiring to contribute to the emergence of a new world view will need to take this issue very seriously and, it must be said, many new thinkers have shunned it.

Thus, because of the taboo on questioning Darwinism, evolutionary biologists have consistently been looking away from the evolution of consciousness, which in my view is the primary factor behind evolution. Instead, they have focused their attention on physical, often superficial, traits having to do with the morphology (shape) of the species in the global fauna and flora. As a result, the very clear creation-based pattern of biological evolution has been blurred. It is only if we shift our attention to what is important from the perspective of the evolution of expressions of consciousness, i.e., significant advances in the size and organization of the brain, that the pattern in Table 9 becomes evident. There we can see that pulse by pulse classes of animals with significantly more developed brains emerge at the beginning of the even-numbered alautuns, the DAYS, of the cycle. The emergence at the beginning of alautun 6 of the vertebrates, distinguished by a cranium providing protection and support for the brain, for instance, is noteworthy as a critical point in cerebral evolution. This midpoint of the cycle marks a turning point in the evolution of consciousness, and from this point and onwards 'real' animals with increasingly intelligent and playful behavior emerge.

THE HERMETIC PRINCIPLE IN BIOLOGY:
THE CONTINENTAL DRIFT AND THE LATERALIZED BRAIN

The aspect of biological evolution that, however, may be the most enlightening to study is that of the lateralization of the brain (creating brains with a left/right duality) during the latter DAYS of the cycle. This development may then be compared to what happened on a continental scale on planet earth in these same DAYS. The mammals, a group that includes us humans, stand out in one significant respect as a class of animals; their brains are lateralized. Although lower genera of animals, such as reptiles and fishes, also have symmetrical brains with left and right halves, it is only in the mammals that these two halves have separate functions. Hence, before the appearance of the first mammals some 200 million years ago there were no organisms around on this planet with lateralized brains. Interestingly, if we look at the continental structure of the earth at that time (Figure 33a) we can see that all land masses were then joined together in what has become known as the Pangaea continent. About 190 million years ago, however, different parts of this giant continent began to drift apart and the result was the initial separation of the continents of the Old and New World. What this means is that simultaneously with the first occurrence, at the beginning of alautun 10, of organisms with lateralized brains the continents of the Old and New World started to drift apart. If we then proceed to the beginning of alautun 12, as the higher placental mammals with brains with considerably larger lateralized cortices first emerge, then another significant change begins in the continental structure of the planet; about 65 million years ago Greenland and Scandinavia started to drift apart. Through the formation of the North Atlantic the two continental blocks then definitely separated, and have since continued to drift even further apart.

Thus, there is a direct parallel between, on the one hand, the rhythm with which animals with lateralized brains have evolved and, on the other, the rhythm with which the main continental blocks of the planet have separated. This seems to indicate that human beings, and in fact all of the mammals, were indeed created in the image of the earth: as above, so below. What happens with the earth, happens with the biological organisms. The yin/yang dualities of the Cosmos operate at different levels simultaneously.

This pattern of dualities also gives a hint to why the dinosaurs became extinct at the beginning of alautun 12. The dinosaurs, in contrast to the mammals, did not have lateralized brains, and so they no longer resonated effectively with the dualistic creation field of the Thirteenth Heaven of the Mammalian Cycle. It is of lesser importance if the immediate cause for their extinction was a meteor, unsuccessful competition with the mammals or something else. If we accept a world view where consciousness is primary to matter then there are no accidents, and the immediate causes for the extinction of the dinosaurs are only secondary.

This pattern of dualistic separations of continents and brains taking place at even-numbered alautuns in the Mammalian Cycle may remind us of how, in the creation of the National Underworld, East/West dualities were introduced at the beginning of even-numbered baktuns. As an example of this, the dinosaurs in fact met their end for a reason that is similar to that of the demise of the German-Roman emperors or the Mayan ahauob: the power of a new duality in the Heavens. Hence, the Mammalian Underworld also created duality, starting with the first emergence of clusters of cells and then DAY-by-DAY developing animals with progressively more polarized brains.

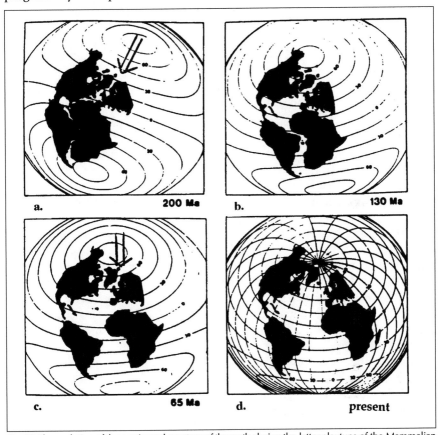

Fig. 33 The evolution of the continental structure of the earth during the latter alautuns of the Mammalian Cycle (Note that for clarity Asia has been omitted from these maps): (a) The Pangea continent shown intact 200 million years ago; (b) At the beginning of alautun 10 some 190 million years ago the continental drift begins and results in the separation of the continental blocks of the New and Old World, here shown 130 million years ago; (c) Greenland starts to drift away from Scandinavia at the beginning of alautun 12; (d) Current continental structure of the earth (Courtesy Bengt Loberg, *Geologi*, p. 24, Norstedts, Stockholm 1980).

Also, because of the introduction of these dualities adhering to the Mayan time cycles for the creation of the Mammalian Underworld, a geocontinental basis for the organization of the planet in the four directions was created. Since the continental structure of the whole planet seems to be determined by invisible creation field boundaries in the north-south and east-west directions and by implication also at 45° from these, the existence of fields such as those studied by dowsers—e.g., Curry and Hartmann lines—seems only natural. These would, however, not be radiations emitted by the earth, but in fact vibrations emanating from the basic creation field that has served to create life in all of its aspects on this planet. The points where these radiation lines intersect would ultimately be resonances with the galactic location called by the Maya the Eight-Partition-Place.

THE SHIVERING OF THE WORLD TREE

The ancient scriptures of humanity, and the Book of Genesis in particular, state that human beings are created in the image of God. Maybe seeing that all mammals, including ourselves, are created in the image of the earth, as was shown in the previous section, may be a first step to understanding that we have been created in the image of God. Above the earth, the next higher level in the organization of the universe is the galaxy, and in Figure 34 our galaxy, and the path of the solar system through it, is shown at an angle. In this picture it can be seen how the solar system, including our own planet, passes in an orbit around the galactic center. The duration of such a cycle is about 240-250 million years and is called a galactic year, which is the time scale of interest in the study of biological and geological evolution. From the perspective taken here, what may be of the most interest is that during the galactic year the solar system performs four cyclical movements up and down through the galactic midplane, and that each such cycle has a duration of 62 million years, i.e., about one alautun. What this indicates is that the dualities created with this very same periodicity on the level of the continental blocks of the earth and the brains of its organisms, respectively, are ultimately resonance phenomena of dualities introduced on the higher level of the galactic midplane: as above, so below. The dualities introduced along the galactic midplane which generate these cyclical movements, in other words, would by holographic resonance be expressed on the planetary level in the separation of continents and on the level of biological organisms in the separation of brain halves. *All three processes adhere to the same alautun-based rhythm.* The continental structure and biological organisms that characterize this earth are then not really the results of an evolution taking place on this earth in isolation. Instead, they have in a very true sense of the word a galactic

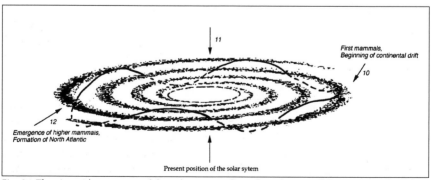

Fig. 34 The sinusoid movement of the solar system about the galactic midplane. Four such cyclical movements about the midplane correspond to a galactic year of about 250 million years. The positions of the solar system at the most recent alautun shifts have been indicated.

origin. This is not to say that they have arrived here from other planets. Rather, they are holographic resonance phenomena generated by the process of creation working through a higher galactic level.

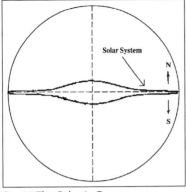

Fig. 35 The Galactic Cross.

For the cyclical movement about the galactic midplane to occur, an invisible creation field boundary along the galactic midplane needs to serve as a wave generator—operating in accordance with an alautun periodicity— generating among other things the cyclic stellar movements about the galactic midplane. Such cyclical movements of the star systems of the galaxy would then be an analogy to the historical movements to and from the planetary midline that we studied earlier. Part of their importance lies in the fact that they are one of the indications that indeed the galactic midplane is active as a creation field boundary. That there also exists a creation field boundary perpendicular to the galactic midplane is shown by the fact that our galaxy has spiral arms whose movement cannot be explained otherwise. Together the two creation field boundaries form a Galactic Cross, but, similarly to how the 12th longitude axis on earth is much more important in diversifying cultural evolution than the equator, the galactic midplane boundary is much more important in creating life than the boundary perpendicular to it. This invisible Cross then is the true World Tree, and it is its trunk, the galactic midplane boundary, that primarily bears fruit.

On our planet the planetary midline at the 12th longitude East is the holographic resonance line for the galactic midplane. We see this in that the separation of the continents emanating from this longitude clearly follows the same periodicity as that of the movement of the solar system about the galactic midplane. The creation of life on this planet in all of its aspects is thus nothing but resonance phenomena of vibrations generated by the Galactic Cross. The creation of human beings from the World Tree is just one example. All that happens on earth is ultimately a reflection of a process of creation operating at a higher hierarchical level, that of the galaxy, and our planet is hence in a very real and direct sense a microcosm of the galaxy. Just as an example, the existence of such a Galactic Cross would explain the extinction of the dinosaurs, whose non-lateralized brains could no longer resonate with its vibrations.

The awesome scale at which creation occurs may be a cause for humbleness on our own part—the diameter of the galaxy is some 100,000,000,000,000 times greater than that of our own planet. In Nordic myth, the World Tree was said to be so huge that its branches would stretch across both heaven and earth. These 'branches' then are the correspondents on a galactic level to Curry and Hartmann lines layered on the invisible sphere surrounding the galaxy. This sphere apparently serves as a kind of projection screen for creative pulses emanating from the roots of the World Tree, which are located at the galactic center. Thus what happens on our own little planet, with its True Cross in resonance with the World Tree, is a reflection of a process of creation occurring on a vastly larger scale which is completely outside of our control.

In this context it is noteworthy that it is not only our own solar system that moves up and down the galactic midplane in a wave-like movement following an alautun rhythm. With a few exceptions, all star systems of the galaxy perform a similar movement, and the logical conclusion to draw is that all the star systems of the galaxy are affected synchronistically by the creation cycles generated by this invisible Galactic Cross. The World Tree is thus truly generating everything in the world, the Galactic World. This means that all the star systems of our galaxy follow the same frequency generated by the midplane arm of the Galactic Cross. This should then mean that all planets with life in the galaxy, and the biological evolution on all of these planets, would be created and develop in synchrony. We on our own planet would be affected by the same sequence of Heavens and Underworlds synchronistically with all life and forms of human-like consciousness on life-harboring planets in other parts of the galaxy. Our cousins on planets in other solar systems would then not be at stages of development all that different from our own, at least not with regard to the nature of their consciousness. If we accept that all life in the galaxy is the result of creation by the same Galactic World Tree, and that its vibrations are affecting life in the entire galaxy, then this is the only logical consequence to draw.

In this way, we may realize that the same Galactic Cross rules the entire galaxy. As we shall see later, this Galactic Cross also holds the potential for generating the return of Christ consciousness. The return of Cosmic Christ will be nothing but a new phase of vibrations generated by the Galactic Cross. For reasons that we will explain later this new phase will be generated in the Galactic Underworld, which evolves according to the rhythm of the tun. This then represents an increase in the frequency generated by the World Tree, going from a frequency of 1/alautun in the creation cycle we have now discussed, the Mammalian Cycle, to 1/tun in the coming Underworld. (And curiously, in Nordic myth it was predicted that as

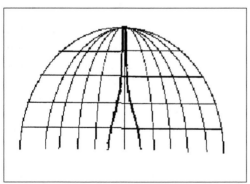

Creation would draw near to its completion the branches of the World Tree would start shivering and shaking much faster than previously.)

Such vibrations, generated by the World Tree with a tun periodicity, have given the revolution of our planet around the sun the particular duration that it has. Since the plane in which the earth and the planets move, the ecliptic, is at an angle with the galactic midplane, pulses through this midplane generated with a tun

Fig. 36 The World Tree with its trunk and branches = A standing Milky Way with 'galactic Curry and Hartmann lines'.

periodicity will result in a planet that revolves around the sun with a similar period. Since, however, the physical manifestations are not always perfect matches of the divine vibrations, the period of revolution of our earth is slightly longer than the tun. Figure 37, adapted from *Cambridge Atlas of Astronomy*, depicts the changing duration of the physical year over time.

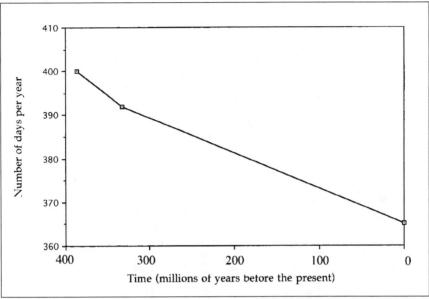

Fig. 37 The change in the number of days in an astronomical year over the past 400 million years (adapted from Cambridge Atlas of Astronomy).

The diagram shows how the number of days in a year has decreased over the past 400 million years, going from about 400 days in a year to 365.2422 today. What this beyond any doubt means is that the number of days in a solar year is not a constant, eternal property of this planet. What the diagram instead seems to indicate is that the solar year is still in the process of approaching the number of days, 360, in a tun, which is the period of some of the pulses emanating from the midplane arm of the Galactic Cross traversing our solar system. Three hundred sixty days is the duration of the spiritual year ordained by the Holy Cross, and generated by the vibrations of the World Tree, and the earth is still in the process of approaching this periodicity. Thus, it is because the pulses of the World Tree follow a tun periodicity that the tun has been recognized as a divine year in many traditions. The tun is the duration of the ideal year existing only in the invisible universe and is thus, in contrast to the physical year, a sure constant of Creation. What this also beyond a doubt means is that if we are to develop resonance with the Living Cross, we can only be aided by a calendar that describes the vibrations of this. Conversely, while calendars built on the physical year may be important for agriculture or for following the seasons, they are irrelevant for our spiritual evolution. This holds true regardless of whether the physical year is described by the

Gregorian calendar or some calendar with a Mayan origin such as the haab (18 × 20 + 5 days) or the Thirteen Moons (13 × 28 + 1 days).

If life in the galaxy, then, is generated by the pulses of creative dualities emanating from the World Tree, this means that the best bet for finding planets with life in the galaxy are those that revolve around stars in an orbit with a duration of approximately 360 days. Hence, the number of planets with life in the galaxy may be much smaller than has previously been thought, possibly as low as ten thousand or fewer.

Fig. 38 A Ceiba tree at Tikal. To the Maya this is symbolic of the World Tree. Its seeds are used for divination and its sap for incense.
(Photo Calleman)

Also, the frequencies of revolution around the sun of the other plants in our solar system would then depend on pulses emitted by the Galactic Cross, creating tones in a symphony played throughout the galaxy. Hence if there is order and harmony in the cosmos, these have to originate at least at a galactic level. The central focus of Kepler's work was to demonstrate that there existed harmonic relationships between the orbits of the planets, and this may be true for reasons that have not previously been recognized. Newton's work may have shown why the planets are accelerated at the rate that they are, but it does not explain why they occupy the orbits with the specific periods of revolution that they do. These periods of revolution are in fact determined by the frequencies of the vibrations— overtones of the hablatun and alautun vibrations—generated by the Galactic Cross, vibrations that may also harmonize with certain colors and sounds important to the human

The Mayan Calendar

experience. This symphony would affect not only the orbital rhythms of the planets, but also the deepest levels of existence in us, since it is linked to the evolution of consciousness.

The tun-based calendars of the Maya may then be recognized as mathematical descriptions of the frequencies of vibration of the World Tree. And indeed, in Mayan myth it is said that some of the fruits of the World Tree were periods of time. Since the pulses of creative dualities generated by the World Tree simultaneously affect both the frequencies of planetary revolutions and the evolution of consciousness, it is not very surprising that sometimes synchronicities between events of a personal nature and planetary movements occur. This does not mean to imply that the planetary movements in some sense cause the human occurrences—which would be a materialist way of thinking—but that the frequencies of the cosmic symphony played by the Galactic Cross affect human events as well as planetary orbits. These would be two independent processes, each manifesting the creativity of the World Tree, which, however, because of their common origin, would sometimes generate synchronicities. Thus, when Mayan ahauob celebrated their spiritual, tun-based birthdays, they really celebrated their own resonance with the World Tree. In the galactic era that we are now about to enter, it may thus be a fruitful avenue for astrologers to focus on the vibrations of the Galactic Cross, rather than on their physical manifestations of creation such as planets or stars.

In light of all of the above the Biblical verse *John 1:1-3*—'In the beginning was the Word, and the Word was with God, and the Word was God. The same was in the beginning with God. All things were made by him; and without him was not any thing made that was made' —may take on a new meaning. If we surmise that the Word is the vibrations of the World Tree, we may realize that God began this Creation by initiating its vibrations, its pulses of creative dualities. The same 'in the beginning' may thus refer to the World Tree, and, indeed, in Mayan myth it was said that the World Tree existed before everything else. The World Tree only required God, the supreme deity beyond all duality, to activate creation by speaking His Word, thus initiating the vibrations of the World Tree.

We may also consider that the trees of our world, and in fact all plants, have been created in the image of the World Tree. As such the trees may all be recognized as holy objects, providing significant support for human life in the forms of fruits and shelter, in addition to the sense that we live on a living planet with something to look up to. Our own lack of respect for the trees, expressed especially in the deforestation of the tropical areas, but in recent years also through large forest fires apparently instigated by humans, is thus a frightening omen.

Hence, all organisms on this planet, including human beings, seem to have been created in the image not only of the earth, but also of the galaxy. It may, however, be possible to go even one step further and demonstrate that in certain respects human beings are created in the image of the entire universe. This may be as close as we now can get to realizing that we are created in the image of God. Figure 39 shows, as we have already discussed, that our lateralized brains are created in the image of the galactic duality. But it also shows that there are noteworthy parallels in a numeric sense. Thus, our brains have approximately 100 billion cells, which is

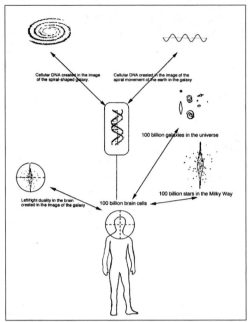

Fig. 39 Human beings have been created in the image of the galaxy and the universe.

close to the number of stars in our galaxy (100-200 billion). It is actually also close to the total number of galaxies in the entire universe (about 50 billion, as estimated by the Hubble telescope). Thus, there exists a direct correspondence between the number of cells in the human brain and the number of stars in the galaxy, as well as with the number of galaxies in the entire universe. Based on this we may tentatively argue that human beings have been created in the image of the universe, since these numeric correspondences may reflect the very processes that condition the holographic resonance between the human brain and the higher hierarchical levels of the universe. Interestingly, it was only as a species, *Homo sapiens,* with a brain size of about 100 billion cells emerged that a creative species, as evidenced through art and crafts, developed on this planet. Our earlier predecessors, such as *Proconsul* or *Homo habilis,* did not have 100 billion brain cells, something that would explain their lack of creativity.

Recent studies have revealed that there is a structure to the large-scale distribution of galaxies in the universe (Figure 40). It is too early to say exactly how this large-scale structure looks. There is, however, a possibility that there are 'sculptures' where galaxies serve as cells. Everything Below in the holographic chain would then be created in the image of these. Of possible significance is a structure shown in this figure, which is reminiscent both of a tree and of a human being. Although it is too early to draw any definite conclusions from this it may certainly serve as food for thought.

It is thus possible that one of the things that have made human beings unique among the species of this planet is that we have been created with a number of

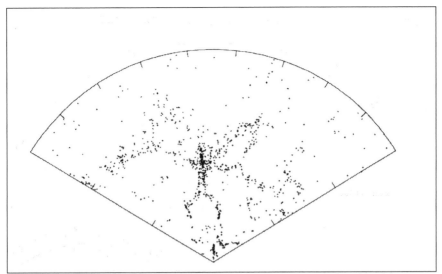

Fig. 40 Sectorial view of the large scale distribution of galaxies in the universe (the radius of the sector is about 400 million light years). The picture shows that the large scale distribution of galaxies in the universe is structured. In the midst of this sector a structure reminiscent of a World Tree of galaxies may be seen. Because this structure has two legs indicated in the lower part, it has jokingly been referred to as a human being (de Lapparent et al., *A Slice of the Universe*)

brain cells that allows our brains to be in resonance with the entire universe and so, through holographic resonance, develop creativity. If so, what led human beings to become creative as we began our resonance with the Heavens of the Regional

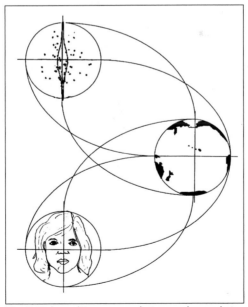

Fig. 41 Holographic resonance between a human being and the galaxy with the creation field of the earth serving as a relay.

The Galactic World Tree and the Star of Bethlehem   107

Underworld, the Fifth Underworld starting 102,000 years ago, was that our brains had then finally attained a size, 100 billion cells, sufficient for unhindered holographic resonance with the universe. As far as we can tell this brain size was attained as a preparation for the beginning of that cycle—with the advent of *Homo sapiens* about 150,000 years ago.

From this we may also understand why our brain size has not increased further since then. As the potential for holographic resonance with the universe cannot be more than complete a further increase in brain size would have served no purpose. If this is true, human beings are indeed special in this Creation, and are, as already argued, what this Creation is all about. Compared to the other species we have a unique role and responsibility as co-creators with God.

This universal perspective on Creation may also be useful when we consider occurrences in our individual lives, some of which we may not like and may even blame on higher powers. What happens in the life of an individual human being is ultimately conditioned by a plan for Creation developed on a galactic scale. It is thus on the galactic and universal scales that the final purpose of Creation will eventually be manifested. Our lives then have purposes laid down by the large-scale purpose of God's Creation. This may not always coincide with our own temporary desires or ambitions, and since the cosmic purpose of God's plan overrides all of our individual ideas of what life should be like, life may not always seem fair. To create a universe with 100 billion galaxies, with 100 billion stars in each of them, where everyone is constantly happy is not necessarily an easy thing to do. This may be something for us to consider as we deliver our complaints.

THE THOUGHTS OF GOD

Einstein once said that his interest in science was based on his desire to understand the thoughts of God. Figure 41 shows a model of how I envision these thoughts of God, which bring the Creation of the world about. In this model, the thoughts of God, the Heavens, are seen as slides which are inserted in the Cosmic Projector (Figure 42) at the highest universal level.

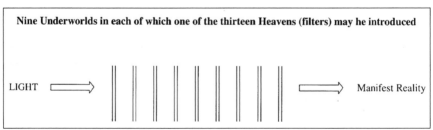

Fig. 42 The Cosmic Pojector.

By means of the LIGHT of God these slides are projected onto the Cosmos and manifested in the Underworlds. Through holographic resonance the projected LIGHT is then dissipated from the cosmic level down to its galaxy components (Figure 41). Since a spiral galaxy is separated into two different hemispheres, it is possible for human beings, as well as other organisms with lateralized brains, 1 receive information through holographic resonance from the highest Heavens with both the galaxy and the earth serving as relays. Part of the explanation as to why the universe is dominated by polarities—polarity of genders, polarity of brains and consciousness—is thus to meet the need for a mechanism to transmit information. Resonance presupposes polarity, and because of the polarity between the hemispheres of our brains these serve as antennas for the reception of information from new Heavens inserted in the Cosmic Projector. Resonance with the Heavens is then partly what propels us to participate in the construction of the Underworlds. We may be more like puppets to the process of Creation than we have liked to think. From this we may also understand the meaning of the term 'Underworld' as a world below created by resonance with the Heavens above.

Such a holographic view of the universe now makes it possible to understand the phenomenon of synchronicities. Since the Heavens affect us all simultaneously, as soon as they are introduced in the Cosmic Projector, it is not very surprising that different individuals independently come up with the same ideas at about the same time. In fact, it would be much more surprising if ideas did not arise synchronistically in different places.

There are also other types of synchronicities where the two individuals are not acting independently, an example of which would be when you run into a person just when you were thinking of him. Such occurrences also become understandable from the above model given that the two persons were in resonance with the same Heaven. Chance meetings that are meant to happen are part of a scenario resulting from divine LIGHT being focused at special evolving streaks in the Underworld, creating 'flows' in the human experience. Synchronicities are currently becoming more common as the frequency of divine creation is now speeding up so as to make seemingly statistically impossible events commonplace. But more about this later.

Incidentally, not many of us ever grow away from thinking that synchronicities are 'strange' and remarkable. This attitude is a logical consequence of our materialist world view and our denial of a divine plan for the evolution of consciousness. Since our consciousness is to us like water is to the fish, we are oblivious to its existence and tend to disregard the changes that it undergoes as the divine plan unfolds. Since this plan governs all material aspects of our existence, including coincidences in the physical universe, it is not queer that many events defy the laws of statistics. What this sums up to is that because we are blind to our own consciousness we fall prey to the illusion that only the material world is real, and in such an illusory material world synchronicities can indeed only seem strange and inexplicable.

PACAL AND THE GALACTIC CROSS

With this background we shall now proceed to discuss how the Galactic Cross has been expressed in Mayan Creation myths. To do so we will travel to the royal capital of Palenque, one of the most beautiful and magical sites built by the ancient Maya, located on the slopes of the Chiapan jungle overlooking the lowlands extending toward the Yucatan. This was the westernmost city of the Classical

Fig. 43 The Temple of the Inscriptions in Palenque in whose crypt Pacal the Great is buried (Photo Calleman).

Mayan world. Its dynasty of rule was founded almost exactly at the beginning of baktun 9, and at the midpoint of this baktun it was ruled by Pacal the Great. Pacal was succeeded by his son Chan-Bahlum, who built a series of extraordinary temples, which may well mark the height of development of the Classical Maya.

Nowhere in the Mayan lands is there to be found such an explicit description of how creation was viewed and how life, death and rebirth was envisioned in the Classical era as in the inscriptions of the Group of the Cross and in the Temple of the Inscriptions of Palenque, the famed nine-storied pyramid in whose crypt Pacal was buried under an even more famous sarcophagus lid. Although these two important rulers of Palenque, Pacal and Chan-Bahlum, may not have founded a new religion, they apparently gave the old one its clearest expression and somewhat changed its emphasis.

The worship of the World Tree was by no means a novelty of Palenque—it can be traced back to a much earlier time—but the Cross is not known to have played such a prominent role at other Mayan sites. And we may wonder: 'Were Pacal and Chan-Bahlum then embarking, if not on a new religion, then at least on a new emphasis on the Cross?' What is interesting here is that in the reliefs of the Group of the Cross, the Cross is presented as distinct from the rulers rather than just identified with them (as, e.g., in Figure 19). Maybe in this we may see a great contribution of Pacal in the evolution of the Mayan religiosity. While being ahauob, he and Chan-Bahlum presented themselves as distinct from the World Tree, and in the mural reliefs they presented the World Tree, the Cross, as an object of worship in itself.

In the temples of Palenque there are several representations of the Cross. One of these is on the sarcophagus lid of Pacal, which, according to its inscription, shows how he, dressed as the First Father, enters 'the road,' the Milky Way, and sinks into an offering plate dedicated to the 'Quadripartite god' (Figure 44). The inscriptions of the Group of the Cross dedicated by his son Chan-Bahlum further

Fig. 44 The lid of Pacal's sarcophagus in the Temple of the Inscriptions. Pacal, dressed as the Maize God, is here seen in front of the World Tree falling in death into its roots. At the roots of the World Tree, underneath Pacal, an offering plate to the Quadripartite god at the galactic center has been placed (Courtesy Schele and Freidel, *A Forest of Kings*).

describe two dates of creation at the beginning of the Long Count corresponding to August 11 and February 3. In *Maya Cosmos* the late Linda Schele and co-workers, through a truly amazing piece of work, pieced together a picture where various symbols of Mayan myths have been connected to specific celestial regions that are evident in the sky on these particular dates.

The correspondences deduced by these authors now allow us not only to understand the Mayan view of the World Tree as identical with the Galactic Cross of the Milky Way, but also how the Maya viewed death and rebirth, as well as the events of Creation at the beginning of the Long Count, in relation to the Galactic Cross. Some of the facets of the two days of Creation have been summarized in Table 10. This is probably as close as we will ever get to a description of how the Classical Maya pictured the events occurring at the beginning of the Great Cycle, the cycle creating the National Underworld.

To understand the two different dates we must realize that the Milky Way, which is generated by the invisible trunk of the World Tree, looks different depending on your point of view. The best picture is obviously gained from a position outside of the galaxy such as the one shown in Figure 45. But someone living on our planet, also indicated in the picture, will gain different views of the World Tree when looking in different directions. One view, which here is called World Tree I (shown in Figures 45 and 46), is gained when looking in the direction of the galactic center, and another, World Tree II, is seen when looking in the direction opposite to the galactic center (shown in Figures 45, 47, 48 and 49). Thus, two different World Trees, each dominating the sky on one of the two Creation dates, have been depicted at the temples of Palenque: World Tree I in the Temple of the Cross and World Tree II in the Temple of the Foliated Cross. To the Maya these two dates in the solar year served to highlight two different galactic locations with different roles in divine creation.

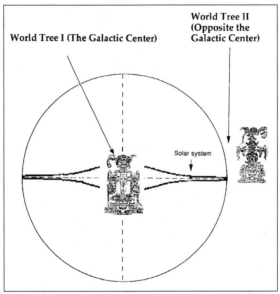

Fig. 45 Cross section of the galaxy indicating the locations portrayed by the Maya as World Tree I (galactic center) and World Tree II (Eight-partition-place, opposite-galactic-center as seen from the earth). The Maya believed that the souls of the dead would enter at the roots of the World Tree, i.e. at the galactic center, in the direction of Scorpio as seen from the earth, and go to Heaven through the branches of the World Tree, i.e. to the Eight-Partition-Place in the direction of Taurus (see also fig. 81).

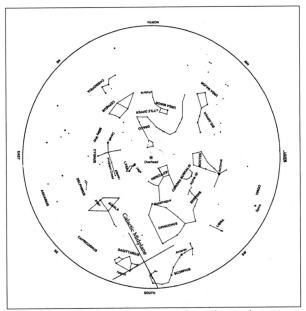

Fig. 46 Star map showing the summer sky in the Northern Hemisphere with the constellations, the Milky Way and the direction towards the galactic center between Sagittarius and Ophiuchus.

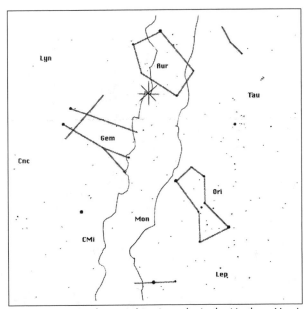

Fig. 47 Star map showing the winter sky in the Northern Hemisphere with the constellation, the Galactic Midplane (visible as the Milky Way), and the point in the opposite direction of the galactic center, the Eight-Partition-House, at the border between Auriga and Taurus.

The Galactic World Tree and the Star of Bethlehem

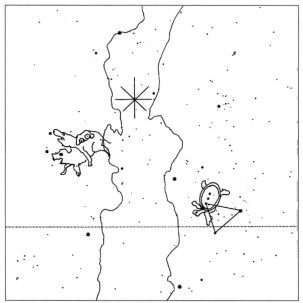

Fig. 48 Star map with the Maya constellations of the Copulating Peccaries (Gemini), the Turtle (Orion's Belt) and Three Hearth Stones (Alnitak, Saiph and Rigel of the lower part of Orion). The triangle of the Three-Stone-Place (where the World Tree was believed to have been raised) points approximately to the opposite-galactic center.

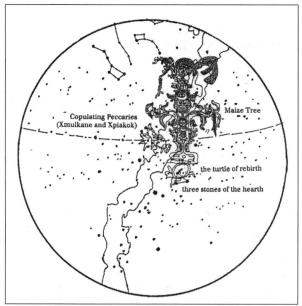

Fig. 49 World Tree II positioned on star map with the cross between the trunk and horizontal arms at the Eight-Partition-Place (Courtesy of Freidel, Schele and Parker, *Maya Cosmos*).

In *Maya Cosmos*, Schele, Freidel and Parker identify the trunk of the World Tree with the Milky Way (the galactic midplane) and the double-headed snake twined around its horizontal arm with the ecliptic. It is very important to realize the distinction between the ecliptic and the horizontal arm of the Cross. The ecliptic is not part of the World Tree, which is an invisible Cross that is constituted by two perpendicular arms that meet in the galactic center. It is upheld by the Quadripartite god, who divides the world according to four perpendicular directions. Since the ecliptic is at an angle with the Galactic Cross it has been represented as a double-headed snake that crawls around the horizontal arm of the Cross. Thus, the World Trees in the Group of the Cross are galactic in nature, and this is a very important point. And if both arms of the World Trees are galactic in nature, then the locations of their points of intersection in the sky become questions of paramount importance.

The point of intersection between the trunk and the arms of World Tree I is actually what we today know to be the galactic center, located in the constellation Sagittarius, above Scorpio, which was used by the Maya as a marker to help indicate its location (see Figure 31). The fact that we may identify the point of intersection of the arms of World Tree I with the location of the galactic center in the sky (Figure 46) shows that the ancient Maya were at least intuitively aware of the importance of this center. Since today very few people, if anyone at all, would be able to point out the galactic center just based on intuition we may realize that the Western consciousness of baktun 9 was quite different from what it is today.

Table 10
The Two Views of the World Tree, Their Locations
and Corresponding Creation Days

World Tree I		World Tree II
	Depicted at	
Temple of the Cross		Temple of the Foliated Cross
	Center located North of	
Scorpius (see Figure 31)		Turtle (Orion's Belt)
	Center of Quadripartite God	
Sagittarius /Ophiucus		Taurus/Auriga
(Actual center of galaxy)		(Opposite to center of galaxy)
		Place of Creation,
		Copulating Peccaries (Gemini)
Place of entering the road		Place of rebirth
(In death Pacal returns to the		(Pacal is dressed as the maize god
World Tree = the Milky Way)		to be reborn North of the Turtle)

August 11, 3114 BC	February 3, 3112 BC
First Father = Maize God = Six-Sky-Lord did an unknown action	First Father entered (became) the Sky and created the Eight-Partition-House
It was made visible, the image at the Lying-Down-Sky	It was made proper the Raised-up-Sky-Place

What may be even more interesting is that the intersection of the vertical and horizontal arms of the Foliated Cross (World Tree II), also called the Maize Tree, represents the point in the sky at the totally opposite direction (Figure 45 and 47). This point the temples in Palenque enigmatically refer to as the Eight-Partition-Place. Although today we do not see any such point in that part of the sky its existence seems to have been obvious to the scribe. The Foliated Cross is thus centered at the point where we arrive if we draw a straight line from the galactic center through the earth and project this onto the spherical creation field surrounding the galaxy. This point is located on the border between the constellations Taurus and Auriga (Figures 48 and 49), somewhat north of the Belt of Orion. Since Taurus is part of the zodiac the ancients surely must have referred to the location as belonging to that constellation, and we will refer to it as such here. This location

Fig. 50 With the help of the Hero Twins, Hunahpu at left and Xbalanque at right, the First Father is reborn from the shell of a Turtle (Orion's belt) (Courtesy of Freidel, Schele and Parker, *Maya Cosmos*).

in the sky, the Eight-Partition-Place, which is opposite to the galactic center, was seen as a point of rebirth. In the Mayan view World Tree II was raised in three stars in the lower part of Orion, called the Three Hearth Stones (Figure 49). The Belt of Orion was, however, seen as a Turtle, the Turtle of Rebirth, from whose shell the maize god emerged after having been brought back to life by his two sons, Hunahpu and Xbalanque (Figure 50).

The nearby constellation of Gemini, called by the Maya the Copulating Pecaries (Figure 48), which borders on the Milky Way was seen as the 'Place of Creation.' Sometimes the constellations of the Turtle and the Copulating Peccaries on the two different sides of the galactic midplane were shown as interchangeable, and so the rebirth of the First Father could be depicted in both constellations. This indicates that the whole region along the trunk of the World Tree was seen as a place of Creation. While the Galactic Cross looked rather plain in the direction of the galactic center (World Tree I, Figure 45) it was seen as fertile in the opposite direction. It is the fruits of the place of Creation that are shown in the Temple of the Foliated Cross. There, the fertile World Tree II is shown not only to produce maize and greenery, but also as manifesting human beings from its branches, as evidenced by small heads. Of course, and this is a crucial point, since we have earlier seen that the various classes of organisms created on this planet (Table 10 and Figure 34) were generated by the pulses emanating from the Galactic World Tree, and the human being in particular first emerged at the cross hairs of the holographic projection of the Galactic Cross on our planet, it becomes difficult to object to the Mayan view of the creation of human beings. Their view is literally true. The trunk of the World Tree II *is* the place of Creation.

The actual reciprocal dates of Creation used by the Maya, August 11 and February 3, seem to lack meaning by themselves, except in that August 11 corresponds to the date of solar zenith in Izapa and February 3 to a time exactly half a year later. Yet the dates are meaningful in that they have served to identify two celestial locations, the galactic center and the point right opposite to it, located in Sagittarius and Taurus, respectively, as corresponding to the roots and branches of the World Tree.

The information in Palenque now tells us that the Maya saw the galactic center as the point of origin of the Heavens, i.e., the Lying-Down-Skies. As these were projected onto the sphere surrounding the galaxy, they apparently were called Raised-up-Skies. Thus, as a Raised-up-Sky was erected, a 'house,' the Eight-Partition-House, was created in Auriga opposite to the galactic center. Through holographic resonance the perpendicular arms of the World Tree were also projected onto the earth and define the four corners of the world, and this is why the Maya identified both a World Tree in the sky (the Milky Way) and another on earth generating the four directions.

This may be an appropriate place to point out that the Maya did not think of the Pleiades as the center of the galaxy, which is a common misconception with no foundation in astronomical science. Together with the stars in the Belt of Orion and several others, the Pleiades form part of a circular complex of novel stars surrounding our own sun called Gould's Belt. This Belt was created as recently as million years ago by a pulse through the galactic midplane as the seventh DAY of the Mammalian Cycle began and the higher mammals replaced the dinosaurs. Although the Pleiades would then seem much too young to have generated biological life, they may serve, together with the Belt of Orion, as parts of a relay for this particular aspect of our consciousness. The Maya saw this star group as a handful of seeds of maize planted by the First Father and thus as part of this Creation. Most importantly, the seven stars of the Pleiades, sometimes regarded as the rattle tail of Quetzalcoatl, may be seen as symbolic of the seven DAYS of the divine process of Creation. The fact that many ancient peoples claim their origin in the Pleiades may thus signify that they see themselves as part of the divine Creation. Because of this symbolism there was much interest in ancient Mexico in calibrating Pleiades-Sun conjunctions, times when the energy of the Pleiades (divine Creation) would be projected onto the earth with the sun acting as a lens.

Almost all Mayan objects of art and worship have been found to have a symbolic meaning in terms of divine Creation, and many of them can be related to the celestial drama that has been described here. The temples of Palenque thus describe what occurred at the beginning of the Great Cycle. They, however, also have another focus. This is the afterlife and the rebirth of human beings generated by their journeys back and forth to the Otherworld. The description of such a journey seems to be the main topic of the sarcophagus of Pacal and the Temples of the Group of the Cross. At the same time as Creation as it occurred at the beginning of the Great Cycle is described, the rebirth of Pacal after he has entered 'the road' is described.

Incidentally, according to *Maya Cosmos*, the reason Pacal on his sarcophagus is dressed as the maize god as he enters 'the road'—actually then the galactic center, the roots of the World Tree providing a doorway to the Otherworld—is that his tomb, the Temple of the Inscriptions, was designed to have him reborn at the place of rebirth. In this, it seems he was aided by his son Chan-Bahlum, who, similarly to the Hero Twins, the sons of the maize god, assisted in the rebirth of his father at the Foliated Cross, the Eight-Partition-Place (Figure 50).

So if we look beyond the planets and the stars we may see a background in reality to the Galactic Cross that the Maya were aware of. This invisible Galactic Cross is the source of everything created in the galaxy and it effects its creativity through the interplay between the Northern and Southern galactic hemispheres that it separates. Having demonstrated the existence of a creative trunk of the World Tree, the question that naturally arises is in what galactic hemisphere our own planet is located. It is known that we are currently located some 68 light years north of the galactic midplane, moving in a direction away from this, and for the entire duration of humanity's existence on this planet it has been located in the same galactic hemisphere (see Figure 34). Is this the male or female hemisphere? Well, in pictures where the Hero Twins (Figure 50) resurrect the maize god in the Turtle of Rebirth, Hunahpu, the male principle, is to the left, and Xbalanque to the right. If the Mayan intuition was correct this would mean that we ourselves are living on a planet in the 'female' hemisphere of the galaxy. An interesting question then is what life is like on planets in the other, 'male' hemisphere of the galaxy.

We may conclude that the World Tree is something that exists on several different hierarchical levels of the universe (see, e.g., Figure 41) that we sometimes need to distinguish from one another. Also, in Biblical myth there is a hint of an awareness of a difference between the Galactic World Tree and the True Cross. After the expulsion of Adam and Eve from the Garden of Eden with its Tree of Life, God decided to seal off this garden from human beings and protect it with cherubs guarding it with a sword of flames. Maybe the sword of flames corresponds to the Cross—how this manifested and was experienced during the Great Cycle—protecting the Tree of Life from the human beings. And we may think of the famous words of Jesus in *Matthew 10:34*: 'I came not to send peace, but a sword.' The sword he is talking about may well be the flaming sword God used for protecting the Tree of Life in the Garden of Eden as, in the beginning of the Great Cycle, this was sealed off. This flaming sword, this razor-sharp duality, would then maybe also be symbolic of the swords carried by the European conquerors, which were almost destined to create disappointment in many peoples of the world, including the ancient Mesoamericans. But maybe time has now come for the flaming sword protecting the Tree of Life to be removed. Maybe as the Galactic Cycle begins we are to embark on a path back to the Garden of Eden.

All of the above calls for a complete revision of how we view the relationship between our lives and the Heavens. It seems likely that modern astrology has been overly tainted by the materialist thinking of the Planetary Underworld, emphasizing the relationships between human life and the physical objects of planets and stars, rather than the invisible creation fields that surround them. Nonetheless, the emphasis on the zodiacal sign of birth of an individual may make sense in that the zodiacal sign is nothing but a definition of what part of the galactic creation field influenced our souls at the time of birth. The message would then be to look beyond the stars for our purpose and destiny.

Fig. 51 The group of the Cross in Palenque (Photo Calleman)

FROM THE OTHERWORLD TO EGYPT

We have now studied some of the Mayan views of death, life and rebirth as well as their view of what happened as the Great Cycle began. Let us then study some of the phenomena that actually occurred in the world around the very beginning of the first baktun of the Great Cycle, i.e., at the time of Creation that was described in the temples of Palenque. This would bring us back to the so-called Thinite kingdom of Egypt, named after the place of birth of Pharaoh Menes, the founder of the First Dynasty at the beginning of baktun 0. We thus have both the Mayan view of what happened at the beginning of the Great Cycle—expressed in spiritual and mythological terms in Palenque—and the historical records from Egypt, such as the so-called Pyramid Texts and other evidence of an archaeological character that describe what happened there during the same period. Could the Mayan view of the dawn of history on this planet help shed some light on some of the historical enigmas associated with ancient Egypt, such as those of the Great Pyramids? Such an approach would probably be unique. Ancient Egyptian history has almost invariably been looked upon through either European or Arabic eyes. Here we will see what we can learn by looking upon it from the perspective of the Mayan view of history, a view that is intimately linked to that of divine Creation. Also, since we ourselves have recently experienced the beginning of a new Underworld, the Galactic, it may be of special interest for us to see what the beginning of another Underworld, in this case the National, beginning some fifty-two hundred tuns ago, looked like. It may be of interest to see how the Heaven of the National Cycle was first manifested as it was projected onto the earth. This is especially so as one of the civilizations that it engendered, that of Egypt of the pharaohs, remained in existence at least until the beginning of baktun 7, that is, for more than half of the duration of the Great Cycle. As the Galactic Cycle has now begun to manifest through the introduction of a new Heaven, we may thus also expect that some of its original expressions will remain in existence at least until the midpoint of that cycle, which will bring us until about the year AD 2006.

Fig. 52 The Great Pyramids of Giza (courtesy of Egyptian Tourist Board).

Our primary focus will be on the very first dynasties after the beginning of baktun 0, as the Egyptian civilization truly emerged. For anyone looking at the sudden emergence of the Egyptian civilization without the Mayan calendar in hand, it is a great enigma how it suddenly appeared almost out of the blue. The institutions of kingship, administration, written language and the ability to perform huge construction works arose almost in a ready form. Thus, since few preliminary forms or preparatory stages of this civilization have been discovered, suggestions have been made that it was developed with the aid of extraterrestrials or survivors of the sunken continent Atlantis. But from the Palenquean perspective there is no need to invoke such external stimuli to explain the rapid flowering of the Egyptian civilization. Instead, the explanation of the sudden emergence of the Thinite kingdom is that the First Father, the Six-Sky-Lord, at this time raised an Eight-Partition-House through which the LIGHT could enter. The human resonance with this new House—generating the sixth (national) level of consciousness—led to the creation of a new civilization. Surely, there must also have existed a relatively high civilization preparing for that of the pharaohs and, based on the tzolkin, we may predict that this went back to about 10,400 tuns before the present. There is, however, nothing to indicate that any such prior civilization would have been more advanced than the one emerging at the beginning of the Great Cycle. The jump taken by civilization at the very beginning of the Great Cycle is very marked and there is really nothing prior to it that compares. After all, the evolution of human consciousness is like the ascent of a pyramid, and there is no indication that it could ever be reversed, like some proponents of Atlantis assert.

How then did the introduction of the new duality created by the Eight-Partition-House affect the religion of the people of Egypt? What was the first experience of the True Cross like? Previously we discussed the effects of the True Cross at the beginning of baktun 12 of the same cycle (in 1617), and we could see how the new duality was expressed in a multitude of ways. But how was the Heaven of the Great Cycle expressed during baktun 0, its twin, before the True Cross was truly dominant? One thing we may note is that, because the Cross had not yet become dominant, the ancient Egyptians were not monotheists. The Egyptian pantheon included a multitude of gods, where the yin/ yang polarity above all seems to have been expressed through the couple of Osiris and Isis, who had a son by the name of Horus. Every pharaoh was believed to be an incarnation of Horus, the progeny of the divine wedlock, and he was thus seen as a personification of the divine. Among the stars Isis, the female aspect, is symbolized by Sirius, and Osiris, the male, by the constellation Orion. We also know that the Egyptian pharaohs were very much preoccupied with their journey to the Otherworld in the life hereafter and their rebirth.

About at the same time that Linda Schele and co-workers published *Maya Cosmos,* two maverick British Egyptologists, Robert Bauval and Adrian Gilbert, published *The Orion Mystery,* whose message is essentially the same although this may not have previously been noticed. The authors of *The Orion Mystery* suggest that the Great Pyramids of Giza (which we now know to have been built in baktun 1) in fact were built so as to reflect the three stars of Orion's Belt. The arguments they present for this theory are convincing, and in Figure 53 we may see how these three pyramids together with four others also built in the Fourth Dynasty form a star map projected onto the ground. Although this star correlation theory fits per-

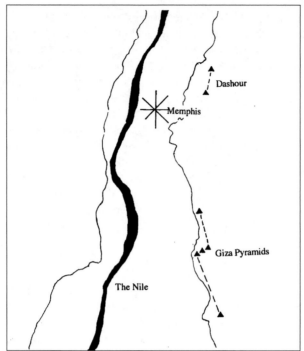

Fig. 53 Map of the Seven pyramids of the Fourth Dynasty with the capital of Memphis.

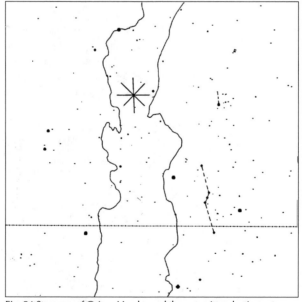

Fig. 54 Star map of Orion, Hyades and the opposite-galactic-center.

fectly for the Giza pyramids and Orion's Belt, it only holds approximately true for the other pyramids, which, however, need not invalidate the theory. From this, and the Pyramid Texts, it seems that the great Egyptian pyramids had been built so that the pharaohs would be reborn as stars, and that a 'star religion' was dominating Egypt at the time these building works were performed. The authors point out that the Egyptian name for the Milky Way translates as 'winding waterway' and they thus find evidence for a correlation between the map of Egypt and the stars in the sky. In this, the Nile was a reflection on earth of the Milky Way.

So far these authors. What may then be added to this from the perspective of the capital of Palenque? First of all, it seems natural that as the new East/West duality was introduced in the sky at the beginning of baktun 0, the Egyptians would see the Nile, flowing from the south, as a reflection of the galactic midplane. It is also understandable that if the Nile god corresponds to the galactic midplane creation field boundary, and if this boundary is what creates the male/female duality, the Egyptians would identify the Nile god as androgynous. It is easy to see how the Nile would be seen as the only source of fertility, as this was the earthly correspondent to the vertical arm of the World Tree, the fertile foliated cross. (Incidentally, also for Moses, who had been placed in a cradle in the river, the Nile was symbolically the place of rebirth.)

Given that the ambition of the pharaohs was to be reborn, it is noteworthy that they built the three Great Pyramids to reflect the Belt of Orion, a constellation that to the Maya was the Turtle of Rebirth where the trunk of the World Tree was erected. From the carapace of the Turtle of Rebirth the maize god was reborn, and it seems that it was in the same location Pacal wanted to be reborn. This means that the pyramids in Giza and Palenque may have been built partly for the same reason, so that the rulers buried in them could be reborn in the location in the sky called the *duat* by the Egyptians and the Eight-Partition-Place by the Maya. At any rate,

Fig. 55a (above)
Eight-partition bowls of rebirth found in Egyptian tombs (E-C Strauss, *Die Nun-schale*, Münchner Ägyptologische Studien 30, 1974).

Fig. 55b (right)
Tutanchamon being reborn from a lotus flower. In the Egyptian Book of the Dead being reborn is described as 'taking shape as a lotus flower,' an eight-petaled flower (Cairo-museum).

both the Egyptians and the Maya, despite the considerable separation of the two cultures in both space and time, considered the same place in the sky, above the Belt of Orion, as a place of rebirth. Since the two cultures arrived at this view independently there are strong reasons to consider that there may be some kind of truth to it.

Judging from Mayan myth it seems that, if we are looking in the direction of the Eight-Partition-Place in Taurus, it is the eastern part of the sky that represents the male hemisphere of the galaxy, which is the one that was lit up by LIGHT during the Great Cycle. Maybe then the Egyptians shared this view since Osiris, ruler of the dead and the darkness, was represented by a figure west of the Milky Way, that is, Orion. It should be noted that ancient Egypt was not only divided into Upper and Lower Egypt, but also according to the eastern and the western riverbeds, and it is described in the Pyramid Texts that the dead were supposed to be buried on the western riverside only. This choice seems natural, assuming that it was on the river-bed corresponding to the DARK galactic hemisphere that the dead would be buried. In this we have further support from ancient myth that our planet is located in the female hemisphere of the galaxy. It seems indeed likely that the people of the Thinite kingdom, who were probably affected by the new duality of the Great Cycle in a very dramatic way, would be best equipped to tell us in what hemisphere we are in.

There are other things that may be added to *The Orion Mystery* from our perspective. If we seek to identify where in Egypt the actual opposite galactic center, the place of rebirth, would be located, it is obvious that it would have to be found somewhere in the Nile, since this river corresponded to the galactic midplane. If we then construct a star map based on the assumption that the three Great Pyramids correspond to the Belt of Orion and look for the opposite center of the galaxy in Taurus, the Eight-Partition-Place, we find that the Giza pyramids point in the direction of the ruins of Memphis. And indeed, the founder of Egypt, Pharaoh Menes, had actually moved the flow of the Nile in order to locate his capital, Memphis, in a position where the Nile had previously been flowing. (The original name of Memphis is Ineb-Hedj, meaning 'the White Wall,' which indicates that indeed he saw it as a reflection of the Milky Way.) Although the location of Memphis is only approximately right according to a star-correlation theory, as is the case also for the locations of some of the pyramids, the correspondence between this ancient capital and the Mayan place of Creation provides additional support for the general ideas of *The Orion Mystery*.

There is further evidence for this correspondence in that Memphis was considered as located at the line dividing Upper and Lower Egypt, which prior to their unification were described as having been ruled by Seth and Horus, respectively. Thus, it was literally localized at a crucial point not only dividing west and east, but also north and south, an Eight-Partition-Place.

We may then understand why the unification of the Two Lands, around 3100 BC, at the beginning of the Great Cycle, was always seen by the ancient Egyptians as an event of cosmic proportions equal to the creation of the world. This unification was described as having come about primarily as a result of the actions of the gods, and since these were identified with different sections of the sky, the pharaohs doing the job on earth were merely seen as representatives of these cosmic forces.

Fig. 56a Eight-partitioned Sun Wheel from Själland, Denmark (Bob G. Lind, *Ales Stenar*).

Fig. 56b Eight-partitioned Christian symbol (the Church of Falun, photo Calleman)

From our perspective such a view actually seems to hold a lot of truth. Without going into detail it seems that the unification of the Two Lands was really brought about by a 90° rotation in the Galactic Round of LIGHT as the National Cycle began on top of the Regional Cycle. This rotation shifting the line of duality to the Nile Valley set an end to the division between north and south that had previously characterized the region. As different as they may at first seem, the Fall of Adam and Eve, the shooting of Seven-Macaw and the cosmic battle between Horus and Seth all describe the same thing: the introduction of a new duality at the beginning of the National Cycle, a duality which superseded the unitary creation field of the seventh DAY of the Regional Cycle.

Until Thebes replaced Memphis as capital of Egypt, the latter served as the undisputed center of this nation during baktuns 0 and 1. It housed the most important temple in all of Egypt, dedicated to the god Ptah, who was the unifying national deity of Old Egypt, the creator of all forms in the world. He was also worshiped as the famous Apis Bull (and the Eight-Partition-Place is in the constellation of Taurus). The god Ptah was, however, part of a triad of gods that also included Sekhmet, a lion goddess, and Nefertum. This triad of gods very likely represented the triangular points setting the limits for a region in the sky, the region between the constellations Orion, Leo and Taurus, in which the Egyptians located the duat, the place of rebirth. We may also note that Nefertum was symbolized by the lotus flower, the eight-petaled flower that among the Egyptians was seen as a symbol of rebirth and the foundation for the creation of the world. This is a very natural symbol of the galactic Eight-Partition-Place, which provided the invisible structure for the creation of the world. This points to the idea that Memphis, the first capital of Egypt, was founded as a center of rebirth and creation, where pharaohs would perpetually be reborn as gods.

It has often been pointed out that not all of the pyramids of Egypt were tombs of pharaohs, and in their grand layout as a star map they may have served a different purpose than we have previously thought. Although part of their purpose may have been to serve as tombs, the star map theory means that they may also have been built to recreate the capital of Memphis as a center of creativity and perpetual rebirth on earth. The pyramids would then have helped focus the spiritual galactic energy to the city of Memphis, so recreating it as the earthly correspondent to the galactic Eight-Partition-Place. Considering that Pharaoh Menes went all the way to move the Nile to build his capital in its midst, it seems entirely possible that very large efforts would similarly have been made to ensure its creativity through the building of the Great Pyramids. In the Eight-Partition-Place we may thus have the true significance of the region in the sky that the Egyptians would call the duat and the explanation of why they would seek to make a star map of pyramids on earth. They wanted to highlight Memphis as the place of creation.

Unfortunately, we may never know if this perspective is true. Memphis became a favorite target for invading peoples who time after time sacked and looted it. The last attack, when the city had long since lost all of its political importance, and its inhabitants had maybe forgotten much of its original meaning, came in the year AD 380. Christian iconoclasts at the instigation of the Roman Emperor Theodosius then destroyed all of its remaining objects of worship. Today, it is little more than a few hills of sand in the outskirts of Cairo, and even if these were excavated it is doubtful that the crucial answers would be found. Yet we may wonder if it suffered so many attacks because the religion upon which it had been built provoked strong reactions from others. The Christians may not have liked to be reminded that there was a prehistory to the Star of Bethlehem.

But even if this large-scale project of recreating the galactic center of rebirth on earth eventually failed, it is still pertinent to ask what is the significance of the galactic location in the direction of the constellation of Taurus. If both the Egyptian pharaohs and the Mayan ahauob recognized the importance of the same location for their afterlife and rebirth, must there not be some kind of truth to this idea? The answer that I have suggested to this is that the World Tree and Eight-Partition-Place described especially in Mayan myth are real phenomena. That is to say that creation works from the root to the branches of the World Tree, where the Eight-Partition-Place indeed is a place of creation and rebirth through the Heavens projected onto the sphere surrounding our galaxy. To what extent it may serve the rebirth of individual human souls, as the ancient rulers seem to have believed, remains an open question.

To bring further understanding to the cult of Osiris and the building of the Great Pyramids, however, it is crucial to also take into consideration how the early Egyptian history was affected by the alternations between DAYS and NIGHTS. To begin with, we should note that the Great Pyramids of the Fourth Dynasty were not built during baktun 0, and that the pyramids built during baktun 0, the first DAY of the Great Cycle, were different from the Great Pyramids. Pharaoh Djoser's Pyramid, dated to the early part of baktun 0, has one very interesting thing in common with the other major pyramid built during the Thinite kingdom, that in Meidum. This is that they were both originally built as step-pyramids in seven terraces. These early pyramids (Figure 22) were in other words built as metaphors for the fundamental design plan for the Great Cycle (Figure 23). The building of the Meidum pyramid, in fact, had as its explicit purpose to serve as a model of the divine process of Creation to future rulers.

It seems, however, as if when the first NIGHT of the Great Cycle came to dominate, the sovereigns forgot the true message of the earliest pyramids of baktun 0. Then, sometime around 2650 BC, around the beginning of baktun 1, the enormous activity that led to the construction of the Great Pyramids at Giza started. This massive undertaking began very suddenly with Pharaoh Sneferu building two pyramids, presumably those of Dashour, and rebuilding the Meidum pyramid so that it became smooth-sided and lost its original step-pyramid character. Why did this pharaoh remodel this old seven-storied pyramid and embark on the huge pyramid construction project of the seven massive pyramids of the Fourth Dynasty? What may be most interesting to note is that he lived close to the beginning of the first NIGHT of the Great Cycle, which began in the year 2721 BC. We have previously seen that baktun shifts have been important in precipitating religious change, and there is no reason to believe that the beginning of this NIGHT was different. Maybe during this NIGHT, which carried a new consciousness, the Egyptian rulers were no longer able to understand the truth of Djoser's Pyramid, that creation was a step-wise project and that DAYS would follow upon the NIGHTS. Maybe in fact Sneferu remodeled the step-pyramid of Meidum as a symbolic denial of the step-wise nature of creation, a denial resulting from the fear provoked by the darkness of the new NIGHT. Maybe the giant pyramid construction work of the Fourth Dynasty, the surge of the cult of Osiris—the ruler of the land of the dead and the night sky—and even the pharaonic quest for rebirth were simply based on a major misunderstanding of the nature of creation that surfaced as the first NIGHT of the Great Cycle began. We may note that the seven Fourth Dynasty pyramids built during this NIGHT were intended to provide a map of the night sky, and maybe the holy number 7 then was also mistakenly thought of as reflecting these seven stars. It seems that the star religion emerging at the time had many elements of a religion of the NIGHT, and that the shift from DAY to NIGHT may have provoked a very sudden change in the thinking of ancient Egypt that led to the giant pyramid works.

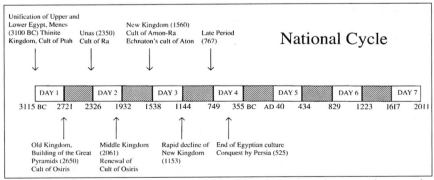

Fig. 57 The evolution of Egyptian civilization and religion during the early DAYS and NIGHTS of the Great Cycle.

The Galactic World Tree and the Star of Bethlehem

Such an interpretation is given further support by the fact that the building of pyramids again seems to have changed character as baktun 2, the second DAY of the Great Cycle, began in the year 2326 BC (see Figure 57). Thus, with Pharaoh Unas, the last pharaoh of the Fifth Dynasty, who lived around 2350 BC, a new era began in which pyramids served more directly as tombs for individual pharaohs buried on the western side of the Nile. In contrast to the seven Great Pyramids of baktun 1, the new and smaller pyramids of baktun 2 do not seem to be part of a huge scheme to mirror the night sky. Instead they were tombs that could be identified by the names of the pharaohs who were buried in them. At the beginning of this the second DAY of the Great Cycle, the pharaohs also began to use the name 'Son of Ra,' the sun god. Thus, as the new LIGHT entered, the worship of Ra, the god of the sun and the day, replaced the worship of Osiris, the god of the dead visible in the night sky as Orion. Such a change of religion was only natural as a new DAY began, but later, in the so-called Middle Kingdom of NIGHT 2, it seems that the cult of Osiris resurfaced. In these shifts between DAYS and NIGHTS we may then find the background to the conflict that many have seen between a solar and a stellar religion in ancient Egypt. With the New Kingdom, emerging exactly at the beginning of DAY 3, Egypt finally became a civilization that seems more easily understandable to us, and, as we mentioned earlier, in this DAY Pharaoh Achnaton even temporarily introduced a monotheistic creed. But even before this the cults of Egypt seem to have alternated with the DAYS and NIGHTS, focusing on the worship of LIGHT and DARKNESS, Ra and Osiris, respectively. Hence, to understand the purpose of the pyramids and Egyptian culture generally we need to be aware of how Egyptian religion changed with the alternations between DAYS and NIGHTS.

THE 'TWELFTH PLANET'

Not only regarding Egyptian mythology, but also Sumerian, may the new perspective gained from the ancient Mayan sources add to our understanding. As previously mentioned, the Sumerian pantheon was ruled by the god of Heaven, An or Anu, who stood above all the other gods and resided in a special abode. He may possibly be seen as a correspondent to the First Father. Below him were his two sons Enlil and Ea, who might be likened to Hunahpu and Xbalanque, as well as a number of their descendants in a special ranking order. This type of heavenly family was worshiped all over the ancient Mediterranean world, by peoples including the later Babylonians and Assyrians, the Hittites, the Greeks and the Romans. Just as in the ancient Egyptian religion, this pantheon underwent considerable change as the Great Cycle with its DAYS and NIGHTS progressed, although this will be left out of this discussion.

Especially following the American moon missions, the idea that extraterrestrials have been visiting our planet has been widespread. This has sometimes included the idea that the early civilizations of mankind had been founded or initiated by visitors from space. Although Erich Von Däniken may have been the most famous writer in this genre, Zecharia Sitchin's ideas in *The Twelfth Planet,* based on his interpretations of Sumerian and Semitic myths, have likewise been widely disseminated. His idea is that our solar system harbors a twelfth planet, whose more advanced inhabitants have traveled to the earth every 3600 years as their planet has come near to it. Here on earth, these supposed extraterrestrials have been the creators not only of human beings genetically, but also of the early civilizations of mankind, and hence they were worshiped as gods.

This theme, the idea that the gods visited the earth, has in the recent decade almost given rise to a literary genre of its own, and purported support for such contentions has been found in ancient sources by several authors. It seems, however, that from the perspective of the Mayan cycles describing the evolution of consciousness an entirely different explanation may be provided to such accounts. Thus, as people at the beginning of the Great Cycle were endowed with a vastly expanded frame of consciousness that dramatically expanded their capabilities, they were also becoming more god-like. The idea of gods visiting the earth may then simply be an expression of the new, more god-like frame of consciousness descending to earth and manifesting in human beings that to some may have appeared as man-gods, demigods or other mythological crosses between men, animals and gods. In our own pre-galactic era such accounts of gods have then come to be interpreted as visitors from outer space or from Atlantis.

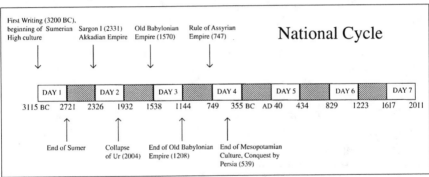

Fig. 58 The evolution of Mesopotamian civilization during the early DAYS and NIGHTS of the Great Cycle.

In light of the Mayan calibration of the pulses of the divine process of Creation there are, however, other much simpler and more likely explanations for many of the phenomena that Sitchin bases his ideas on. To begin with we may look at how the early events in Mesopotamian cultural development conform to the various creation cycles described by the Maya. The settled culture in Sumer took its beginning at the same time as the seventh DAY of the Regional Cycle (about 5900 BC, see Figure 28). The first writing was then invented shortly before the beginning of the Great Cycle (Figure 58), and the various civilizational rises and falls in the Land of the Two Rivers conform very well to its alternations between DAYS and NIGHTS. And, like the Egyptian culture, the Mesopotamian culture lost its distinct character at the midpoint of the cycle. The conclusion to draw from this is that there is absolutely no need to invoke extraterrestrial visitors to explain the sudden emergence of the Sumerian civilization or the following civilizational shifts in the area. The Mayan calendar, a matrix for the divine process of Creation, by itself provides enough of an explanation for the emergence of human civilization. As we saw in the previous section, this was true for Egypt and it is also true for Mesopotamia.

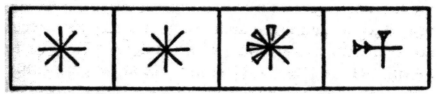

Fig. 59 Symbolism of the Sumerian god of Heaven (from left to right: An = Star = Heaven = God) (Anu) (Courtesy of Sitchin, *The Twelfth Planet*).

As mentioned, the ancient Sumerians identified a celestial abode for Anu, the god of Heaven. Although Sitchin labels this abode a 'twelfth planet,' it seems immediately clear from his discussion that the Sumerians did not only include the nine planets commonly recognized today, but the sun and the moon as well, among their twelve celestial objects. So there is no a priori reason to believe that the 'abode of Anu' was a planet. What distinguishes stars from planets is that only the stars twinkle, and the ancient Sumerian logogram, and later Babylonian cuneiform, clearly shows that Anu had been identified by an apparently twinkling Eight-Partitioned center. This logogram (Figure 59) gives the impression that the abode of Anu was a star rather than a planet. To further emphasize this, the abode of Anu was described as the most shining of the gods, a description that hardly applies to a planet, especially not one in the darker, more remote regions of the solar system.

Could the 'heavenly abode' mentioned in ancient Sumerian sources then actually be the same as the Mayan Eight-Partition-Place and the Egyptian duat? Its logogram is certainly consistent with such an interpretation and there is fairly strong additional circumstantial evidence that this is the case. To begin with, the zero point of the Sumerian zodiac—the prototype of the modern Western zodiac—was located between the constellations of Gemini and Taurus, what we now from Mayan sources know to be the trunk of the World Tree. Symbolically, the Sumerians would link the 'heavenly abode' to the Tree of Life, and, quite in contrast to Sitchin's speculations of a twelfth planet, Von Waarden relates that the ancient Babylonians referred to the constellation of Taurus, GUD.AN.NA, simply as 'star', meaning that the abode of Anu had a set location in this constellation. Thus, in ancient Sumerian sources it is said that the abode of Anu, the 'star', divides the Heaven in two halves, where Enlil sat on the right side of Anu (presumably then facing us) and Ea to the left, which again may be interpreted as a parallel to the galactic polarity created by Hunahpu and Xbalanque that we have already discussed.

The 'beloved star' of Anu then really seems to be located at the Eight-Partition-Place of the Maya, and, in contrast to planets, it does not move. In fact, it seems that in a host of ancient representations from the Near Orient, a Cross has been depicted either in immediate proximity to a bull (Figure 60) or between Taurus and Leo (Figure 61). The most obvious interpretation of these is that the abode of Anu

Fig. 60 Babylonian picture of bull together with cross (Courtesy of Sitchin, *The Twelfth Planet*).

Fig. 61 Babylonian picture showing cross in between a bull and a lion, presumably reflecting the constellations of Taurus and Leo (Courtesy of Sitchin, *The Twelfth Planet*).

was located in the Eight-Partition-Place in the upper part of Taurus, between on the one hand the constellations of Leo and Gemini and on the other that of Taurus. The heavenly abode, which also went by the name of Niburu, was also described as a celestial center that penetrated everywhere with its Cross, a view that does not seem to have been all that different from that of the Maya.

Localizing the abode of Anu—also referred to as the 'pure place'—above Taurus is even further strengthened by later varieties of the heavenly family developed in other cultures. Hence, Marduk of the Babylonians, Teschub of the Hittites, El, the father god of the Canaanites, Zeus of the Greeks and Jupiter of the Romans were all widely represented standing on the backs of bulls sending lightning with a hammer (Figure 62). This indicates that divine lightning was striking from a position in the sky left of the constellation of Taurus. It may also be typical that wearing the horns of a bull on the head would often be a symbol of divinity in ancient pictures and statues, and the link between Taurus and the heavenly abode may be at the root of this practice. It seems that several peoples of antiquity saw the

Fig. 62 The Greek father god Zeus sending lightning from the back of a bull (courtesy of Sitchin, *The Twelfth Planet*).

Eight-Partition-Place as a location of lightning and assumed that their respective father gods were residing there.

If the bull on which all the father gods of the Mediterranean world were standing in fact was a representation of the constellation of Taurus in the sky, then this logically identifies the source of their lightning as the Eight-Partition-Place. The lightning observed by these peoples must then have been generated by the creation field boundaries that separated the LIGHT and DARK galactic hemispheres and created the cosmic interplay between yang and yin, which had repercussions also on our own earth. The lightning created by the father god in Taurus would not fit a 'twelfth planet,' but very probably would fit the Eight-Partition-Place, which separates the yin and yang of the Heavens ruled by Enlil and Ea. The only reason we normally are not able to see such phenomena today is that the consciousness of the Planetary Underworld has blinded us to divine LIGHT.

The father god's residence in the Milky Way applied also to Nordic mythology, in which the ancient god of heaven, Heimdall, had his abode in the World Tree Yggdrasil. In a similar way as the abode of Anu was referred to as the 'heavenly heights,' his was referred to as the 'heavenly mountains.' And as Anu would later come to be replaced by Marduk, the Bronze Age father god of the Scandinavians, Heimdall, would later be replaced by Oden.

As an aside, the name of Pacal, ruler in Palenque at the crucial time when the understanding of the workings of the World Tree was elaborated, is sometimes linked to the name of Votan, Pacal Votan. Legends, and even prophecies today, of good men clad in red arriving from the East are commonplace in Native American traditions (note that in Figure 7 red is the color of the East), and one such legend refers to a Votan who came from across the Atlantic to found the city of Palenque. Although the historicity of this legend may rightly be questioned, it is this that has sometimes given the Great Pacal the name Pacal Votan.

The curious thing about this name is that Votan may refer to the father god of the Vikings. Votan is another form of the Swedish Oden, which also exists in the forms Woden, Wodan, Wotan or Wuotan. Oden was believed to be the protector of the huge ash Yggdrasil, the World Tree in Nordic myth. Here we thus have a connection to Pacal, who on his sarcophagus lid is seen with the World Tree. The name Wodan is also linked to the English 'wood,' which in Swedish is *ved.*

Interestingly, in Swedish the words for both 'knowledge,' *vetande*, and 'consciousness,' *medvetande*, are linked to the same root, namely *ved*. Thus, in very ancient times, as the Indo-European languages came into existence, there must have existed an understanding of the links between Wotan, the wood of the World Tree, knowledge and consciousness. And indeed, as we have seen here, it is through our resonance with the Galactic World Tree that we gain both knowledge and consciousness. In addition, in English we have the words 'world' and 'word' of Germanic origin, *värld* and *ord* in Swedish, which are then linked to 'wood.'

The Vedic scriptures derive the origin of their name from the Indo-European *vid*, linked to the Latin *videre*, 'to see,' which recurs in the English word 'vision.' It has even been suggested that the word Buddha, meaning 'the enlightened one,' is the same word as Wuotan. So 'the world' (the entire creation), 'the word' (creative vibrations), 'seeing' (especially in the spiritual sense of the Vedic scriptures) and 'enlightenment,' 'knowing' and 'being conscious' etymologically all seem to be linked to 'ved,' the World Tree guarded by the Nordic god Wuotan.

Fig. 63 Raising the Maypole at midsummer in Vinäs, Mora, Sweden. Curiously, the word Maypole is derived from the verb 'maja', which means covering the pole with leaves (Photo Bärsgard).

Returning to Mesopotamian culture, this also provides some information that may add to our understanding of the creation cycles that we have already gained from the Mayan perspective. To begin with, we know that the numerical system of the ancient Sumerians was hexagesimal, that is to say that it was based on the number 60, and our practice of dividing the circle into 360 degrees has been inherited

Fig. 64 Viking age textile from Överhogdal, Härjedalen, Sweden, depicting the World Tree with a bird at the top (Trotzig, *Vikingar*).

The Galactic World Tree and the Star of Bethlehem   133

from their culture. In Sumerian, the words 'solar system member' and 'whole circle' and the number 3600 are all written in the same way, as a circle. Although Sitchin interprets this circle as meaning that the orbit of the 'twelfth planet' is 3600 years, this does not make sense. How could the Sumerians possibly have monitored such a time span? What makes perfect sense, however, is to interpret the cycle of the 'heavenly abode' to be 3600 days, 10 tuns or, in other words, half a katun, a cycle which is a direct overtone of a baktun. Since the Sumerians did describe the increasing and decreasing LIGHT from this Eight-Partition-Place, we may fully understand why 3600 became such an important number for them, and why they divided the circle into 360 degrees.

Maybe then the increasing and decreasing LIGHT from the 'beloved planet' is what led to the emergence of astrology in the first place. Ancient Mesopotamians described various events on earth as associated with the increasing LIGHT from the heavenly center, and indeed the katun, and obviously then also the half-katun, is in a very real way linked to civilizational development as this is effected by the divine process of Creation. Considering that at this early time astrology was used only for predicting the fates of whole nations or civilizations, the monitoring of the LIGHT from the Eight-Partition-Place must have been seen as tremendously important (and it actually was!). From this, then, it may not have been such a big step to believe that other celestial phenomena, such as the positions of the planets, also influence civilizational changes. This is, however, a much more questionable idea, which has never been demonstrated through systematic empirical studies.

Fig. 65 Ancient Sumerian plate of clay showing an Eight-partitioned star in between the moon and seven suns, a probable reference to the Seven DAYS in the NIGHT, and their relationship to the 'lightning' at the Eight-Partition-Place (Courtesy of Sitchin, *The Twelfth Planet*).

The understanding of the basic rhythm of Creation as seven DAYS and six NIGHTS actually had its origin in ancient Mesopotamia, and was inherited by the Jews from there. In various contexts we see the seven DAYS symbolically represented in early sources, although in these the rhythm of Creation was described as seven pulses of LIGHT in the DARK. This is what is represented in Figure 65. There we see seven stars (DAYS) on one side of the Eight-Partition-Place and a moon (NIGHT) on the other, with a symbol of the earth mother who provides the stage for the new Creation. This description probably comes close to the truth, since what we have called the six NIGHTS of Creation really is nothing but six periods when there is no LIGHT. The four ancient symbols signifying the seven pulses of LIGHT, the night that provided the background, the Eight-Partition-Place creating the duality and the earth providing the stage really tells all we need to know about a Creation cycle— other than the exact calendar to describe the changing tides of LIGHT.

Since in the ancient Babylonian view there were seven pulses of LIGHT in the DARK, the seven stages of their step-pyramids, or ziggurats, were really symbolic of the seven DAYS of Creation. It is then interesting to see how they described the seven stages in which these were built: stage 1 (DAY 1): the Ruler of Heaven, Holy House, (rule of new Heaven); stage 2 (DAY 2): where the fields divide (yin/yang duality becoming evident); stage 3 (DAY 3): facing the heavenly abode, lord of the inextinguishable fire (divine LIGHT); stage 4 (DAY 4): Holy place of destiny, lord of the storm (destiny of new cycle comes to dominate); stage 5 (DAY 5): road of travel, where the Word of the Shepherd is revealed (see next section); stage 6 (DAY 6): the boat of the traveler, the lord of the chosen gateway (easy traveling for the chosen); stage 7 (DAY 7): the house for the building of life on earth (completion of the creation cycle). It seems evident then that the Mesopotamian way of describing the seven DAYS of Creation is straight to the point and captures the essence of these very well. Regardless, it seems that the notion of a process of divine Creation moving through different stages existed from the very onset of human civilization, among the Egyptians and the Sumerians, who built their earliest pyramids to reflect this fact.

THE STAR OF BETHLEHEM

For a long time it has been considered as near certain that Jesus was born at some time other than at the beginning of our chronology. Two lines of reasoning have seemed to support such a contention. First, the calculations of Dionysios Exiguus, on whose correlation with the Roman calendar our present Gregorian calendar is based, seem to have been erroneous, and it has thus been assumed that the beginning of our chronology has been arbitrarily set. Second, the few historical facts upon which we may estimate the time of birth of Jesus Christ have been contradictory. Hence, King Herod the Great, during whose reign Jesus was born, according to the Gospels of Matthew and Luke, died in the year 4 BC, meaning that this would be the very latest time that he could have been born. On the other hand, it is said in the Gospel of Luke that Joseph and Maria were obliged to register themselves for indiction in Bethlehem when Quirinius was Roman governor. Since Quirinius held this position from AD 6, Jesus could not have been born before this year.

Since Jesus could not have been born both before 4 BC and after AD 6, the historicity of the Gospels has been questioned, apparently on good ground. So it has been asserted that the tale of Herod killing infant boys goes back to old Semitic legends and is reminiscent of the beginning of the life of Moses. To claim that the life of Jesus would have been threatened by Herod, who at one point did kill his own sons, would then have been a typical way of creating a Messianic legend in the Jewish tradition. Similarly, it has been claimed that the Biblical passage where Joseph and Maria were subject to the indiction of Augustus really was added to emphasize that for this purpose they needed to go Bethlehem. This was where earlier Jewish prophets had claimed that the Messiah would be born, and the gospels thus wanted to suggest that this was where Jesus was born. To have this story fit, Jesus would need to have been born when Quirinius was governor of Syria.

To sort this contradiction out, many attempts have been made to identify the star of Bethlehem, which had guided the three magi from the East to honor the newborn king of the Jews. What then was this star and when did it appear? Kepler made an attempt at studying planetary orbits to look for special events around the time of the beginning of our chronology and suggested that a conjunction of Jupiter and Saturn in the year 7 BC could have been the star of Bethlehem. Countless others have followed in his footsteps with somewhat different ideas. The thing is, however, that etymologists maintain that the Greek word *aster,* used to describe the star of Bethlehem, can only mean 'singular star,' and absolutely not a planet, nor a conjunction of planets or a constellation of stars. This would exclude the conjunction hypothesis, which incidentally would also make Jesus an unlikely forty years old at the time of his crucifixion.

To identify the true time of birth of Jesus it is necessary to provide some further background. It is generally believed that the three magi were from Mesopotamia, presumably Babylonian court astrologers or the like. Ever since the Babylonian captivity a Jewish community had existed in the Land of the Two Rivers that had disseminated its view of the coming appearance of a Messiah in their land of origin. However, there existed among the Chaldeans also a prophetic vision that a King of Peace would be born in the West. The existence of such a prophecy is by itself not very surprising, given that the Mesopotamians were aware of the basic rhythm of Creation of seven DAYS and six NIGHTS. The students of celestial phenomena especially must have been intuitively aware of the workings of the True Cross and how this was now driving the focus of the process of Creation in a Western direction. Intuitively, or even quite consciously if they kept a 3600-day count, they must have been aware that the new LIGHT should break through around the beginning of baktun 8, in the year AD 40. In this context we should, however, remember also that the katuns represent waves of LIGHT and DARKNESS, albeit of a higher frequency than the baktuns. The katun is an overtone of the baktun, and every other katun would be LIGHT and every other DARK, relatively speaking.

Furthermore, according to the Maya, the first half of a katun was ruled by one deity and the other half by another, which means that in AD 1 a half-katun, a lahuntun of 3600 days, of increasing LIGHT would begin. Assuming that the magi were well aware of the prophetic implications of the changing LIGHT of the abode of Anu, and the ancient Sumerian and Babylonian knowledge of its tidings (its 3600-day cycle), it seems very reasonable that the star of Bethlehem was indeed the abode of Anu, which in the millennia before Christ had been depicted on so many tablets from the Near Orient. We know from the inscriptions in Palenque that the Eight-Partition-Place was still visible in the seventh century AD (and probably at least until AD 730), meaning that it must also have been visible around the time of birth of Jesus. What other 'star' would just appear in the way it is described in the Gospels? All regular physical stars have fixed positions in the sky, which the Chaldeans were well aware of, and do not vary so much in their output of light that it would be visible to the naked eye. And of course the only reason that the star of Bethlehem could guide the three magi to Jesus is that it provided a divine LIGHT unlike that of the regular stars, a LIGHT that through holographic resonance they would also perceive as an inner LIGHT, as a guiding star.

If we think about it, given the knowledge the Chaldean magi must have had about the divine process of Creation, at the very least being aware of its basic structure of seven DAYS and six NIGHTS and the 3600-day cycle of the LIGHT emanating from the abode of Anu, what else but an increased LIGHT from this source could possibly have motivated them to go on a journey to honor the coming Messiah in Israel? They must have been aware that all planetary movements were cyclical and repetitive, and thus that no planetary event could be important enough to motivate honoring a King of Peace, a wished-for one-time occurrence in the history of mankind. Moreover, the common idea of the star of Bethlehem as radiating is not consistent with a planet, since these do not twinkle. It is impossible to tell how well the Babylonian knowledge of the seven DAYS and six NIGHTS of divine Creation was correlated with the 3600-day cycles of LIGHT from the abode of Anu, but I would like to highlight one very important fact in this regard. This is that in the Babylonian view of the seven DAYS of Creation it was maintained that in the fifth DAY (what we now know to be baktun 8 beginning in AD 40) 'the Word of the Shepherd would appear.' This is a truly remarkable prophecy, and given their position as keepers of this knowledge it is no wonder that the three magi would set out on a journey to the West, since, according to their own view of Creation, this is where they expected the Shepherd to be born.

So when was Jesus born? The katun when the heavenly abode must have begun to increase its LIGHT began February 9 in AD 1. Assuming then that this was the sign that sent the magi on the move, and that it took them about a month to travel from Mesopotamia to Israel, Jesus most likely was born sometime in March of that year. This would also explain why he has often been symbolized by a fish: he was born in the sign of Pisces. After years of suggestions that Jesus was not born at the time of the beginning of our Gregorian calendar, the somewhat surprising conclusion is then that indeed he was. Hence the intuition of Dionysios Exiguus seems to have guided him exactly right in correlating the years of the Roman and Christian calendars. As a further consequence, humanity is celebrating the new millennium at essentially the right time (although the bimillennium of the birth of Christ should really be celebrated in March of 2001).

That Jesus was born in the year 1 is also consistent with a claim made in the Gospel of Luke (3:23) that Jesus was thirty years old at the time he began his mission to teach. Since his active mission is not believed to have lasted for more than three years, and he was crucified when Pontius Pilate was governor in Palestine (AD 26-36), the time of birth that has been proposed here is also consistent with the estimate most commonly made for the year of his crucifixion (AD 33).

It thus seems that the Egyptian duat, the Sumerian and later Babylonian heavenly abode of Anu and the Jewish star of Bethlehem are all identical to the Mayan Eight-Partition-Place. If this heavenly abode increases in strength with a tun (360-day) and a lahuntun (3600-day) periodicity, it does not seem so surprising that many ancient peoples of the world used the 360-day period as the basis for their spiritual calendars. Indeed, what the peoples recognizing this center in the sky all seem to have in common is that they had calendars built on the 360-day cycle. This seems like more than a coincidence, and establishes a link between these two cultural characteristics. Incidentally, the Sumerian god Enlil was, like his Mayan counterpart Quetzalcoatl, seen as the wind god and the bringer of civilization and culture. This may give us a hint of how the Maya calibrated their calendars, and how these were related to Quetzalcoatl.

CHAPTER 8
QUETZALCOATL AND THE
CREATION OF THE MAYAN CALENDAR

Allah is He Who created Seven Heavens,
and of the Earth the like of them.
Qur'an Surah 65:12

After these excursions into the Cosmos and journeys to the Otherworld we shall now return to a more earthly perspective on the course of human history. So far I have said little that may shed light on the cult of Quetzalcoatl, other than to indicate that one of his aspects seems to have been the White Tezcatlipoca, the LIGHT, Western aspect of the Creator duality, i.e., the Aztec correspondent to Hunahpu. This description, however, hardly explains that he is a deity that has been likened to Christ, or why he was represented as a Plumed Serpent, or why Hernan Cortes was initially believed to be one of his incarnations. Some readers may also have begun to wonder how the arrival of the Spanish in the early sixteenth century fits into the scheme of the seven DAYS and six NIGHTS presented earlier. To shed light on these questions, and on the role of Quetzalcoatl in creating the calendar, we will now take a look at the history and religion of ancient Mesoamerica. But before doing so it is necessary to somewhat complicate our analysis of the Thirteen Heavens.

Are the Seven Heavens mentioned in the quote above from the Qur'an identical to the seven DAYS of the divine process of Creation that have been described? Well, not quite, it seems, and the very year of the consecration of the Holy Qur'an, AD 632, may give us a further key to understanding the wave movement of a creation cycle. AD 632, the year when Mohammed died and the Qur'an was presented to the world, is the exact midpoint of baktun 9, and it marked the beginning of a revitalization of the Mediterranean region which occurred in the midst of this NIGHT. What was it that the followers of Mohammed began to see that made his message spread with such speed?

Fig. 66 The Maize god – the First Father – shown in the dark being prepared to go to the place of creation (courtesy of Freidel, Schele and Parker, *Maya Cosmos*).

Quetzalcoatl and the Creation of the Mayan Calendar   *139*

What I suggest is that they saw a new Heaven, the Heaven of baktun 10, although the LIGHT did not yet shine on this. It was not yet dawn. There is a parallel to this in the Mayan Creation myths, where it is said that before the DAY of baktun 0 began the sky was already there, only there was no LIGHT, so the Heaven was not really visible. This is why on ancient pots depicting the First Father, the gods were shown in the dark before the creation of the Great Cycle had begun (Figure 66). Also, in the time cosmology of the Maya, it is said that the deity ruling the upcoming time cycle already rules during the second half of the preceding time period, such as the second half of a baktun. This would mean that the second half of baktun 9 was actually ruled by the Heaven of baktun 10, although in the latter half of baktun 9 the LIGHT did not yet shine on this Heaven. This setup, where periods of LIGHT and ruling Heavens overlap, may serve to explain why history does not manifest as a staccato-like movement with complete breaks in continuity between DAYS and NIGHTS, but as a smooth wave-like process whose movements are more like the wriggling of a snake than sudden discontinuous jumps.

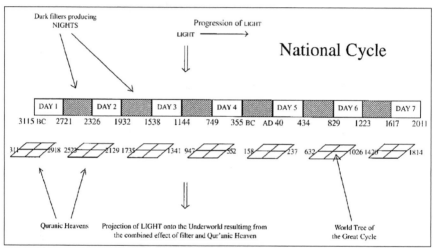

Fig. 67 The Seven Qur'anic heavens and their relationship to the Thirteen Heavens of the Maya (Seven DAYS and six NIGHTS).

Thus it is that the midpoint of a NIGHT is a turning point, when the deity of the upcoming DAY already begins to assert its rule. The emergence of Islam at the midpoint of baktun 9 is a clear expression of this. The expansion of this mono-theistic religion in the midst of this NIGHT was a reflection of one of the Seven Heavens (in the sense of the quote above) beginning its rule and creating the earth the like thereof. To avoid confusion I will in the following reserve the term Heaven for the Thirteen Heavens of the Maya, and the Seven Heavens in Figure 67 will be referred to as Qur'anic Heavens.

Another example of the effects of this overlap between Qur'anic Heavens and filters of DARKNESS is that the nations of western Europe had begun to expand west already at the midpoint of baktun 11 (1420), half a baktun before the new DAY actually began. England, for one, had, during the first half of baktun 11, been enmeshed in a protracted war in France, but with the appearance of the divinely inspired Jeanne d'Arc (1412-1431) its invasion began to be rolled back. From this point and onwards the attention of both nations began to turn west and later; in the beginning of the sixteenth century, France would start to colonize North America, and with Henry VIII Britannia would be set to sea. It was, however, only with baktun 12 that the buildup of the British Empire would begin with the founding of its colonies in North America.

In a parallel development on the Iberian peninsula, Henry the Navigator, prince of Portugal, initiated the bold travels of his nation when Madeira and the Azores were discovered in 1419 and 1431, respectively. These represented the first evident effects of the Cross propelling discoveries and conquests from the Iberian peninsula in the western direction. This process would be increasingly strengthened by the discoveries of America (1492) and India (1498) and culminate with the crushing of the Aztec and Inca empires by Cortes and Francisco Pizarro, respectively. As a result of the looting of its colonies in the New World in the early and mid sixteenth century, Spain came to be the most powerful nation of Europe. But as the Cross also drove history north, and brought about a new duality between spiritual and worldly power, Protestant Britain and the Netherlands would defeat Spain. Initially, after the beginning of baktun 12, this led to the era of power of the Dutch, but later, in the eighteenth century, Britain, located further to the west, would come to rule the seas, only sometimes in competition with the French. Regardless, the point to see here is that the development that led European colonialism to dominate the entire planet during baktun 12, had, in less spectacular ways, taken its beginning already at the midpoint of the previous baktun, baktun 11.

By the same token, we may understand that the waves of history seem to crest at the midpoints of baktuns that are DAYS. The Roman Empire reached its greatest expansion in the year 211, only twenty-five years before the midpoint of baktun 8, DAY 5, of the Great Cycle. After this point the tide turned and the empire's decline began until, at the beginning of baktun 9, it collapsed. Somehow it had already lost the wind at its back at the midpoint of baktun 8, as its expansion then ceased and its contraction began. We may find parallels in a multitude of ways in the rise and fall of civilizations in the European-Mediterranean region. Thus, DAY 1 saw the rise and fall of Sumer and the Thinite kingdom of Egypt; DAY 3 the rise and fall of the New Kingdom in Egypt; DAY 4 the rise and fall of the Persian kingdom and the Golden Era of the Greeks; DAY 5, as mentioned, the rise and fall of the Roman Empire; and DAY 7 the rise and fall of the monarchic nation-states of Europe.

All of this alerts us to the importance of the midpoints of cycles, either as times when the innovations of DAYS are cresting, or, at the midpoints of NIGHTS, when the first signs of innovations begin to be visible. In Figure 67, it is shown how this overlapping arrangement of Qur'anic Heavens and filters of DARKNESS might look. This overlap produces the kind of wave-like, rise and fall movement of history that indeed is its hallmark. The Seven Qur'anic Heavens combine with seven transparent and six dark filters to produce a total of 26 half-baktuns of the Great Cycle. As we now seek to understand the history of Mesoamerica, and the relationship of Quetzalcoatl to the calendar, this more complex view of overlapping Heavens will turn out to be useful. Those desiring an even more complex analysis of Creation are referred to Figure 89 and the discussion of this in Appendix I.

A BRIEF HISTORY OF MESOAMERICA

When discussing the history of Mesoamerica it is important to keep in mind that the peoples of this region have indeed had a very rich and varied history with both ups and downs. Its history traces its roots back at least to the emergence of the Olmecs around 1500 BC, i.e., to the beginning of baktun 4, and surely, albeit in less developed ways, also to the very beginning of the Great Cycle. Many still talk about 'the Maya' as if this was a culture that remained essentially static throughout its existence, which is a false picture. The Mayan culture collapsed and was reinvigorated several times during the course of its history.

Table 11
Important Events in Mesoamerica
Related to Baktun and Mid-Baktun Shifts

mid-baktun 6 (552 BC)	First known use of writing and the tzolkin (Zapotecs, sixth century BC)
mid-baktun 7 (158 BC)	First appearance of sculpted Mayan temples, and of writing, *Popol-Vuh* mythology (Izapa, second century BC)
baktun 8 (AD 40)	Desertion of several prehistoric sites (AD 50) Rise of Teotihuacan and the cult of Quetzalcoatl
mid-baktun 8 (237)	Beginning of the institution of kingship (c. 220) and of Classical Mayan culture (c. 250)
baktun 9 (434)	Founding of Palenque (431)
mid-baktun 9 (632)	The Great Pacal (616-690)
baktun 10 (829)	Collapse of Teotihuacan (~750), Collapse of all southern Mayan cities (800-830), Founding of Chichen-Itza (842)
mid-baktun 10 (1026)	End of rule of Ce Acatl Tipiltzin (999 or 1063), Height of cult of Quetzalcoatl in Chichen-Itza (around 1000)
baktun 11 (1223)	Desertion of Chichen-Itza (1223), Desertion and collapse of Tula (1224), Beginning of Aztec Empire (1350)

mid-baktun 11 (1420)	Fall of the League of Mayapan (1451), Arrival of the Spanish (Columbus 1504, Alvarado 1512, Cortes 1519) and fall of the Aztec Empire (1521)
baktun 12 (1617)	Fall of the last independent Mayan kingdom (1697)

Although the best-known such occurrence was the abandonment of the southern temple cities at the beginning of baktun 10, several other points of civilizational rise and fall marked the evolution of the Mayan region, as well as the Mesoamerican region generally. A number of crucial events in Mesoamerican history have been summarized in Table 11. Although this summary is far from exhaustive and includes some uncertain datings, it may give a general idea of this history.

In Table 11 we may see that significant breakthroughs took place in the Mesoamerican culture during some of the DAYS of the Great Cycle. The first written language and recorded use of calendars in Mesoamerica were found among the Zapotecs of the state of Oaxaca in Mexico, and have been dated to about the midpoint of baktun 6, which actually also represents the midpoint of the entire Great Cycle. Then, after some preliminary developments in Izapa beginning around the midpoint of baktun 7, the significant characteristics of the Classical Mayan culture—the Long Count calendar, the written language, pyramid construction and the institution of ahauob—were developed at the beginning of baktun 8, DAY 5, of the Great Cycle. At about the same time the city of Teotihuacan with its majestic pyramids rose to a population of about 60,000-100,000 inhabitants and became a major center at the Mexican high plateau, and it was then that the worship of Quetzalcoatl began.

At the beginning of baktun 10 Chichen-Itza, located in the northern Yucatan peninsula, became the leading Mayan center. Thus, at the beginning of the sixth DAY of the Great Cycle this city developed several significant innovations, such as the state religion of Quetzalcoatl, a more elegant architecture and a system of rule that was not based on shaman kings. The rule of Chichen-Itza covered a whole empire of cities in the northern Yucatan. In a parallel development the city of Tula, the capital of the Toltecs, which was also very much focused on the cult of Quetzalcoatl, became the leading center in northern Mexico, replacing Teotihuacan, which had collapsed toward the end of baktun 9. Historians debate whether the Toltecs actually invaded Chichen-Itza or not. Regardless, Tula and Chichen-Itza show common traits, partly in the predominant role that was given to the worship of Quetzalcoatl, and legends link the two cities in positive acts performed by an incarnation of Quetzalcoatl around the midpoint of baktun 10.

Despite such advances at the beginning of the new DAYS, it seems that Mesoamerican culture was also very easily disturbed by these very same beginnings, as well as by baktun shifts generally. Thus, for instance, around AD 50, right at the beginning of baktun 8, the Maya deserted several prehistoric centers, including Cerros and El Mirador. Another example of the sensitivity of Mesoamerican culture to the beginning of new DAYS is the widespread and simultaneous collapse of the Classical Mayan sites shortly prior to the beginning of baktun 10, for which I have already suggested an explanation. But through cultural innovations, the Maya were able to successfully respond to the spiritual challenges represented by the beginnings of DAYS 5 and 6. It was only with DAY 7 that no such innovative cultural transformations were developed, and instead the last small independent Mayan kingdom was destroyed at the hands of the Spanish. Mesoamerican culture proved unable to respond successfully to the challenge of the beginning of DAY 7 and was for the most part crushed and assimilated by the European culture driven west from the midline by the Cross.

In Table 11 we may also note that in both Chichen-Itza and Tula the worship of Quetzalcoatl crested at the midpoint of baktun 10. At the beginning of baktun 11, the two cities then simultaneously collapsed, Tula because of the invasion of the Aztecs, and Chichen-Itza for unknown reasons. The last 'empire' of city-states in the Yucatan, the League of Mayapan, was destroyed in 1451, around the midpoint of baktun 11, supposedly because of internal warfare. Although the last major Mesoamerican civilization, the Aztec Empire, was crushed by the swords of steel and the horses of the Spaniards, as well as the lack of immunity on the part of the natives to the diseases carried by the intruders, it is equally evident that independently of this, and even prior to the arrival of the Europeans, these civilizations were very sensitive to the ups and downs of the divine process of Creation. Thus, it was not only in European history that the changing tides generated by the Cross caused the rise and fall of civilizations. We can see evidence of parallel effects in Mesoamerica and, despite the fact that the Maya had calibrated the baktun shifts of the Great Cycle fairly exactly, their culture was equally, and in fact probably more, sensitive to the changing Heavens. The advanced cosmic resonance that their culture was based on offered no protection against its eventual collapse.

We may speculate as to the reasons for this collapse. One strong contributing factor seems to have been the already discussed duality between the worldly and the spiritual realms introduced by the Cross; another is that the Cross with every new DAY tended to push the evolution of human history north. It is a common reaction among visitors today to be surprised at the advanced intellectual culture and science that once reigned in the tropical climate of the Maya, especially since in recent centuries most scientific and technological innovations have been initiated much further north. It is necessary to realize that the creation field of the earth, generated by the particular Heaven that reigns, was in fact different during baktun 8, as the first signs of high culture among the Maya developed, compared to today. Under the Heavens reigning during baktuns 8 through 10, the location close to the creative tension of the equator made the tropics a hot spot of cultural development that it no longer is. As the Cross of baktun 12 pushed history north from the equator, the last kingdom of the Maya lost its independence as the focus of the creative tension then moved all the way up to North America. Although the architectural masterpieces of the Maya are still hidden in the jungles of Guatemala and Chiapas, the creative tension that produced them is no longer present in this tropical region.

This sensitivity of Mesoamerican civilization to the ups and downs of the divine process of Creation indicates that the outcome of the confrontation with the Europeans was perhaps predictable, and indeed several native prophets had forecasted the arrival of Christianity and the Europeans. Given how we now may understand the whole global creation field as a unified structure where interdependent spiritual winds synchronistically affect people in all the corners of the world, it does not seem so surprising that such prophecies indeed had been made. The prophecies simply served to give words to the trends and developments inherent in the divine process of Creation, and for the Mesoamericans, knowledgeable in the varying nature of time cycles, and with a world organized according to the four directions, the ability to prophesy was only natural. So even if Mesoamerica was indeed very sensitive to the waves created by the divine process of Creation, we may also speculate, however, that there was another side of the coin of this sensitivity, one which made them better equipped to develop calendars that described this very process of divine Creation.

In the final DAY of the Great Cycle, Mayan culture has very much gone underground, seemingly having accepted the new cross brought by the missionaries. But through much persecution, also in recent times, the Mayan people have survived and seem increasingly willing to give away their wisdom to the world. Part of this wisdom is embodied in their calendrical system, and maybe the very sensitivity their culture displayed in relation to the wriggling, wave-like process of history may give us a clue to how they were able to calibrate the Great Cycle with such great accuracy—and why they worshiped the Plumed Serpent, the 'creator' of the calendar.

THE DESCENT OF QUETZALCOATL
AND THE SEVEN DAYS OF CREATION

In Table 11 we may note that the worship of Quetzalcoatl in Mesoamerica developed especially during the DAYS of baktuns 8 and 10. The great city of Teotihuacan that became important during baktun 8, simultaneously with the first pulse of Christianity taking place in Europe, was focused on the worship of Quetzalcoatl. We also know that the establishment of the leading role of Chichen-Itza, whose oldest date goes back to the very beginning of baktun 10, meant a surge in the worship of Quetzalcoatl. This was in contrast to the earlier Classical times, when this mythic figure did not among the Maya play the role of an independent object of worship, but seems to have been important mostly in ceremonies performed by the ahauob. In the southern areas the Vision Serpent had been a means for the king to communicate with the ancestors and the gods.

In Chichen-Itza Quetzalcoatl no longer was held as just one of the many gods of the Maya. There he apparently came to be worshiped above everything and became a symbol of the divinity of the state. The high priest of the 'state cult' of Kukulcan in Chichen-Itza carried the title of Ah Kin Maix, Priest of the Cycle, emphasizing the link between Quetzalcoatl and the calendrical cycles. Quetzalcoatl was usually hailed as the bringer of civilization and the calendar, and yet no inscriptions exist from Classical times to indicate that he was a person. But if we are not talking about a person, what does it mean that Quetzalcoatl created the calendar? We may find a first clue in the fact that the worship of the Plumed Serpent was most pronounced during the DAYS—during baktun 8 in Teotihuacan and during baktun 10 in Tula and Chichen-Itza. Thus its worship paralleled the evolution of Christianity in Europe, a very important point.

We have now already started to use the Jewish-Christian-Muslim concept of seven DAYS and six NIGHTS of Creation in the Mesoamerican context, and we must then ask if there is not any evidence from Mayan culture to support the Creation equation presented in Chapter 6. Considering how preoccupied the Maya were with these types of questions, it would be very surprising if they did not know about this identity and leave some sign of this knowledge.

And yes, there seems to be one such sign, which, although it may be the only one we know of, is all the more telling. There is a sign that the Maya, at least those of baktun 10 in Chichen-Itza, had identified the Thirteen Heavens with the seven DAYS and six NIGHTS of Creation. This sign is the descent of the Feathered Serpent along the staircases of the Pyramid of Kukulcan, becoming visible only at the spring and autumn equinoxes (Figure 1). There, in the most spectacular way possible to the ancient Maya, the rhythm of the process of Creation is made evident as seven triangles of light on the back of the Serpent. Together with the six triangle-shaped shadows that are then formed from the terraces, these seven triangles of light give rise to a wave-like pattern consisting of thirteen different triangles, Thirteen Heavens. In the otherwise 'silent' city of Chichen-Itza, which generally lacks written inscriptions, the descent of Quetzalcoatl along the Pyramid of Kukulcan was the most spectacular and educational way to convey, through the architecture of the pyramid, that seven scales of the Serpent were light and six were dark. The astro-architects of Chichen-Itza had indeed been able to construct its central pyramid in such a way that the message of the wave-like descent of the Heavens to earth through the movement of Quetzalcoatl was conveyed. It tells us that the seven DAYS of Quetzalcoatl was considered a most profound revelation.

Through this, the Epic of Creation becomes complete. These triangles on the side of the Pyramid of Kukulcan bring the Creation stories of the Old and the New worlds together. To my knowledge, the descent of the Feathered Serpent from the Pyramid of Kukulcan of Chichen-Itza is the only direct evidence originating from the Maya that links their Thirteen Heavens to the Jewish-Christian-Muslim Creation story, according to which God created the world in seven DAYS and six NIGHTS. What the descent of the Feathered Serpent reveals is that the Maya who built the pyramid at Chichen-Itza were aware of history as a wave-like process created by seven pulses of LIGHT interspersed with six intermediate periods of DARKNESS. Since baktun 10 was an era of LIGHT, this new insight was very likely the result of a new revelation generated by resonance with the new Heaven of this baktun. Considering this concordance between the Christian and Mayan Creation stories, the thought that the cult of the Feathered Serpent in the New World was a parallel phenomenon to Christianity in the Old World no longer seems implausible.

It is well known that among the Maya the Cosmic Serpent is a metaphor of Creation, and, given the wave-like, wriggling process of history, what could possibly be a more natural symbol for this process than a snake? Given the predominant role that Quetzalcoatl had in both Teotihuacan and Chichen-Itza, it is in fact hard to imagine that he would signify anything less than the divine process of Creation. To the ancient Mesoamericans Quetzalcoatl was thus a symbol of the divine process of Creation, progressing through the seven DAYS and six NIGHTS.

Quetzalcoatl was, however, especially a symbol of the LIGHT aspect of Creation, also called the White Tezcatlipoca. Since the even-numbered baktuns—when the cult of Quetzalcoatl was the strongest—were also the eras of LIGHT in the West when the most cultural innovations took place in Mesoamerica, it would then also be natural to regard Quetzalcoatl as the deity of culture and the arts—the bringer of civilization. This role was, as we have seen in previous chapters, the one that the DAYS of the divine process of Creation indeed played. The Maya built the Pyramid of Kukulcan in a new DAY to signify the optimism that this initially brought following the collapse of the Classical culture. At the beginning of baktun 10 the LIGHT aspect of the divine process of Creation had brought a new civilization to the Maya.

Thus, the Maya who built Chichen-Itza were aware that the process of divine Creation progressed through seven DAYS and six NIGHTS. The same obviously was true also for the Christians, whose religion in the Old World was built on the same LIGHT, only symbolized in a different way, by a Cross rather than a Plumed Serpent. Considering this, the idea voiced by many that Quetzalcoatl and Christ were the same has a real foundation. Both were reflections of the LIGHT emerging at even-numbered baktuns.

QUETZALCOATL AS THE ORIGINATOR OF THE CALENDAR

When we previously studied the wave-like nature of the process of Creation during the Great Cycle, we mainly followed large-scale migrations in the east-west direction and the rise and fall of civilizations on the Eurasian continent. We must, however, assume that these events were unknown to the ancient Maya, and could not have been the basis for their calibration of the Long Count. How, then, were they able to develop a calendar that described the changing winds of history? Well, what the Mayan seers probably saw as they looked in the eastern direction of the Heaven was the vertical arm of the Cross.

Over time, movements by this vertical arm of the Cross must from a Western perspective have appeared as the wriggling of a snake. The overlapping of the Seven Qur'anic Heavens, each of which was dominated by a Cross, with the seven periods of LIGHT must have produced the appearance of a flying arm of the Cross in the eastern direction that was especially evident during the DAYS of the Great Cycle. The wriggling movements of this flying arm of the Cross made it appear as a Flying Serpent, and hence the name the Plumed Serpent. And so Quetzalcoatl was not only a symbol of the LIGHT, but also of the duality that distinguishes it from the DARKNESS. In many cultures the snake has been a symbol of duality, and the Plumed

Serpent introducing the yin/yang duality along the vertical arm of the Cross serves exactly such a role.

I have previously claimed that the True Cross is invisible. If this was the case, how could the Maya then have seen the movements of its vertical arm, which they came to call the Plumed Serpent? Well, although the True Cross is invisible its effects are not, and some of these are the historical migrations. Others are caused by vibrations of other frequencies emitted by this wave generator. These overtone vibrations could readily have produced colors, which at least could be seen by the inner vision of the sages. We should recall that the ancient Mesoamericans would associate the various geographic directions with colors, and given that their lives were ruled by a LIGHT/DARKNESS duality generated by the World Tree wave generator, this is not very surprising.

When we consider the expanding and contracting LIGHT emanating from the midline in phase with the various baktun and mid-baktun shifts of the Great Cycle (Figure 67), it seems absolutely logical that from Mesoamerica—that is, from a Western perspective—the vertical arm of the Cross would look like the wriggling movements of a serpent. Then it also becomes understandable that people living in this part of the world would think of Quetzalcoatl as the father of the calendar. It must have been by observing the movements of the Flying Serpent, the vibrational overtones of the Cross, that the Maya were able to calibrate so precisely the calendar of the divine process of Creation.

At katun or tun shifts the ahauob would climb to the top of the pyramids, where they would attain a state of trance reminiscent of a cosmic consciousness, and by contacting the Vision Serpent they would find out in what direction the spiritual wind would blow in the time period ahead. They would see if the LIGHT from the Vision Serpent in the sky expanded or contracted. They would ponder what this would mean for their respective peoples, whom it was their responsibility to guide into the new katun. Such a trance-like contact with the Vision Serpent would be the main source of their prophecies.

Most likely the Mayan seers were not only sensitive to vibrations of the Cross linked to the baktun periods, but almost certainly also to wriggling linked to the shorter katun and tun periodicities. What would then be more natural than for the ahauob to ask the Vision Serpent, i.e., the winding movement of the divine process of Creation, for guidance? This would happen especially at the celebration of katun shifts, when the serpent seemed to change direction. This the Mesoamericans could see, and they could see it throughout the period of domination of the National Underworld, since in this period the creation field of the earth was dominated by the East/West duality of LIGHT, generated by the vertical arm of the Cross.

It would thus be vibrations of a high frequency rather than any material manifestations of the Cross that would provide for the calibration of the Mayan calendar. To see the wriggling movements of Quetzalcoatl it was, however, probably necessary to attain a trance-like or meditative state. Why then have people living today not been seeing this deity? It is for the same reason that we may no longer see the celestial Eight-Partition-Place; because of the Planetary Round of LIGHT the consciousness of human beings has been altered since baktuns 8 and 10, so that we no longer have the same experience of reality that the ancient Maya had. Another yin/yang duality dominated consciousness then compared to in our own time. It is also likely that the well-known use of hallucinogenic mushrooms altered the consciousness of the Mayan seers and that these helped them see the Feathered Serpent more clearly. In the Classical Mayan culture this seeing was probably the special task of the ahauob, but could obviously have been accomplished by other priests or day-keepers as well. After all, the Plumed Serpent was real; it was only a matter of finding the right tools for seeing him.

Fig. 68 Lady 6-Tun communicating with an Ancestor through the Vision Serpent. Note the six dark triangles on the Serpent interspersing the LIGHT areas (Courtesy of Schele and Freidel, *A Forest of Kings*).

The Plumed Serpent is then a symbol or, literally, animation of the divine process of Creation as this moves through the Thirteen Heavens. It would be seen as holding all knowledge about what had occurred in this process. Thus, the ancestors would also ceremonially be brought back and contacted through the mouth of the Vision Serpent (see Figure 68) in Classical times. Thus, although the worship of the snake goes back to the earliest time of Mesoamerican culture, it was only with the rise of Chichen-Itza that the cult of Quetzalcoatl became elevated to the status of something like a religion in the Mayan area. It was only then that it took a place that outshadowed all other objects of worship. And we may understand this on two levels. On the spiritual level, we have now found Quetzalcoatl to be identical with the vertical arm of the True Cross. Since we saw earlier that this Cross became increasingly dominating with every new DAY of the Great Cycle, it becomes logical that the same is true for its vertical arm, Quetzalcoatl. On a more worldly level, it is evident that by concentrating on a cult of a divine principle—Quetzalcoatl as a spiritual emanation of the divine process of Creation—the state of Chichen-Itza avoided the problems, such as the cult of the ahauob as divine, that had led to the downfall of the southern cities. In the same way as the European rulers at the same time sought legitimacy from the Cross, the rulers of Chichen-Itza sought legitimacy directly from Quetzalcoatl. This rule worked well until Quetzalcoatl started to disappear in the East and seemed to remove his protection from the city.

Fig. 69 The temple of Quetzalcoatl in Teotihuacan (photo Calleman).

Fig. 70. The Pyramid of the sun in Teotihuacan (photo Calleman).

After the midpoint of baktun 10 the tide thus began to turn for all the innovations that had been introduced at Chichen-Itza and Tula at the beginning of the baktun. Chichen-Itza began to decline and in Tula the priesthood of the Dark Tezcatlipoca became increasingly powerful. After the expulsion of Ce Acatl Tipiltzin human sacrifice began to rise. The mood now started to shift, as indeed Quetzalcoatl started to disappear, but, as the seers in this culture of pulsing time would know, he would one day return. The scribes knew from their books that Quetzalcoatl would reappear about a baktun later, and maybe take manifest form in a human reincarnation. Yet, since the LIGHT that Quetzalcoatl, the White Tezcatlipoca, provided was the source of their culture, it is easy to understand that his disappearance frightened the ancient Mesoamericans. They knew that the Dark Tezcatlipoca would rule at least throughout their own life spans, and they could only long for the return of Quetzalcoatl, the innovative principle of LIGHT in a relatively distant future. At the beginning of the following NIGHT, baktun 11, Chichen-Itza was, as mentioned, apparently deserted. The city of Tula simultaneously encountered the same fate as it was destroyed by the Aztecs.

Fig. 71 The 'Crucifixion of Quetzalcoatl' (Codex Borgianus).

The Aztecs, whose fierce rule dominated Mesoamerica throughout the first half of baktun 11, seem to have been perpetually worried about the future of the world, especially since it had been prophesied soon to come to an end. Much of the human sacrifice at the time seems to have had as its aim averting such an end. Yet the ancient Mesoamericans would still have their hopes up that Quetzalcoatl would one day return from the East and bring about a renaissance of their culture. Given this background, it is not very surprising that the Aztecs believed Hernan Cortes to be an incarnation of Quetzalcoatl as he planted his cross on the eastern coastline on Good Friday 1519. In fact, it would have been truly remarkable if they did not.

Quetzalcoatl was a symbol of the divine process of Creation. It was the Cross as seen from another angle, meaning that the Christians and the Mesoamericans did not in reality worship different manifestations of the divine. They just looked at the same manifestation from different angles. Maybe then there is also a link between Quetzalcoatl and the snake in the Garden of Eden, since in Biblical mythology the snake was also seen as something that set about the divine process of Creation by luring Eve to enjoy the fruits of the World Tree. But, as mentioned, in the Bible this was portrayed as a crime and God cursed the snake, which came to be considered an evil animal. It was thus suppressed as a symbol, and while the Maya continued to talk to the snake communication with it was broken in the Jewish-Christian tradition.

The lesson for us to learn is that the same reality may look very different from different perspectives. It seems that the European and the Mesoamerican tradition both held places for the Serpent and the Cross, albeit in widely different proportions. In Europe, the Cross came to be all-dominating and it would top the crowns of the kings, while the snake was cursed. In Chichen-Itza, the temples and the kings were subordinated to the Plumed Serpent while the Cross was hardly present. In the invisible universe, however, the two symbols reflect the same reality.

THE TWIN MYTHS OF THE WORLD

This scenario for the rise and fall of Quetzalcoatl, however, points to an inherent weakness in the ancient Mesoamerican spirituality. Thus, as the tide started to turn toward the new NIGHT of baktun 11, so did the priests and their cults, who now became focused on the Dark principle, Tezcatlipoca. The priests of Tezcatlipoca came, at least in the Toltec capital of Tula, to be dominating in the later half of baktun 10. If there were different priesthoods, and their relative strength varied with the Heaven ruling at a particular time, then it seems that these priesthoods failed to realize the basic unity of Creation. When human beings start to worship deities that are seen as independently acting and sometimes competing forces, as evidently was the case with the Toltecs and Aztecs, then they can no longer be qualified as monotheists. Ultimately, this polytheism and inability to see the unity beyond the changing tides of manifest Creation became a paramount spiritual factor behind the downfall of Mesoamerican culture.

The Europeans, in contrast, partly by denying the existence of the yin/yang duality and an ongoing divine process of Creation with its ups and downs, were able to maintain the belief in the basic unity of Creation and in the One God even during the darkness of the NIGHTS. It seems obvious that the belief in one god has the advantage of maintaining social unity as well as cultural and religious continuity. Such a unity may be a strength, both on the part of a nation and on the part of a human individual, in a reality whose evolution appears to be determined by the alternating power of Tezcatlipoca and his twin, Quetzalcoatl. To recognize, as the Christians did, that there is a supreme deity even beyond the LIGHT/DARKNESS duality, and seek a direct relationship with Him, became a prime factor in strengthening the Europeans in the conquest of America. This is by no means to say that the conquistadors were not brutal, but it may serve to explain why small bands were successful in bringing about the downfall of huge empires.

The theme of twins is important also in the *Popol-Vuh*, whose main figures, Hunahpu and Xbalanque, are twins. Hunahpu is transformed into the sun and Xbalanque into the moon, meaning that, similarly to the Quetzalcoatl/Tezcatlipoca pair of twins, they represent principles of LIGHT and DARKNESS interacting in a cosmic drama of the yin/yang type. Such myths of twins are common in Native American Creation stories, but exist in many other cultures as well.

An important European creation story involving twins is that of Romulus and Remus, but there is a curious difference between the Mayan and Roman creation myths. In the *Popol-Vuh*, the two twins seem almost inseparable (as are yin and yang) and they both participate in the attempts to outsmart the Lords of Death. Romulus and Remus, on the other hand, were not inseparable. When Romulus (presumably the counterpart of Hunahpu) has decided where the city is to be founded, and Remus mocks him by crossing the line he has drawn to show this, Romulus simply kills his twin. In this Roman myth no more games are played between yin and yang, presumably since under the midline there is only room for one person.

Fig. 72. Serpent on the wall of the nunnery in Uxmal (photo Calleman).

This reflects a difference in attitude between, on the one hand, midliners, Europeans, and on the other, peoples living on either side of the Cross, Maya and Chinese alike. In the yin/yang philosophy and the mythology of the Hero Twins it seems that the existence of both principles, the principle of LIGHT and the principle of DARKNESS, may be recognized and accepted, and in fact, that human existence cannot be imagined without the two of them. In the midline tradition, on the other hand, there is a thought that the Dark principle should not exist, and hence there has often been a desire to deny or erase it. This attitude has created some very intolerant wars against evil in the name of Christianity, especially, perhaps, on the part of the Papacy and its Inquisition. This type of 'there is only one right way—destroy the dark forces' attitude is thus reflected already in the creation myth of Rome. Satan, the Christian view of the dark force, is viewed as something that should not be.

From a wider perspective it seems, however, that the very duality between LIGHT and DARKNESS has to exist in order for Creation to take place. Unless there was duality, and a Cross maintaining this duality, nothing would ever be created. Yet it seems like the myth of Romulus and Remus would be a fairly good start for a city with the ambition to rule the world, an ambition that the Roman emperors, and during certain periods also the Papacy, have inherited.

Nothing in the Classical records tells us that Quetzalcoatl was ever a man. Yet as the Spanish arrived they heard the legends of Ce Acatl Tipiltzin and possibly even earlier individuals going by the name of Quetzalcoatl. And indeed, this may be an appropriate way of looking at certain individuals, some of whom carried the title of Quetzalcoatl. Although Quetzalcoatl is a divine principle, the yang of the Creator duality, we may of course consider persons who did good works as Quetzalcoatls, as incarnations of the LIGHT principle of the process of divine Creation, in the same way as we may consider Jesus of Nazareth as an incarnation of divine LIGHT. Jesus, as well as the legendary early bearded Quetzalcoatl, may then be seen as an incarnation of the LIGHT of the fifth DAY of the Great Cycle, while Ce Acatl Tipiltzin would be an incarnation of its sixth DAY. Creation not only needs Heavens and their LIGHT, but individuals to carry out the work of LIGHT as well.

This means that if a new Underworld generating pulses of LIGHT visible to our inner vision would return to rule the Heavens, then the consciousness of Christ and of Quetzalcoatl will also return in the form of human incarnations. Maybe one day we will again see visions of Flying Serpents in the sky. If Quetzalcoatl could disappear he can also reappear. If he could sacrifice his heart to become Venus, then that heart can also return to the human beings when Venus returns to the Underworld. And such a return to the Underworld was believed to take place at every inferior conjunction of Venus with the sun, or, in other words, as Venus passes between the earth and the sun, when it is neither evening star nor morning star. In Mesoamerican mythology the passage of Venus through its various phases was a metaphor for the alternations between DAYS and NIGHTS. Maybe one day, then, as Quetzalcoatl is reborn as the morning star, he will sow the birth of the new human being, expressing the new consciousness of Christ. But before we arrive in the future we need to visit the present and look at how its particular frame of consciousness has been developed.

CHAPTER 9
THE PLANETARY UNDERWORLD
AND THE RISE OF THE UNITED STATES

THE DISAPPEARANCE OF QUETZALCOATL

Thus, to summarize, as baktun 11 came to rule and the new NIGHT began, the LIGHT aspect of the Creator duality disappeared, and so Quetzalcoatl, the vertical arm of the Cross, bringing about the yin/yang duality of the DAYS, could no longer be seen in Mesoamerica above the eastern horizon. The creation field boundary in the East from whose wriggling LIGHT seemed to emanate faded away. As a result, without the nurturing influence of the divine LIGHT of Quetzalcoatl, Mesoamerican culture declined and lost the wind of history it previously had at its back.

We may then wonder why the disappearance of the creation field boundary in the East had a more negative effect on the intellectual level of Mesoamerican culture at the beginning of NIGHT 6 than it seems to have had at the beginning of previous NIGHTS. The reason for this intellectual decline of Mayan science is to be found in the Planetary Round of LIGHT. As we saw in Chapter 6, the distribution of LIGHT in the planetary creation field, and the location of the ruling yin/yang duality line, came to be different in the Planetary as compared to the National Underworld, and already as this Underworld was approaching it started to influence the consciousness of human beings all over the world. Although it did not become dominant until AD 1755, the approach of this Underworld had started to make itself clearly felt already in AD 730, and even more markedly in AD 1499. These four 13-katun cycles preceding the Planetary Cycle are discussed briefly in Appendix I regarding the tzolkin (see Figures 89 and 90).

The Planetary Underworld does not have a creation field boundary in the East, and its LIGHT does not fall on the Western Hemisphere but on the European back side of the planet (Figure 29). Hence, as the Heavens preparing for the Planetary Underworld began to make themselves felt, the Maya were no longer able to clearly see Quetzalcoatl, the vertical arm of the Cross, which they had been using for their calendrical calibrations. If they did, the picture was no longer clear, but confusing because of the overlay of the new yin/yang duality. Thus, the knowledge they had inherited from their ancestors about cyclical processes no longer quite seemed to apply. Above all, these preparatory Planetary Underworlds created an awareness among the Mesoamericans that a new age was now to begin, an age that would bring all the cultures of the world together but would also lead to the end of their own distinct civilizations. This slow, preparatory change in consciousness may well have been what prompted the prophecies about the arrival of the Spanish and Christianity, and the fear among the Aztecs of the impending end to their own world.

The emerging influence of the Planetary Underworld and the disappearance of Quetzalcoatl also directly affected the Mayan calendar, which was now reformed. The last stele with a Long Count date had been erected in the year AD 909, and its last known use is reported from AD 1752, a few years before the Planetary Underworld definitely began its rule. The Maya of Chichen-Itza replaced the Long Count with so called Short Counts, rounds of 13 katuns, and later even with the 52-year calendar rounds. Thus, at the beginning of the tenth century AD, the creation field of the Planetary Underworld had already started to obscure the vision of the day-keepers and calendar priests, since the LIGHT of Quetzalcoatl was no longer there for guidance and calendrical calibrations. The 52-year calendar rounds, much emphasized by the later Aztecs, especially seem to represent a deterioration compared to the spiritual calendars. It is highly significant then that the Lords of the 13 katuns in the *Book of Chilam Balam of Chumayel* are shown as blurred and that this book describes that these Lords of Time had been blindfolded (Figure 73). By holographic resonance the blindfolding of these 'Lords' on a cosmic scale then also resulted in a blindfolding of the planet, and the human beings in resonance with this. This blindfolding markedly increased with the beginning in AD 1755 of the Planetary Cycle, which is truly the last in a series of cycles of 13 katuns.

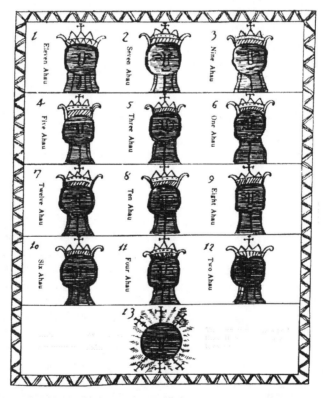

Fig. 73 The (apparently blindfolded) Lords of the Thirteen katuns in a katun round from the *Book of Chilam Balam of Chumayel* (R. Roys).

This is also why we have reasons, in our attempts today to develop a new calendar appropriate for our own time, to emphasize the calendrical knowledge of the Classical Maya the most strongly. The reason is that before AD 730 they had the best vision of the pulsating movements of the Cosmic Serpent for guidance, and in the centuries that followed much of this knowledge was lost. The blurred vision was shared also by their direct descendants, who were as blindfolded as people everywhere else on the planet. For us who live today there are thus strong reasons to think twice about replacing, for instance, the Classical tzolkin count with those that have emerged at later times or have simply been invented in the last decade. Such disregard of the calendrical knowledge of the Classical Maya is not likely to lead to the truth.

TELECOMMUNICATIONS:
THE NERVE THREADS OF THE GLOBAL BRAIN

The Underworld that was created on top of the National Underworld in the step-wise construction of the cosmic pyramid of nine terraces was the Planetary Underworld. Since the creation of each new Underworld is accomplished in a time twenty times shorter than the creation of that below, the creation of the Planetary Underworld is accomplished in 5200/20 = 260 tuns, or, in other words, 256.4 years. This cycle thus began in AD 1755 and will be completed at the end of the year 2011.

Generally speaking, the mid eighteenth century was a time when very great changes occurred, and even if it may not have been described as a 'new age' at the time, a new civilization—the civilization of planetary industrialism—was then seeded. Hence, the beginning of the industrial revolution is usually identified with James Watt's invention of the steam engine in 1769. Paralleling this, the beginning of the Planetary Cycle was in Europe the height of the Enlightenment, emphasizing empirical science and religious tolerance. The first cosmopolitans—persons who did not identify exclusively with their own nations, but with humanity as a whole—also emerged at this time. The first katun, the first DAY, of this Planetary Cycle saw the beginning of the politically and philosophically important American Revolution, and hence the process of making the New World into something other than an area dominated by European colonial powers began.

Similarly to the other Underworlds, this one was also created through a progression through Thirteen Heavens, with the difference that, since we have exact datings for important events throughout this cycle, this Underworld is much easier to study than the previous. The Planetary Cycle develops many things that many have not thought of as being the results of a divine plan, such as industrialism. To understand why we do not always think of the products of this era as the results of a divine plan, we may again take a look at its distribution of LIGHT in the Planetary Round (Figure 29). There, we can see that the Planetary Cycle is a non-dualistic, unitary cycle where none of the LIGHT falls on the vision side of the planet, as is also symbolically shown by the Maya in Figure 73. This means that throughout this cycle human beings are more or less blindfolded and fail to see the existence of a divine process of creation. As a result, human creativity, rather than divine guidance, has been strongly emphasized in explaining the course of events of this cycle.

We may gain a view of the evolution, both of technology and of a planetary frame of consciousness, generated by this cycle by following the emergence of telecommunications. When we discussed the Great Cycle we pointed out the critical role that writing had for its development, and as long as human beings lived in a national context—which evolved with a reasonably slow baktun-based rhythm—it was adequate to communicate by written messages. Nations usually were not so large than that their entire area could not be reached by courier within a few days, and rarely were communications faster than this necessary. However, as a result of the evolution of the planetary frame of consciousness, the whole planet has gradually developed into a common network of communication. As the rate of the process of creation, and hence that of technological development, has speeded up twenty-fold, writing is no longer a sufficiently rapid way of communicating. For this reason telecommunications—using the field of electricity, which was essentially unknown in the National Underworld—has been developed in the Planetary Underworld. But for the very reason that during this creation cycle no LIGHT falls on the Pacific side of the planet, it seems that we have often confused cause and effect in this process, and have failed to see its origin in the divine plan. Thus, in reality, it is not the inventions and development of telecommunications that have caused the emergence of the planetary frame of consciousness. It is exactly the other way around; the new Heavens of this creation cycle have caused the evolution of the planetary frame of consciousness and thus inspired the inventions of means of telecommunication.

Table 12
The Evolution of Telecommunications during the DAYS of the Planetary Cycle

DAY 1:	1755-1775	Theory of telegraph (Anonymous 1753, Bozolus 1767)
DAY 2:	1794-1814	Optical telegraph (Paris-Lille 1794, Sweden 1794)
DAY 3:	1834-1854	Electrical telegraph (Morse 1835, Washington-Baltimore line 1843)
DAY 4:	1873-1893	Telephone (Bell's patent application 1876, First telephone station in the US 1878)
DAY 5:	1913-1932	Radio (First regular broadcasts in the US 1910, Belgium 1913)
DAY 6:	1952-1972	Television (First public broadcast in England 1932, Color TV in US 1953.
DAY 7:	1992-2011	Computer networks (World Wide Web 1992, Global television channels, Mobile telephones)

What is shown in Table 12 is how the development of telecommunications has characteristically taken its greatest steps forward very close to the beginnings of the DAYS, which are the even-numbered katuns, of the Planetary Cycle. This development was seeded with the first thoughts and theories of making a telegraph during DAY 1, when, according to the Aztecs (see Appendix I), the god of time and fire ruled. It continued with the first telecommunications of practical value, as the optical telegraph was invented as it was watered by the goddess of water in DAY 2. The seed that was planted and received warmth and water during DAYS 1 and 2 grew to the electrical telegraph, as it was nurtured by the goddess of love and birth in DAY 3, and even further by the god of sustenance, which produced the telephone during DAY 4. During DAY 5 Quetzalcoatl furnished light, which resulted in radio broadcasts. Following the rule during katun 9 of Tezcatlipoca, the god of darkness (and the destruction this rule produced through Hitlerism, Stalinism and the ensuing World War II with its atomic bomb), television came to conquer the world during DAY 6 as the goddess of birth dominated (which in many ways was a period of rebirth and optimism). Finally, as Ometeotl, the supreme Creator duality, came to rule during DAY 7, this process was completed by the Internet, global TV channels and mobile telephones. Thus, the Net, which became more widely available only after the seventh DAY of Creation had begun in 1992, represents the highest manifestation of this development of telecommunications. Given this progression through the rules of the various Aztec gods, we may wonder who is right. Is it the average person today who thinks that technological development is unguided, unplanned and just the result of fortunate human inventiveness? Or is it the Aztec and Maya who saw history as the result of creation cycles governed by different deities. Well, apparently the creationists have a strong case.

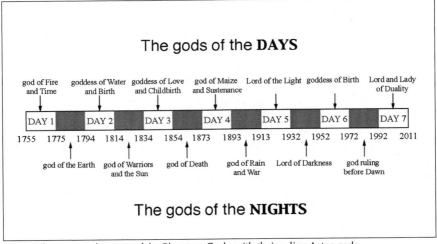

Fig. 74 The DAYS and NIGHTS of the Planetary Cycle with their ruling Aztec gods.

In tracking this evolution we may also note how the potential for global contacts provided by these different types of telecommunications has expanded DAY by DAY. During the first DAY, things were only on the stage of ideas; during the second DAY (optical telegraph) certain special individuals could communicate with other special individuals. During the third DAY, the telegraph was open to any individual, but it could only be used to reach other single individuals, and needed a skilled operator as mediator. The telephone of DAY 4, however, allows for true conversations without the requirement of outside assistance, although only between single individuals. During the fifth DAY, then, certain individuals (radio broadcasters) could reach all other individuals with their messages, and the same was true for the sixth DAY, although the potential for communication was then much expanded as living pictures also were transmitted through television. The emergence of the computer networks of the seventh DAY, however, meant that in principle all individuals could reach all other individuals with pictures, still or moving. This is why we may talk about the Internet as the highest manifestation of the tele-communications generated by the Planetary Underworld, the completion of the process, although mobile telephones are also a clear expression of its frequency increase.

HISTORY OF THE UNITED STATES

Telecommunications is one example of how technology has taken its most important steps as the new DAYS of the Planetary Cycle have begun, but there is a multitude of others. Everything that evolves, regardless of if we are studying art, science, democracy, industry, physical communications or financial exchange, can in a similar way be tracked forward from the beginning of the Planetary Cycle. To be able to see this is mostly a matter of sitting down with the chronicles of modern history and the katun shifts of the Planetary Cycle in hand. If we do, we find that all innovations ultimately are conditioned by the evolution of consciousness according to a rhythm determined by changes in the invisible universe, a rhythm that has been set by the Creator. Here the tracking of these evolutionary trends will be very limited.

Another example of the emergence of this consciousness is the evolution of the United States (Table 13), a nation that was seeded during the first DAY of the Planetary Cycle. Following the Gulf War and the collapse of the Soviet Union shortly prior to the beginning of DAY 7 of this cycle, this country reached a position as the most powerful nation of the planet. The United States, of course, is not a nation in the same sense as the monarchic nations of Europe whose emergence at the beginning of baktun 12 was described in Chapter 4. In contrast to these nations, the United States does not find its origin in a people sharing a common heritage, language and a certain geographical region inhabited for generations. Rather, the emergence of the United States is based on the Cross driving immigrants west from the various nations of Europe ever since the beginning of baktun 12 of the National Cycle. Then, gradually, as the creation of the Planetary Underworld has progressed, people from many other regions of the world such as east Asia and South America have been attracted as well.

Table 13
The Expanding Power of the United States
during the DAYS of the Planetary Cycle

DAY 1:	1755-1775	Consolidation of the thirteen states. Declaration of Independence (1776).
DAY 2:	1794-1814	Louisiana Purchase.
DAY 3:	1834-1854	Conquest of Texas and northern Mexico (CA, NM, AZ, OK, etc.). Incorporation of the Pacific Northwest.
DAY 4:	1873-1893	Expansion of railway system. Massive development of industry and agriculture.
DAY 5:	1913-1932	Victory in World War I. Rise to world power.
DAY 6:	1952-1972	Leader of the Western bloc.
DAY 7:	1992-2011	Only superpower.

Thus, the emergence of the United States is an inherent aspect of the evolution of the Planetary Underworld. The very fact that the nation has evolved through the mixing of people from the various nations of the world means that it reflects the transcendence of the nation as a frame for human life. Moreover, it reflects the development of the left-hemisphere functionality of the global brain. It is true, as we mentioned earlier, that the ancient culture of the Maya also had many traits of a left-brain culture; the ball game was one and its mathematical-analytical descriptions of Creation another. But the ancient Maya did not have ties to the rest of the world, and, in contrast to the North Americans of today, they thus did not represent the left-hemisphere culture of a more or less integrated planet. It is because of this dominant function that we can see how the power in the global context of the United States has increased DAY by DAY during the Planetary Cycle. This development is just as inherent a part of the divine plan of the Planetary Underworld as the emergence of the monarchic nation-state was of the National. The Planetary Underworld is a non-dualistic one serving to create the planet as a unified whole, where the United States has gradually come to play the politically leading role. As a parallel to how the left hemisphere of the brain is the one predominating in the interactions of the present, and is responsible for the external relations of an individual, the present leading role of the United States in the planetary context becomes understandable. Of course, in accordance with the Hermetic principle, this function of the nation as a whole has affected the mentality of the majority of its inhabitants, who are typically very action-oriented and little chained by their past.

Fig. 75 Great Seal of the United States. Note the thirteen stars, thirteen arrows, thirteen olives, thirteen letters and thirteen olive leaves. The flag shows seven light areas interspersed by six dark areas, below which there are nine eagle feathers (from US dollar bill).

Thus, in certain significant regards the Planetary Cycle has developed American ideals from mere seeds in the first DAY to phenomena dominating the world in the seventh. The link between the United States and this creation cycle is particularly evident in much of the symbolism developed as this nation was founded. Thus, for instance, the Great Seal (Figure 75) of the United States contains seven LIGHT and six DARK stripes, almost as if its founding fathers were intuitively aware that the upcoming creation cycle of 13 katuns would come to be dominated by their own nation.

A curious effect that the Planetary Round of LIGHT has had on the United States is the location of its capital. After a short period in Philadelphia, the capital of the United States was moved to Washington, located at the 78th longitude West, which is exactly 90° west of the planetary midline through Rome. This location is linked to the yin/yang duality dominating the Planetary Underworld (Figure 29), and it is by this yin/yang duality its present strength in the world has been generated.

HISTORY OF ATHEISM AND MATERIALISM

The study of the different Underworlds may give a new perspective on atheism and materialism as human attitudes toward the world. Thus, in the National Underworld, as I pointed out in Chapter 5, atheism hardly existed until the beginning of the construction of the Planetary Underworld. When the Heavens of the National Underworld ruled, most everyone believed, if not in God, then at least in 'the gods' or the existence of a spiritual reality, and we could identify certain common traits in the evolution of human religiosity. During the Planetary Cycle, however, this evolution has been moving essentially in the opposite direction. This could first be seen in Europe, where the initial signs of questioning the existence of God appeared in the early eighteenth century as British philosophers questioned the value of revealed knowledge. Although he was placed in the Bastille for voicing such ideas, Voltaire then also came out, if not as an atheist, then at least as a non-Christian. But it was not until very shortly before the beginning of the rule of the Planetary Underworld that some thinkers started to advocate materialism in an explicit way. Thus, in 1748, Julien La Mettrie published his enormously influential book, *L'Homme Machine*, which went all the way in claiming that human beings were like machines that had no souls. In 1751, Helvetius, one of the Encyclopedists, maybe for the first time openly advocated atheism. His article provoked the Papacy to excommunicate anyone reading *La Grande Encyclopédie* from the Church, but this move only backfired as a wave of anti-clericalism swept Europe around the time of the beginning of the Planetary Cycle in AD 1755.

The rest we know. During the evolution of the Planetary Underworld people have step by step adapted to a materialist world view. This has been punctuated by certain important philosophical stepping stones, such as Charles Darwin's *The Origin of Species,* purporting to prove that human beings have come into existence by accident; Karl Marx's claim that the religions were mere reflections of the economic conditions of society; and finally Friedrich Nietzsche's exclamation: 'God is Dead!' Concurrently with this development, the attitudes of people at large, and of their rulers, have gradually changed, so that belief or non-belief in God has turned into a private matter. No longer is religion to influence matters of economics and politics as it used to in the olden days when kings would see themselves as carrying out missions awarded to them by divine providence. Today, mankind has on a massive scale adapted to a materialist, producer/consumer life-style, and no politician would now have the audacity to claim that his actions were inspired by divine intelligence. Although a large proportion of the population, for instance in the Muslim world or the United States, still believe in God, this is not necessarily reflected in the way they live their lives or in the way society at large is organized. Regardless of whether this serves divine creation or not, money (Figure 75), rather than divine inspiration, rules the world in this Underworld.

Thus, in the history of mankind atheism and materialism first appear in a clear and consequent form simultaneously with the onset of the creation of the Planetary Underworld. Its own proponents have usually explained the materialist, or secular, world view that emerged then by the improved material conditions of human life resulting from industrialism. However, atheism actually appeared on the scene somewhat before the material conditions of human life began to be substantially alleviated due to the advent of industrialism. What one would suggest is thus that the emergence of atheism was the result not primarily of changing human societies and habits, but of the very consciousness developed by the Planetary Underworld, blinding us to the LIGHT of God (Figures 29 and 73).

So clearly the major historical religions of humanity have been generated by the consciousness and filters for viewing reality that belonged to the National Underworld. Equally evident is the rise of materialism in the Planetary Underworld. Yet a spiritual evolution also took place during the Planetary Cycle, although its extension was much more limited than during the National Cycle. A predominant trait of this spiritual evolution was its eclecticism, that is, its ambition to unify the religions of the world, point out the commonalties between them and bring together thoughts from different currents; and in this way it has been much less dogmatic than the religions of the past that have a long history of warfare and intolerance among them. This is a natural, and positive, trait given the very fact that the planetary frame of consciousness tends to transcend the borders created by the national frame. Also, it can probably be said that in this evolution the role of God has been less predominant than previously and that there has been an ambition to unify science and religion. These different traits are easily understandable from the perspective of the blindfolded frame of consciousness of the Planetary Cycle. The very limited scope, relatively speaking, of the spiritual evolution that it has carried is also understandable from this. This spiritual evolution can very loosely be called theosophy and has developed mostly outside of the framework of the organized historical religions. These lines of thinking have also developed in a pulse-wise fashion with an emphasis on the DAYS of the cycle:

DAY 1:	1755-1775	Swedenborg (*The True Christian Religion*, 1771)
DAY 2:	1794-1814	?
DAY 3:	1834-1854	Founding of Bahá'i (1844)
DAY 4:	1873-1893	Founding of Theosophical Society (Blavatsky, 1875)
DAY 5:	1913-1932	Anthroposophy (Steiner, 1913); Bailey, (1919)
DAY 6:	1952-1972	Zen, Hinduism, Transcendental meditation
DAY 7:	1992-2011	Eclectic world spirituality

Emanuel Swedenborg was a typical representative of the spiritual evolution as the Planetary Cycle was seeded, being a cosmopolitan living both in Sweden and in England, and being a noted scientist as well as a seer. As Blavatsky and Olcott founded the Theosophical Society at the beginning of DAY 4, the midpoint of the cycle, they also reiterated as one of its goals the unification of science and religion. And clearly, several theosophists were intuitively aware of the rhythm of creation as it may be described according to Mayan calendrics; Helena Blavatsky talks about cycles of seven and Alice Bailey about the seven rays. Nonetheless, at the time that these theosophists were active, science had not progressed to a stage where an exact dating of such cycles of seven was possible. Most importantly, the Big Bang theory was not proposed until 1927 and proved in 1965, and almost all the datings of biological evolution and historical cultures that had been made at the time of Blavatsky and Bailey were very inexact according to what we now know from carbon[14] techniques. Obviously this lack of data affected their thinking, and at the time a unification of science and religion was hardly feasible. Yet they had the intuitive awareness that the universe evolved according to cycles of seven stages and of the holiness of the number 7.

It should also be pointed out that the overwhelming interest of the early theosophists was directed toward the East—to the traditions of Hinduism and Buddhism —for inspiration. While this might have brought valuable ideas to the Western world, the Hindus and Buddhists were never in possession of calendars that could serve the unification of science and religion through accurately charting the spiritual cycles of the Cosmos. At the time of Blavatsky the Mayan calendar was virtually unknown, and its correlation with the Gregorian calendar, a prerequisite for serious work with it, had not yet been worked out.

Why would God then have created a consciousness that has blinded the majority of people to His/Her existence? The answer may be that this disbelief is not part of the primary purpose of this Underworld, but a spin-off effect. There is a certain logic to Creation as it passes through all of its phases of Heavens and Underworlds, which may only be understandable in terms of the intended end result. As we do not know exactly what this final purpose of Creation is—only that there is one—it is not always easy for us to understand how it has been designed. What we do know, however, is that the creation of each Underworld serves as a foundation for the next higher Underworld, meaning that whatever happened during the Planetary Cycle is at least partly understandable as providing a foundation for the Galactic Cycle. Creation unfolds according to a preset pattern for the evolution of consciousness that involves periodic alternations between unity and duality and LIGHT and DARKNESS. This pattern serves the emergence of higher frames of consciousness, and in this way the Planetary Cycle is perfectly designed to prepare for the Galactic. Unfortunately, it is not always easy to see how much of the actual course of events directly depends on our choices and how much of it has been prescribed by the divine plan.

THE BEGINNING OF THE
FINAL KATUN, FEBRUARY 10, 1992

In Table 14 I have summarized a few critical events that took place close to the katun shift that marks the beginning of the seventh DAY of the Planetary Cycle on February 10, 1992. These events all represent the completion of the evolutionary process of consciousness that began in the first DAY of this cycle, beginning in 1755, and are examples that are typical of some of the tendencies that we see in today's world. Thus, for instance, the final coming down to earth of the British monarchy, the last monarchy with some remaining formal power, represents the completion of a process that had begun on the first DAY of the Planetary Underworld, as the United States proclaimed itself a republic. Today, at its seventh DAY, the whole world is in practice ruled as republics, while monarchies, which are intimately linked to the national frame of consciousness, have tended to obstruct the emergence of a planetary frame. This movement toward republics and existential, if not economic, equality between human beings is one of the most important manifestations of the planetary frame of consciousness. Thus, while many may be surprised to see that World War I began DAY 5 of the Cycle, this war becomes partly understandable in that it precipitated the collapse of a whole range of autocratically governed empires, which in many countries paved the way for democratic republics to emerge.

Table 14
The Transfer from the National to the
Planetary Frame of Consciousness around the Beginning
of the Seventh DAY of the Planetary Cycle

National ------------>	*Planetary*
National armies	Multinational forces; US/ NATO/ UN (Gulf War, 1991)
National TV	Global TV channels; CNN (Gulf War, 1991)
National economies	Privatization of the Eastern bloc. Free trade agreements; EU (1992), APEC/NAFTA (1994), EU expansion (1995), WTO (1995)
Monarchies	Republics (*Anno Horribilis* of the British monarchy, 1992)

The restructuring of the military organization of the world—going from nationally controlled military forces linked to either of the Cold War blocs to today's world police composed of forces from different countries in various combinations of the UN, NATO or the US—is another example of the transfer to a planetary frame of consciousness. This change was decisively brought about during the Gulf War in the year prior to the katun shift.

A third very important event linked to the particular katun shift in Table 13 was the final collapse of the Soviet Union. On Christmas Day 1991, the flag of independent Russia was waving above the Kremlin, thus marking the end to seventy-five years of Soviet rule. From that point and onwards the various former republics of the Soviet Union would be governed as independent states. As a result, the world became one integrated whole, which no longer was separated into two distinct camps, as had been the case during the Cold War. The collapse of the Soviet Union was then the decisive step, taking place some six weeks prior to the katun shift. The stage was set for the beginning of the final katun of the Planetary Underworld, whose purpose it was to transcend the East-West polarity of the National Underworld.

Another noteworthy event occurring close to the katun shift was the signing, on February 7, 1992, that is, four days before the actual katun shift, of the Maastricht Treaty. The Maastricht Treaty committed the nations of the European Union to the creation of a common currency, the euro, which was implemented on January 1, 1999, and went into effect as the banks opened on January 4. What this meant in practice is that the member nations sacrificed their national sovereignty to begin the creation of a new planetary center. But more of this later. Simultaneously, in 1992, the EU completed the creation of its common market and was expanded to include also some nations that had previously stood outside of it. This was the first in a series of common market and free trade agreements that have been instituted globally after the beginning of the seventh DAY of the Planetary Cycle. The result is a global market with very few obstacles for the exchange of goods and people, all representing expressions of the planetary frame of consciousness that has now come to dominate the world.

There is another aspect of the evolution of different levels of consciousness that may be appropriate to discuss in the context of the Planetary Underworld. This is that of the levels of maturity of human beings. Students in the field generally acknowledge that as late as in the seventeenth century childhood did not exist as a distinct phase in the development of the human individual. At least until then human beings of an age less than fifteen years were simply seen as small adults. This attitude decisively changed in the mid eighteenth century with the emerging dominance of the Planetary Underworld. Thus, in 1761, Jean Jacques Rousseau wrote his epoch-making book *Émile,* claiming that children had special needs distinct from those of adults. Moreover, in 1763 Prussia, as the first nation in the world, introduced compulsory schools for children. Thus, at the beginning of the Planetary Cycle children were effectively sealed off from the lives of adults. Both of these occurrences point to the emergence of a 'new age,' that of children, as the Planetary Cycle began.

At about the same time populations in Europe started to increase fairly rapidly. The population of England and Wales increased 10% in the first half of the eighteenth century, but as much as 50% in its second half. This increase in population took place all over Europe, even in countries unaffected by industrialism and improvements in agriculture. Thus, this population increase may very much be linked to the emergence of childhood as a distinct phase of human development. In a sense, by having many children, adults in the Planetary Underworld may have wanted to compensate themselves for the loss of the part of themselves that had been sealed off.

Without tracking the full development of childhood in the Planetary Underworld, we have at the beginning of its seventh DAY arrived at what Robert Bly has aptly termed in the title of his book *The Sibling Society.* In the Sibling Society of the seventh DAY of the Planetary Cycle every one of us, regardless of age, tends to live our life as an 'adolescent.' This represents the resolution of the distinction between childhood and adulthood, which had emerged at the beginning of the Cycle. What we then may expect of the Galactic Cycle is a definite end to childhood. We will then all, regardless of physical age, make a new start at the beginning of a creation cycle whose purpose it is to develop us into mature adults, and in this we also have a new angle on the advent of a new age. This change will have numerous repercussions, one of which will be an end to the phenomenon of schools as distinct places to keep younger people. Another will be a decrease in birth rates. This will happen not only because of the disappearance of childhood as a distinct age, but also because as we approach an eternal life the need for inheritors will disappear. The whole idea that 'the children are our future' will no longer be true, as everyone, regardless of physical age, will belong to the generation of the future, a future with a potential for an eternal life.

TRANSCENDING THE DUALITIES OF THE NATIONAL UNDERWORLD AND PREPARING FOR THE COMING

The consciousness of the Planetary Underworld is a non-dualistic consciousness, and it has served to create the planet as a global brain, a planetary whole without distinctive lines between its various component parts. Its unitary creation field has been evident in, among other things, the decline of wars. Thus, before the Planetary Cycle had began, Europe, for instance, was perpetually ravaged by war, and it was only around the beginning of the Planetary Cycle that the first idealists appeared who suggested that a world without wars was possible. At the time, this was considered an utterly naive thought since it implied that people should be encouraged not to fight for what they then considered as the highest good, their countries. Although the Planetary Cycle has since seen the outbreak of a number of very large wars, such as the Napoleonic Wars and World Wars I and II, a marked decline in warfare took place as the cycle reached its seventh DAY. Despite much tension and many minor conflicts the Cold War never resulted in World War III. Between the time the Cold War came to an end around the beginning of the seventh DAY of the Planetary Cycle (February 10, 1992) and the beginning of the Galactic Cycle (January 5, 1999), there were in fact few, if any, instances of wars between two different nations. Concurrently there was a decline in the number of civil wars, and while the United Nations in 1987 counted 38 wars, this was down to 15 in 1997. While we have still not seen the successful completion of this Creation, it is clear that shortly before the beginning of the Galactic Underworld the world was more peaceful than it had ever been before. This was the manifestation of a process that started on DAY 1 of the Planetary Cycle, when the first cosmopolitans appeared and when some advocated the notion of perpetual peace. Ultimately, the decline of warfare during the seventh DAY of the Planetary Underworld goes back to the fact that it has endowed humanity with a planetary frame of consciousness. Its members are now able to see things from a higher perspective than the national, and hence, toward its end they have been less willing to go to war in the name of their nations or ethnic groups.

From the perspective presented here the origin of wars thus seems more complex than has generally been thought. To simply blame wars on human evil or greed does not quite explain their roots. Although warfare has persisted throughout the Planetary Cycle, the conflicts generating them have mostly had their origin in the dualities inherited from the National Cycle and the limited frames of consciousness human beings had in that cycle. So the solution to bringing a definite end to wars seems to be to expand the frame of human consciousness. However, increasing our frame of consciousness seems to be beyond our own control, since it is expanded according to a preset schedule given by the Mayan calendar. Thus the relationships between the divine plan, free will and human action still need to be pondered. If our actions have been, if not determined, then at least conditioned by the divine plan, what is the limit of our own responsibility? Is our own responsibility now about to increase?

Even if we are not able to raise our frame of consciousness, it seems that we may, as an act of choice, develop meta-consciousness, i.e., awareness and understanding of the origin of our consciousness. If we can develop meta-consciousness, or, in other words, an awareness of how the evolution of our consciousness is conditioned by the divine plan—and how this proceeds according to the rhythms of the Mayan calendrics—could this change things? Can the emerging meta-consciousness set an end to our previous stages as puppets of the process of Creation? Can we by developing a meta-consciousness become truly free, responsible to create and not under the control of the ever-changing dualities of the divine process of Creation? Only time can tell, but we may already now pose the question of how we are to attain meta-consciousness, which is still extremely rare in today's world. Yet, at this point at least three paths seem possible: study of the Mayan calendar, use of the Mayan calendar and meditation to create resonance with the highest possible Heavens.

Since duality tends to create wars, we may wonder why duality, as the ancient Mesoamericans were so well aware, is an inherent aspect of many of the Underworlds. The answer is that on the most fundamental level the introduction of dualities is the only way of creating distinctions, and without distinctions nothing would ever exist. Without LIGHT there is no DARKNESS, etc. All that could exist without distinctions is either nothing or everything, which could not be distinguished anyway. Thus, distinctions are necessary for Creation, and to evolve to the next level it is necessary to create distinctions. Creation is a climb of Nine Underworlds, and the only way of evolving from the consciousness of a cell to that of a human being is through a series of frames of consciousness which alternate between unity and duality.

For instance, as we studied the progression through the Thirteen Heavens of the Great Cycle, we saw that this developed the frame of human consciousness from ancient Egypt to the modern nation-state through a series of alternations between dualistic and unitary Heavens. The reason it was designed in this way is that it would be impossible to jump directly from baktun 0 to baktun 12. Thus, to make it possible for us to participate in this evolution a ladder has been created on which we may elevate our consciousness in step-wise fashion and which, during the NIGHTS, gives us a chance to rest from the steep climb. Similarly, it may not be possible to make the jump directly from the frame of consciousness of the Cellular to that of the Universal Underworld. Rather, it seems necessary to progress through a series of Underworlds alternating between duality and unity, and obviously then some of these Underworlds need to be dominated by duality. In climbing the nine-storied pyramid we have one more round of duality/unity to go, and the Underworld now beginning, the Galactic, is a dualistic one.

At the current time (2000), our consciousness is still essentially limited by the Planetary Underworld. We cannot yet see the full truth of Universal Man, and this is the reason we still need to go through a dualistic-unitary pair of Underworlds. To realize that our evolution is not yet completed, we need only consider the number of different viewpoints that exist today regarding the nature of God. This is because from the limited perspective of the Planetary Underworld none of us can see the full truth. Even if today there is a marked absence of wars in the world, there is no safe and stable unity either. Rather, conflicting viewpoints merely coexist, and to realize the true nature of God and find true peace we will need to ascend through one more round of duality/unity. Only in this way, only by seeing the truth in the new LIGHT of the emerging duality of the Galactic Underworld and the distinctions this will teach us, will we be able to arrive at an inclusive unity of all the religions of the world in the Universal. Such a unity would not be one of mere coexistence, or imposed by one group of humans on the others, but one which is based on us actually seeing and recognizing the same truth. This will appear only with the Universal Underworld when Creation, with the emergence of the true human being —the Universal Human Being—will be completed.

The completion of the process of Creation does not mean that a new cycle will begin, as has sometimes been implied. Instead it means the end to all governing cycles, the end of human serfdom to the divine process of Creation. It means that humanity will have attained a state of evolution where there is no further need for divine guidance. The transcendence of the dualities of the Galactic Cycle by the unitary frame of consciousness of the Universal Cycle will mean the final end to all experience of separation: separation between science and spirituality, between matter and consciousness, between the feminine and the masculine, between the inner and outer, between man and God, and so even between life and death—a return to the Dreamtime.

CHAPTER 10
TOWARD THE REVIVAL
OF THE MAYAN CALENDAR

CALENDARS AND CONSCIOUSNESS OF TIME

We have now seen how each Underworld develops a special frame of consciousness and how it is possible to identify certain general patterns in the evolution of these frames. Consciousness of time is a special aspect of the frame of consciousness associated with a specific Underworld, and hence a specific consciousness of time will dominate in each of the different Underworlds. We may notice, for instance, that the consciousness of time of the animals in the Mammalian Underworld is less developed than our own, meaning that animals have a less developed sense of the long-term direction of time than we do. Thus, animals do not plan. A cat, for instance, does not start out his day by planning how he is going to spend it. It takes each day as it comes, catches mice as they appear and seems to be unaware of death.

Although in the Familial and Tribal Underworlds that were built upon the Mammalian a more directional consciousness of time gradually developed, it seems that it was only with the Regional Underworld that a long-term perspective of time, including an awareness of death and a possible afterlife, first emerged. Such awareness is evidenced by the so-called Flower Burial in Iraq dated to sixty thousand years ago. In parallel with the human creativity emerging in this Underworld, a more advanced consciousness of time was developed. Thus, for instance, the use of canoes to reach Australia some fifty thousand years ago and the crossing of Bering Strait twenty-six thousand years ago must have required a certain amount of planning. Nonetheless, during the Regional Cycle the frequency of the process of creation, with DAYS and NIGHTS replacing one another only every eight thousand years, was so low that an awareness of human evolution hardly could have existed at all. Because of this low frequency of creation, very little change that was noticeable within a human lifetime occurred in these early cultures. Thus, while during the seventh DAY of this cycle, as agriculture was established, the need for and interest in keeping track of the changing seasons of the solar year surely must have emerged, there was still no need to develop a long term-calendar, a chronology, to distinguish between different years.

As the Great Cycle with a twenty times higher frequency than the Regional began some five thousand years ago this all started to change. During the National Cycle, human life became organized on such a large scale that people's activities needed to be coordinated. The building of the pyramids, for instance, seems to have required that specific points in time, such as a given day or a given hour to deliver stones from a quarry, could be identified. Thus, the national frame of consciousness, with its particular consciousness of time, promoted the creation of calendars.

With the invention of writing at the beginning of the Great Cycle we may also see that indeed a new consciousness of time emerged then. Hence, writing was developed in response to the need to preserve information. But the need to preserve can only arise among people who at least subconsciously are aware of evolutionary change, which in turn can only arise in a creation cycle with a relatively high frequency. To distinguish between the different days of the solar year, and hence allow for the coordination of human activities, the Sothis calendar, based on the yearly rising of Sirius, was thus developed in ancient Egypt. In this calendar, five feared days when no feelings of sorrow or joy were allowed to be expressed distinguished the holy 360-day year from the astronomical year.

Despite these advances in timekeeping, however, the history of ancient Egypt may never come to be correctly sorted out as no long-term calendar was implemented there. Years were described merely as 'the third year in the reign of Pharaoh Amenhotep IV' or the like. It was only later, at the beginning of baktun 6, that the need for long-term calendars, that is, calendars counting time beyond the life span of a ruler or a dynasty, arose. Curiously, it was at the same time that the first chronicles of history began to be written, again providing evidence of a growing awareness that things change with time. The original long-term calendars from baktun 6, the Greek and Roman, were then later replaced by the Jewish, the Gregorian and the Muslim chronologies that are still in existence.

Also, as the Planetary Underworld began in AD 1755 the consciousness of time seems to have altered among the people living then. The last remnants of calendars based on the divine 360-day year disappeared. Since the divine reality could no longer be perceived, there was no need for a calendar based on the 360-day year that described the evolution of the divine plan. With the blindfolded consciousness of the Planetary Underworld time came to be seen as a physical phenomenon. Instead of exactness in the calendars of the divine, a high precision was developed in physical measurements, and this pertained also to such cycles as the year and month, etc. As a result of the increase in the frequency of the process of creation, and the materialism reigning in today's global civilization, an exact timekeeping to coordinate economic activities was required. In the increased frequency of this Underworld, where changes take place between DAYS and NIGHTS every twentieth tun, such activities take place at a considerably higher pace than, for instance, was the case in the beginning of the Great Cycle. As a result of this change in function the actual meaning of the Gregorian calendar has changed beyond recognition. While in the National Underworld its various years were expressed as Anno Domini, in the Year of the Lord, and time was regarded as having a holy origin, this is no longer evident today. Today, the very same calendar is nothing but a physically exact coordinator of the economic activities that, taken together, at an increasing rate are destroying the resources of the earth.

Although today most people are not aware of the origin of the increased pace of life in the increased frequencies of the vibrations of the World Tree, we are still all very much affected by them. While in the Regional Underworld people's fashions might have changed very slowly—a change in one's way of decorating the body from teeth of saber-toothed tiger to mammoth ivory took ten thousand years or so—we are in the Planetary Underworld presented with two collections of fashion every year. The high frequency of this Underworld has created an obsession for people to have things that are new, an obsession that is even further promoted by economic interests favoring a rapid turnover of things rather than the preservation of the resources of the earth. Over the past 250 years the industrial output and productivity has increased enormously and the emphasis on speed is present everywhere.

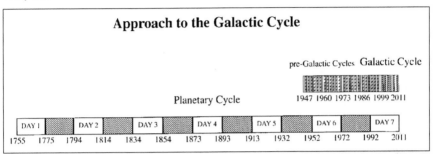

Fig. 76 Approach to the Galactic Cycle with the last five preparatory Galactic Cycles (5 x 13 = 65 tun) overlapping with the DAYS and NIGHTS of the Planetary Cycle (13 x 20 tun).

This frequency increase has become the most evident since the pre-Galactic Cycles began to make their presence felt in 1947 (see Figure 76), and the experience of this frequency increase has been accentuated by the onset of the Galactic Cycle in 1999. Thus, today it is a common experience among people that time is accelerating, and that things now go much faster or even that time disappears. Long-term planning has become more difficult. People who are not clear about their purpose in life especially may easily fall prey to this frequency increase and be worn down as slaves of time, 'burn out' since the pressure to rush affects also the most irrelevant things. To avoid this, the frequency increase does require that everyone make priorities, and to do so we need to know what we are here to do. From the perspective of the Mayan creation cycles this experience of an acceleration of time is completely logical. Time, evolutionary time, *is* accelerating; the shifts between DAYS and NIGHTS *are* happening at an accelerated rate. All we need to do to realize this is to distance ourselves from the materially based calendars.

Also, the calendars used by the Maya have undergone a change that has paralleled the change in consciousness of time that we have described here. Thus, while the baktun-based Long Count was predominating during Classical times, this was replaced in the tenth century AD by the so-called Short Counts of 13 katuns. Later, these in turn were replaced by shorter physical cycles, such as the 52-year calendar round, and the tun was replaced by the haab. Thus, as human consciousness has made the transition from the national to the planetary frame, with a concomitant increase in the frequency of creation, the calendars of the Maya have also changed from spiritual to materialist. Among the non–physically-based calendars it is only the short-term tzolkin that has remained in use until our day, d among some groups of Maya, for this too, the original count used in Classical ..mes has been lost.

This has consequences for how we are to regard the Maya. This was not a superior race, or a group of people that was exceptionally developed spiritually. It was a group of people whose geospiritual placement on the earth endowed them with a possibility of calibrating the spiritual calendars more exactly than the other peoples of this planet were able to. But this ability was given to them through a specific frame of consciousness, the Western consciousness of baktuns 7, 8 and 9, and as this frame of consciousness changed so did their ability to follow the movements of the divine.

The point to realize from this is that human methods of timekeeping in general, and our calendars in particular, are directly conditioned by the frequency of the True Cross in the particular Underworld in which we are living. It is in this perspective that the transfer to a new calendar today needs to be discussed. Ultimately, the need for a new calendar now arises because we are entering the Galactic Underworld, which carries an altered consciousness of time. It is from this that we may understand the current rise in interest in the Mayan calendar.

Three things can be said about the coming change in consciousness of time as we enter the galactic context. First, we will become aware of the evolution of the divine plan proceeding according to a tun-based rhythm, something that will require us to complement the physical calendars with a calendar describing this rhythm. Human beings will again become aware of the LIGHT/DARKNESS duality (Figure 29) and hence become aware of the rhythm with which this pulsates. The Mayan calendar of the future will serve to describe this exactly. Second, as we see the new DAY we will become aware of the basic frequency of creation increasing from 1/katun to 1/tun. This frequency increase will affect not only our experience of time, but our ability to see colors and hear sounds as well. The result of the third thing is somewhat paradoxical; although the new frame of consciousness will be transmitted to human beings with an increased frequency this frame will, as such, carry a more 'eternal' experience of time. As we pass from a planetary frame of existence, where our experience of time has largely depended on the earth's 365-day revolution around the sun, to a galactic, where it depends on the earth's revolution around the galactic center in 250 million years, the basic physical rhythm will increase 250 million times, thus creating an experience of quasi-eternity. Regardless, the new consciousness of time will set a resurgence of the tun-based calendars on the agenda.

THE SPIRITUAL BIRTHDAY

The idea that the day we were born is important for who we are as individuals, and what our destinies will be like, is shared by most human cultures. Also, the most basic facts authorities always ask for today when identifying an individual, is time and place of birth. Because of the presumed importance of the date we started out in life, it has been common to celebrate birthdays, which in some sense are a repetition of the particular day we were born. But what day should we really call our birthday? This depends on what calendar we use. In modern society we have come to take it for granted that our birthdays are to be celebrated on the date in the Gregorian year that we were born. Our birthday in the Gregorian year may then be called our astronomical or biological birthday, since it corresponds to the same point in the change between the seasons as the day when we were born.

This practice of basing our birthday on the physical, or seasonal, year is, however, by no means to be taken as a given (consider for instance that sometimes 365 days and at other times 366 days elapse between these birthdays!) and a number of other possible days exist for celebrating our births. The Classical Maya would, for instance, celebrate their birthdays every tun, at every 360-day period after they were born, and among these the katun periods of 20 tuns were the most important. We may call such days spiritual birthdays, since our individual spiritual evolution follows a 360-day periodicity with a special emphasis on every fifth, tenth and twentieth tun. What this means is that while the common birthday in the Gregorian calendar may correspond to our biological phases, the spiritual birthday marks the beginning of a new spiritual phase of 360 days. In the Gregorian year spiritual birthdays will thus fall on different dates from year to year.

That the spiritual birthday was important to the ancient Maya is evident in a number of ways. To them the spiritual birthdays of kings would typically be reasons for celebration. Not only that, they would also celebrate 'tuniversaries' of important political events such as accessions to thrones. Although in the Planetary Underworld the practice of celebrating tuniversaries has completely disappeared, even among the Maya, it is now likely to return. As we are entering a new creation cycle, the Galactic, whose basic period is exactly a tun, our consciousness of time will again change as we start following a rhythm of 360-day periods. For this reason our own individual tun-based rhythms, starting at our day of birth, will dramatically increase in importance. Appendix III describes how to calculate spiritual birthdays.

The fact that each of us has an individual spiritual rhythm, starting on our tuniversaries, is part of the reason there is so much individual variation regarding the aspects of the Heavens we are in resonance with (another factor causing individual variation is where we were born). Unless such a variation existed human beings would all be affected simultaneously as soon as a new Heaven was introduced in the Cosmic Projector. What this means is that there exists both universal phases for the evolution of the divine plan that are common to the entire universe, presented in Table 20 (Appendix I), and individual phases conditioning how this plan is manifested through individuals. These latter phases will then obviously take their beginnings on the different days on which different individuals are born.

Another important non-physical period followed by the Maya is the 260-day tzolkin, which is discussed in Appendix I. For twenty-five hundred years this has been used without interruption to define the energy of the day of birth of an individual. How to calculate your tzolkin day of birth is also presented in Appendix III. It should be noted that there is a difference between the spiritual birthday and the tzolkin birthday. While a tuniversary defines the beginning of a new 360-day spiritual phase in your life, the tzolkin day defines the energy of the day you were born. While the modern revival of interest in the Mayan calendar has focused mostly on the tzolkin, the archeological evidence from Classical times points to the tuniversaries as the most celebrated birthdays.

THE MAYAN CALENDAR:
THE CALENDAR OF THE NEW AGE

One of the names of the upcoming Galactic Cycle is the New Age, an idea that has generated a widespread movement in Western society during recent decades. From the previous we may conclude that in at least one way this current has proved to be right: A new age is now beginning. Here the New Age is then meant in a literal sense since, as we pass from the Planetary to the Galactic Underworld, and from an essentially katun-based to a tun-based rhythm, the 'age' of time will decrease twenty times. The same amount of transformation will come to be accomplished in one tun as was previously accomplished in twenty tuns. This shift from the planetary to the galactic consciousness of time is thus brought about by a frequency increase, ultimately generated by the vibrations emanating from the True Cross.

But, of course, the New Age movement has only to a small degree preoccupied itself with the phenomenon of time. Instead it has focused on a wide range of phenomena relating to human development and healing of diseases and traumas. In a sense, however, these things also can be directly traced back to the increased rate of shivering of the World Tree, which has caused an increase in a wide range of other frequencies as well. Take such phenomena as aura seeing or healing techniques using colors or sounds. These phenomena are linked to the overtones of the basic frequencies of creation generated by the wave generator of the World Tree, and emerge in parallel with the new frequency of time.

The lowest frequency generated by the World Tree is $1/13$ hablatuns $= 1/(13 \times 1,280,000,000 \times 360 \times 24 \times 60 \times 60 \text{ sec}) = 1.9 \times 10^{-18}$ Hz. Another very basic frequency is $1/\text{hablatun} = 1/(1,280,000,000 \times 360 \times 24 \times 60 \times 60 \text{ sec}) = 2.5 \times 10^{-17}$ Hz. Then any multiple of twenty of these basic frequencies, and countless types of overtones in the invisible universe, may serve to generate our experience of wave phenomena such as light, sound, earth radiation and planetary orbits. While many of the most basic frequencies, such as those of the planetary revolutions, were presumably set already during the Cellular Underworld, others have come into existence since then. And so we are likely to experience many new frequencies as a result of the arrival of the Galactic Underworld. As the True Cross starts to vibrate with a higher frequency, new colors and sounds and countless other phenomena will be generated, or, maybe more precisely said, perceived for the first time. All of these phenomena are linked to the arrival of a new age, and their early forms have been expressed by the New Age movement.

Nonetheless, the whole concept that the New Age has been based on, the precession of the equinoxes moving the point of the spring equinox from the constellation of Pisces to that of Aquarius, may now be recognized as an illusory notion based on a materialist understanding of time. In the galactic context that we are now about to enter, the precessional movement of the earth will be recognized as nothing but a spin-off effect of the tun-based vibrations of the World Tree (see Appendix V).

Astrology in general will at the very least be relegated to a lesser role. Astrology is in two significant ways conditioned by the planetary frame of consciousness. First, because it emphasizes the role of planets in determining the human fate, and second, because of its physicalist way of thinking. Thus, the movements and place-ments of the planets in the sky is determined exactly by Kepler's and Newton's laws for material bodies, and hence astrology is based on an assumption that the physical determines the spiritual. In the galactic frame of consciousness, on the other hand, it will be recognized that the spiritual is primary to the material world. While the planetary frame of consciousness has fostered a perspective, e.g., astrological, from the inside looking out, the galactic frame will foster one from the outside looking in.

Generally speaking, I feel the use of the tun-based Mayan calendar may serve as an aid in the development of meta-consciousness, that is, for creating an awareness of the processes governing the evolution of human consciousness. To allow people to follow and be in phase with the evolutionary process determined by the divine process of Creation will be the chief purpose for the Mayan calendar during the Galactic Cycle. For those now beginning to use this calendar, above all by noting its tun and half-tun shifts, but also the Classical tzolkin, it will mean the development, at least on an intuitive level, of an ability to predict the future. We may thus also say that the Mayan calendar will provide guidance for the future and an improved understanding of the course of events as they unfold.

To what extent the Mayan calendar will allow a person to surf on the waves of creation, however, will depend to a large degree on how he or she uses it in prac-tice. To spend some time every day to sense and meditate on the energies of a particular day in the Mayan calendar may play an important role in the develop-ment of meta-consciousness. Also, the short 13-day count is the result of a wave-like process generated by the True Cross. By experiencing the energies corres-ponding to this count we may learn to surf on the waves of time, i.e. the creative processes pervading the universe, and so align our own projects of creation with the large-scale waves. Following the tun-based phases linked to our spiritual birthdays will generate the same kind of result.

What may be most important, however, is following the alternating DAYS and NIGHTS of the Galactic Cycle, since this will allow us to identify the new LIGHT, and the new phenomena propelled by this LIGHT. The same is true for the 20-day uinals, which are also characterized by alternating periods of LIGHT and DARKNESS, meaning movement forward and rest, respectively. Following the tun-based calendar of the Galactic Cycle will allow us to identify the true LIGHT of the future and make crucial choices with regard to this. Although the use of the Mayan calendar is not to be regarded as an entrance ticket to Heaven, it may aid us in making the right choices and chart a path forward in phase with the new energies. The Mayan calendar will provide a time schedule for the descent of the Kingdom of Heaven, the Ninth Underworld, to earth. Such a time schedule—in fact a map of time—will allow us not only to see that Creation is going in the direction of the

Kingdom of Heaven, but also not to expect this to arrive earlier than scheduled. It will tell us that in the large-scale picture of creation everything has its own time and that there is no step in the evolution of the universe that can be omitted if the end result is to be accomplished. The pyramid of creation needs to be climbed one step at a time. In this sense the Mayan calendar may be a very useful tool for grounding us in the reality of time, where the energies of all days need to be played out because they all play a role in the larger scheme of things. The Mayan calendar does tell us the rhythm of human progress, but it also tells us not to feel frustrated because things do not move as rapidly as some of us may wish.

During the past five hundred years or so humans have been engaged in developing maps of their spatial reality, previously mostly of the earth and more recently in outer space. The Mayan calendar which now emerges, on the other hand, represents the beginning of a mapping of time, and if the need arises this map may be brought to a much higher resolution than what has been presented here. In the temporal landscape of the Galactic Underworld that we are now about to enter, a map of time may be even more important to us than a spatial map, as our frames of reality will dramatically change. Time will no longer be what it used to be. And it is for this very reason that we will need a new calendar, a calendar that accurately describes spiritual, rather than physical, time and thus the exact progression through energies. Regardless of whether or not we use the map provided by the Mayan calendar, living through the Galactic Cycle is likely to be like riding a roller coaster. The difference between using the Mayan calendar as a time map and not doing so is like that between riding a roller coaster with open eyes or blindfolded. Those that ride with open eyes will at least see where the train is going and be prepared for its ups and downs.

As we saw earlier, the Planetary Underworld has been one of extreme materialism where the highest good, as defined by politicians and other public representatives of society, has been to keep the wheels of industry going, and even growing. The calendar of this materialist philosophy and life-style is the Gregorian calendar, which is based on the physical year. In the Planetary Underworld the Gregorian calendar has lost its originally holy character and turned into a tool for coordinating the rat race, and it is this rat race, and its associated philosophy of materialist growth, that is threatening to destroy the earth. If growth, of material wealth or of populations, is seen as a desirable end result in itself, then the earth will obviously eventually be destroyed, since the resources that were meant for humanity's spiritual evolution and the entry into the Kingdom of Heaven will no longer be at hand.

Thus, the two calendars, the Gregorian and the Mayan, will come to represent two different cultures, a materialist and a spiritual, one that represent economic growth and another that represents the true spiritual destiny of humanity. The Mayan calendar, therefore, may be seen as a tool for those seeking to break out of the rat race and the physical time of the Planetary Cycle. It will allow us to come into phase with the waves of the divine plan, the vibrations of the World Tree and the True Cross, the waves that ultimately will bring us to the Universal Underworld.

In this way the choice of calendar is a political question that is linked to different views of what human life on this earth is meant to be like.

Of course, this does not mean that any Mayan calendar will work. For one thing, the true traditional tzolkin count will need to be used (see Appendix IV). It is also necessary that the 13 tuns of the Galactic Cycle are correctly calibrated, and for this the traditional tzolkin count will ultimately provide the master (Appendix II). The Galactic Cycle needs to begin and end on a day that in the traditional tzolkin count is 13 Ahau. Finally, to use any of a number of Mayan calendars that are physical, based on the revolutions of the moon around the sun or the earth around the sun or the precession of the earth (Appendix V), will lead the user astray regardless of the tradition such calendars have been part of. Consciousness is primary to matter!

We should note here that the Galactic Cycle is a dualistic cycle where the divine LIGHT will fall predominantly on the Eastern Hemisphere. What this means is that a bifurcation of consciousness will be introduced, separating the Western and Eastern Hemispheres of the planet, and for this reason the ensuing consciousness of time may not necessarily be homogeneous all over the planet. Maybe, if it is in the Eastern Hemisphere where the LIGHT of the Galactic Cycle will predominantly fall, people there will be more inclined to change calendars, whereas in the Western Hemisphere they may to a higher degree be stuck in the physical concept of time characterizing the Planetary Underworld. Hence, in the era to come different types of calendars may come to be introduced in different areas of the world.

In addition to the above arguments for transferring to the Mayan calendar, there is another and more tangible one. This is that we need a calendrical system that is useful all over the galaxy, something that disqualifies the current Gregorian calendar, which is based on particularities of our own planet. Hence, the Gregorian calendar is based not only on the time of birth of a prophet on our particular planet, Jesus Christ, but also on its astronomical particularities, notably the duration of its revolution around the sun, 365.2422 days. There is, however, no reason to believe that these constants of time, so ingrained in our consciousness, have any relevance on other planets of our galaxy. The same may be said about the precessional cycle of the earth, whose duration, about 26,000 years, is determined by particularities of our own solar system and lacks relevance in the galactic context.

In contrast to the Gregorian, the tun-based calendar of the Maya is in principle valid all across the galaxy and probably even across the universe. Thus, wherever you are in the galaxy you are affected by the same vibrations of the Galactic World Tree, whose invisible branches envelop the galaxy in its entirety. A calendar describing these vibrations is then valid all across this.

Thus, in terms of Mayan time, the number of Heavens and Underworlds that have ruled since the beginning of creation some 16 billion years ago will be the same everywhere. In the creation-based time the 'now' defined by the particular Heaven ruling is universal in nature. Thus, although physical calendars are likely to differ between planets, the spiritual calendars may be universal. This would mean that the tun-based Mayan calendar is more suitable than the Gregorian calendar for facilitating interplanetary communications. This will be especially so as during the upcoming Galactic Cycle the very evolution of the means of intragalactic communications will, all across the galaxy, be developed in phase with the DAYS of the cycle. Wherever there is human-like consciousness in the galaxy, it will now, like ourselves, be waking up to the possibility of using a tun-based calendar to describe the divine process of Creation.

CHAPTER 11
PREDICTIONS FOR
THE GALACTIC CYCLE

This cycle (of thirteen tun) will begin in 1999 and may have to do with the emergence of some kind of self-generating global computer intelligence. In the same way as the written language was used only by a small part of the human population 13 x 20² tun ago, and only today is something that the whole world is in possession of, we may assume that the possibility that will emerge in 1999 will make a start that is relatively little noticed and then rapidly spreads across the planet to prepare for the end of the cycle in 2011.
Maya-hypotesen (Carl Johan Calleman, 1994)

THE NEW GALACTIC CIVILIZATION

Nothing is new under the sun. Nothing emerges from nothing and everything has a prehistory. It is sometimes difficult, therefore, to pinpoint exactly the first time something manifested on this planet. Some would say that the beginning of the Web in 1992 was what really changed things. Others would point out that even this has a prehistory, that e-mails have been sent in the academic world since the mid 1980s and that the Internet may be traced to a computer network for military purposes going back to 1976. Maybe even the invention of the computer in 1946-1948 or Charles Babbage's analytical engine in 1834 or Blaise Pascal's invention of the mechanical calculator in 1643 was the real demarcation line. The many possible starting points is why no theory can be based on a single event but must consider the total evolutionary picture.

Yet it seems that, at least in northern Europe, 1999 was the year when people became aware that the computer technology had led to a new civilization, a new civilization that would leave the industrial society behind. This was the year when it became evident to most everyone that evolution now takes places through computers and that it develops according to a self-generating logic of its own, and that this evolution is about to transform human society in all of its aspects. This change, it was typically said, will be as great as that brought by the industrial revolution. Yet among all the new inventions and applications of information technology (IT) it may still be difficult to pinpoint exactly what corresponds to the steam engine (if indeed such an exact correspondent must exist).

The predominant trait of the Galactic Creation Cycle, at least initially, is what is commonly referred to as the IT revolution—the emergence of a new civilization driven largely by the evolution of the new means of communication and information processing provided by the computer technology in its many different aspects. Much of its exact course may be unpredictable, but it is already obvious that it develops according to a rhythm that conforms to that of the Mayan calendar.

Hence, the mature fruit of the development of telecommunications brought about by the Planetary Cycle was manifested at the beginning of its seventh DAY with the emergence in 1992 of the World Wide Web of the Internet. In 1999, the initiatory year of the Galactic Creation Cycle, it has become evident that this has provided the foundation for the beginning of a new type of civilization. And in several places it is now heard that the current change is comparable in scope to events at the beginning of the industrial revolution. What this in practice means is that the new information technology civilization is a reflection of the new consciousness carried by the Galactic Creation Cycle.

Looked upon from the perspective of Mayan calendrics, the emergence of the IT civilization is indeed a parallel to the industrial revolution: The scientific revolution, and the means to disseminate written information more widely, postal service and newspapers, emerged around the beginning of the seventh DAY of the National Cycle in 1617. These new ways of thinking and communicating were what paved the way for the industrial revolution around the beginning of the Planetary Cycle in 1755. As a direct parallel, the World Wide Web, with its vastly expanded means of exchanging information, emerged at the beginning of the seventh DAY of the Planetary Cycle in 1992, thus paving the way for the IT civilization that emerged with the Galactic Cycle in 1999. The feeling that IT is now bringing about a new civilization and a new economy became widespread in 1999.

An interesting consequence of this link between the Galactic Creation Cycle and the IT civilization is that the great steps forward will be taken by the latter, during the DAYS of this cycle. There will be very obvious parallels between this rhythm and the rhythms with which writing developed during the National Cycle or telecommunications developed during the Planetary Cycle (Table 12). Hence, also for this new process, the NIGHTS will be periods mostly for widening the distribution of the phenomena developed during the previous DAYS and for preparing for the new to come during the following DAYS. A marked difference between the development of the IT revolution and the previous developments of writing and telecommunications, however, is that it will develop at a much higher frequency, with a tun-based rhythm rather than the earlier baktun- and katun-based rhythms.

We may expect that this evolution of IT will develop via broad band technology to wireless computer communications. After a few DAYS the current IT may come to look as obsolete as the steam engine may look to us who live today. It also seems clear that it will be developing in a galactic direction. More than a million people downloaded the SETI program for aiding in the search for extraterrestrial radio signals in the seminal year for the Galactic Cycle, and, combined with the new techniques for studying extra-solar planets, the serious search may be said to have begun. But for this to be successful it seems obvious that cosmic fields other than electromagnetic will have to come into play. And of course information technology reflects a new relationship between consciousness and matter. Thoughts that human beings have are immediately manifested on the computer screen as if it is a mirror. Although it is a technology that is considered scientific by the mainstream it is at the same time magic.

Another predominating aspect of the upcoming Galactic Cycle is that it will bring about the unification of Europe. The political, economic and military unification of Europe is in turn an aspect of the unification of the entire planet, with Europe in a central position, which in turn is an aspect of the galactification of human life. At first sight it might be thought that European unification is simply an economically motivated project which has little to do with Mayan calendrics or Revelation. Yet, it is profoundly conditioned by the switching of places of yin and yang in this new Underworld. This shift will favor a new creativity along the planetary midline and also set an end to the dominance of the Western Hemisphere over the Eastern. As a result of this, a new creative tension will be generated in the midst of the planet, and Europe will again come to play a central role. This is not to say that Europe will come to dominate the world. Rather it seems likely that, as the dominance of the Western Hemisphere over the Eastern will come to its end, the geospiritual location of Europe will endow it with a coordinating role.

As we saw earlier, the line separating the Eastern and Western Hemispheres along the 12th longitude East is the primary resonance line for the galactic mid-plane, the creative trunk of the World Tree. In the Galactic Underworld this line will, however, not be like the razor-sharp flaming sword it was in the National Underworld. Instead, the entire central European area will be dominated by the projection of the galactic disc, the whole trunk of the World Tree (which then will have to be imagined as standing up; see Figure 77a). Ultimately, this is the geospiritual background to the formation of the EMU (European Monetary Union).

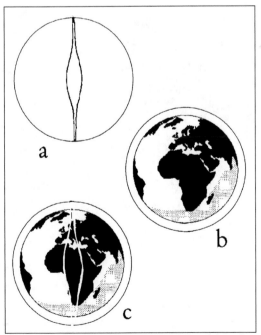

Fig. 77 Holographic resonance projection (c) of the galactic disc (a) on the earth (b).

The nations located in the region with the predominant holographic resonance with the World Tree trunk will, because of this shared resonance, form a new center. The repercussions of this may come to be felt the most strongly in the direction that the LIGHT will be expanding during the Galactic Cycle, toward the east.

If we look at Figure 77 we may wonder why it is not Africa that will be playing such a coordinating role. On the planetary level, the reason seems to be that during the National Cycle the equatorial arm of the Cross with every DAY has tended to push the edge of civilizational development north away from Africa. In a wider galactic context, it can also be said that it is the trunk rather than the root of the World Tree that is the place of creation. Thus, while the stars in the central bulge of the galaxy have irregular orbits and behave like swarming bees, the peripheral ones adhere to a smooth creation-based alautun rhythm that may be necessary for the generation of life. It would thus seem that it is in the peripheral regions of the galactic disc, closer to the branches of the World Tree, that the galactic biosphere is located. Since it is Europe rather than Africa that is most directly in holographic resonance with the peripheral galactic biosphere, it has more often played an initiating role in the civilizational development of the planet.

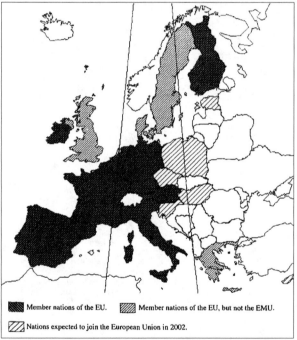

Fig. 78 Close-up of approximate holographic resonance lines of the galactic disc, The World Tree trunk, in Europe.

The inauguration of the EMU, which occurred at the very beginning of the first DAY of the Galactic Creation Cycle, was the first and decisive step toward the creation of a European 'super-state.' The common currency of Europe, the euro, was instituted on January 1, 1999 (taking effect as the banks opened on January 4, 1999 (0.0.0)—the creation day of the Galactic Cycle; See Table 15). NATO, which provides for the military integration of Europe, later in the same year expanded eastwards to include also the Czech Republic, Hungary and Poland. Soon these same nations, joined by Estonia, Slovenia and Cyprus, will also enter this European super-state, emerging as a result of galactic resonance. This resonance will serve to create a superstructure which is balanced with regard to the planetary midline, extending to an area of approximately the same size on both sides of this midline (Figure 78).

Table 15
Tun and Half-tun Shifts of the Galactic Cycle
in Gregorian Dates (Ahau Days)

0.0.0	January 4, 1999	7.0.0	November 28, 2005
0.9.0	July 3, 1999	7.9.0	May 28, 2006
1.0.0	December 30, 1999	8.0.0	November.23, 2006
1.9.0	June 27, 2000	8.9.0	May 22, 2007
2.0.0	December 24, 2000	9.0.0	November.18, 2007
2.9.0	June 22, 2001	9.9.0	May 17, 2008
3.0.0	December 19, 2001	10.0.0	November. 12, 2008
3.9.0	June 17, 2002	10.9.0	May 11, 2009
4.0.0	December 14, 2002	11.0.0	November. 7, 2009
4.9.0	June 12, 2003	11.9.0	May 6, 2010
5.0.0	December 9, 2003	12.0.0	November. 2, 2010
5.9.0	June 6, 2004	12.9.0	May 1, 2011
6.0.0	December 3, 2004	13.0.0	October 28, 2011
6.9.0	June 1, 2005		

As part of this process, much of the warfare and conflicts that surfaced on the Balkans in the wake of the breakup of Yugoslavia and the Soviet Union have their origins in the divisive eastern line of resonance with the disc of the galaxy. Since some nations are inside of the area created as a manifestation of galactic resonance, and others will be outside, ethnic conflicts have surfaced along this. In addition, the re-emergence of the Cross on a planetary scale has tended to reactivate conflicts between Muslims and Christians living in the affected region. Thus, conflicts between Muslims and Christians in Bosnia and in Kosovo-Albania resurfaced.

The emerging unified Europe is not only an economic and political project, however. It is likely to have religious aspects also, where the Vatican may seek to play a leading role. And we shall note that the upcoming cycle carries a more spiritual consciousness than our present, something that will reactivate old religious expressions in a new galactic context. As part of this process a new unity is likely to be established among the Christian churches, with the Vatican playing the leading role.

The path to such a reunification of the churches has already been prepared in a joint declaration between the Vatican and some Lutheran churches signed in Augsburg in October 1999, which in principle heals the rift that was created some five hundred years ago. The emerging new expression of the Christian religiosity is likely also to make overtures to New Agers, as can already be seen in discussions on UFOs by leading members of the Vatican.

Similarly to how at the beginning of the National Cycle an entirely new civilization, influencing all aspects of life—economic, political, religious, etc.—emerged in Egypt as a result of the Heavenly duality introduced at the time, human life is also now about to undergo a tremendous change among an essentially unsuspecting public. The essentially false materialist world view touted by media, schools, churches and universities means that many people will be taken by surprise, and a situation may emerge that powerful economic and religious forces could profit from.

The birth of the unified Europe may be what the Book of Revelation refers to as the woman with twelve stars in her hair who went out into the desert to give birth to a child. (Significantly, despite the fact that there are now fifteen member nations of the European Union, it has chosen to retain only twelve stars in its flag.) It also says there that the Beast makes itself ready to swallow her child as it is born, possibly a reference to a good cause that is threatened by materialist forces seeking to dominate this new union. These forces may seek to create a new 'Empire' of the Galactic Cycle, generated through a synthesis of the materialist civilization inherited from the Planetary Underworld, NATO and the EU and a galactified Christian religiosity. Ultimately this could develop into a world empire increasingly centered in Europe, but whose power is linked intimately to that of the US. It would be an empire without an emperor, based on a tremendous economic power, which develops according to the interests linked to this. It would hold awesome means for electronically controlling its citizens.

What there is to know, then, is that if such a rule of the Beast materializes, it will not last. The entirely new synthesis of worldly and spiritual power of pharaonic Egypt that had been unified by Menes did not last. It only lasted until about the midpoint of the Great Cycle (Figure 57), when the rule of the last native pharaohs came to an end. What this seems to imply is that even if the creation of the Galactic Underworld will begin with the rule of a new civilization, a new synthesis of spiritual and worldly power in the galactic context, this original synthesis will not last. Also in this new civilization people will, as a result of the effects of the True Cross, increasingly become able to distinguish between worldly and spiritual power. Thus, the rule of the Beast will disintegrate with a rhythm that parallels that of pharaonic rule in Egypt during the Great Cycle, with the significant difference that now the rise and fall of the original synthesis will be measured in tuns, rather than in baktuns.

Why then will the world ultimately be developing in the direction of deepened democracy and peace? Most profoundly because in the widened galactic context people will in a much deeper sense recognize themselves as equals. Since the days of the pharaohs there has been a trend in human development toward a deepening realization that we are all equals. In the now beginning cycle, with the emerging information technology providing potential means for an expanded grass-ro control, demands will be raised for a deepening of democracy, even to the point of the replacement of the current representative rule with a direct democracy, utilizing computers for this purpose.

In parallel with this deepened democracy and end to representative rule we will see an end to right-left political polarity. The conflict between right and left, which had its origin early in the Planetary Cycle in the French Revolution, has already lost much of its meaning. In several European countries the Social Democrats (the so-called left) simply took over the political programs of the Conservative parties (the so-called right) and now rule on such a platform. To some extent the opposite exchange has also taken place. Especially because the number of people employed in industry is decreasing, the old contradiction between workers and employers is currently losing much of its original meaning. And this by itself is a part of the rationale for a deepened democracy.

Industry will also be very profoundly transformed by the emerging galactic consciousness and its expression through IT. The leading role of industry in the development of human society will disappear. There is little or no reason to expect new fundamental household inventions such as the car, refrigerator, etc., which were all results of the materialist consciousness of the Planetary Cycle. Instead, the existing inventions and production/consumption will be transformed by the current IT, which will be the driving sector of society. From an environmentalist point of view there is actually a lot of hope inherent in the fact that industry will lose its driving role. There is currently a strong trend in industry toward developing more energy-efficient and environmentally adapted products, and much of the development in the manufacturing sector of society is taking place with this purpose. As new fundamental inventions of appliances, etc., are not to be expected, environmental concerns will become increasingly important factors in the competition.

Because we are already in the seventh DAY of the Planetary Cycle, and economic depressions seems to occur around the beginnings of NIGHTS—1932 (the Great Depression) and 1972 (the oil crisis)—there is little reason to expect a worldwide industrial crisis in the future. What may be expected is an economic roller coaster following a tun-based rhythm with regard to the IT-linked economy. In times when DAYS are approaching, or during DAYS, stock markets, etc., will be optimistic, while during NIGHTS, or when NIGHTS are approaching, there will be downfalls. The tun beginning November 18, 2007, ruled by the god of darkness and corresponding to the Great Depression in the Planetary Cycle, will, however, most likely bring a more serious crash in the IT economy.

New fundamental ways of thinking regarding value and economics will also emerge. There is now a school of thought in economics advocating the notion of 'de-materialization,' placing the value on the service rather than on the material product, and all such new ways of thinking carried by the new cycle will aid in the preservation of the planet's resources without necessarily creating the kind of tensions around the issues that may previously have been the case. Hence, the age-old Christian and Marxist visions of a classless communitarian society without private property may enter the world through the back door, so to speak. Without conflicts or clashes people will simply shift what they place value on. De-materialization may become a key word also for the technological development in the future, and I will return to this in the next chapter.

So there is a lot of hope for human survival in the very fact that the economy will become based on new values (this is already evident within the IT world, which sometimes operates according to a very different logic than the industrial world), and that the resources of the world may be safeguarded by a much more energy-efficient industrial sector. Nonetheless, as mentioned earlier, it is not necessarily true that everyone will approve of this shift in values and the trend toward existential equality and deepened democracy. A new type of hate crime seems to have surfaced both in Europe and the US in 1999, as well as political parties of a very dubious character, to say the least, in France and Austria, for instance, that have rallied large followings of industrial workers. This is part of the reaction against the largely positive transformation of society that is a result of the Galactic Creation Cycle and its influence on human consciousness. Given that the Galactic Cycle is a dualistic cycle we may expect that certain types of conflicts may be exacerbated, especially during its DAYS.

Clearly, the unification of Europe is going to be paralleled by similar integrative tendencies in other parts of the world, especially in the Western Hemisphere, where all the nations of Latin America are soon to form parts of an expanded NAFTA, thus creating a common Western Hemispheric market. The unification of Europe is thus really nothing but the most visible aspect of a restructuring of the world for a galactic context. That the planet is becoming one single market where movements of capital are unhindered will be even more evident than previously. What the repercussions of the adaptation to the galactic resonance will be in Russia—currently experiencing social difficulties—is more difficult to tell. The greatest change generated by the Galactic Cycle is likely to take place in the Eastern Hemisphere, since this is where the divine LIGHT of the cycle will preferentially fall. It is to be expected that the new LIGHT, as well as its concomitant political structures, with each new DAY of the Galactic Cycle will expand its effects eastwards from the center of the duality in Europe, thus most immediately altering life in that hemisphere. Initially, as people seek to adapt to and give room for the new LIGHT, we may also expect the most unrest in the Eastern Hemisphere. The conflicts in the Balkans in recent years (along the resonance line of the galactic disc) may be seen as the first signs of an upcoming transformation of the Eastern Hemisphere. To the extent that people are unaware of the ultimate causes of this change they may come to engage in bitter struggles.

The new LIGHT falling on the Eastern Hemisphere already has had visible effects. The extent of the Chinese Falun Gong movement and the crackdown by its government on this is one example pointing to a spirituality carried by the Galactic Cycle on a larger scale. And generally, the halt to the rapid economic expansion in east Asia and a set of conflicts, often with religious undertones, are signs, not necessarily optimistic, that people there are coming out of the materialism generated by the Planetary Cycle and are shifting their focus elsewhere. Russia is the big unknown in this picture. While on the one hand its people have suffered serious economic difficulties and the disintegration of social structures following the collapse of the Soviet Union, this collapse of social structures may also be cause for optimism since it could allow for a relatively direct transition into a society based on spiritual principles.

In the DAYS of the Galactic Cycle we may expect to see conflicts along the resonance lines of the galactic disc, expressed notably in Ireland and the Balkans, but also further south in Africa. Pulse by pulse the forces transcending national borders will, however, strengthen their hands, and since what ultimately drives the process forward is the resonance with the Galactic Cross, there will be no possibilities of turning back to national rule or a national frame of life. This is already visible in the reactions of NATO and the EU toward Yugoslavia and Jörg Haider's Austria. Whatever one might feel about the latter regimes, the fact is that in diplomatic relations the sovereignty principle no longer applies and it is not likely to come back.

A trend that will be more prominent than any other is that toward a greater scale of everything generated by the wider frame of human consciousness. This obviously is true for all aspects of business organization, where currently several multinational companies are greater economic entities than many nations. But such an increasing scale of things, and transcendence of borders, is likely to be seen in all kinds of activities.

It may be added that the United Nations is likely to play a decreased role in the new cycle although this drives the nations of the world in the direction of a new larger context. The reason is partly that this organization is built on the union of nations, and the roles of the nation-states will constantly decrease in importance as the Galactic Cycle progresses. Thus, the most important players in the new empire will initially be multinational corporations, military pacts and economic communities.

Some form of a Galactic Empire (which is not like in a *Star Wars* movie, but on this planet) will dominate life on earth at least until DAY 4 (approximately the year 2005) of the Galactic Cycle, when, because of the increasingly strong effects of the returning Cross, its power will start to recede and gradually disintegrate. However, we may not now be able to see this rule as illegitimate as little as the Egyptians of baktun 0 saw their pharaohs as usurpers of divine power. Much of what is now called democracy will in the new emerging LIGHT with a deepened democracy come to appear as dictatorship with a tightly regulated framework for the human existence. However, this rule, which we are probably subordinated to right now, will also have a purpose in that it will provide an institutional framework for the expansion of human life and consciousness into the galactic context. As we have seen before in the creation of different Underworlds, however, the seeds set at the first DAY include both negative and positive aspects, and one effect of the returning Cross will be to separate the two, create distinctions and pave the way for a cosmic Christ consciousness. The breakthrough of this new consciousness of LIGHT will most dramatically be seen at the beginning of DAY 5 of the cycle, corresponding approximately to the year 2007 (Figure 79), but it will have to be prepared for much earlier than that.

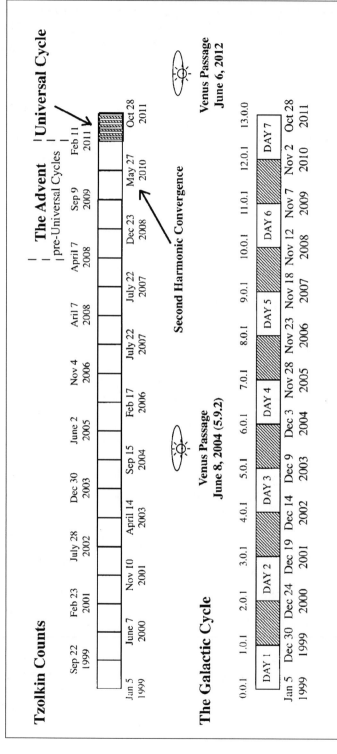

Fig. 79 The Galactic Cycle divided into eighteen tzolkin rounds ending with four pre-Universal Cycles and the Universal Cycle or into thirteen tun with Seven DAYS and Six NIGHTS. Shown are also the upcoming Venus passages.

The fact that some of the new energies, the new LIGHT and the new Christ consciousness will seem to emanate from the new European super-state, or even the Papacy in Rome, centered under the 12th longitude East, does not mean that these institutions are the carriers of the True Cross. Many powerful institutions may in fact seek to keep the existence of the True Cross secret so as to be able to usurp its power. To what extent the new planetary civilization centered around the European super-state will be positive or negative will thus depend on how the struggle between opposing forces plays out, which in turn depends on the level of meta-consciousness that has been attained by humanity. In the absence of meta-consciousness all kinds of narrow and particular human interests will, in their own ways, seek to profit from the emergence of the new civilization in a galactic context. Also, they may seek to present the emerging Christ consciousness as a doctrinal monopoly, or even as their own creation.

So how will the struggle between opposing forces end? The answer given by the *Book of Revelation* is that the Beast will be cast down from the Heaven and Satan destroyed by God. The true Christians (which is not to be understood in a narrow sense of the word, but as anyone with an open heart seeking to serve God) will be placed on thrones as measures for the others to be judged by. Eventually those passing Judgment Day will enter the Kingdom of Heaven, an eternal life upon which the LIGHT of God will shine forever.

An important thing to realize is that the Beast cannot win. It may initially come to be very powerful, as the new galactic civilization starts to develop from the foundation of the materialist culture of the Planetary Underworld. Yet, as the Galactic Cycle progresses, the True Cross will DAY by DAY become increasingly dominating. It is because this evolution of consciousness is in God's hands only that it becomes logical that Satan and the Beast eventually will be destroyed, unable to survive the new LIGHT.

A PROPHETIC PROGRESSION
THROUGH THE GALACTIC UNDERWORLD

Following the establishment of the new galactic civilization on DAY 1, the first NIGHT of the Galactic Cycle began on December 31, 1999 (1.0.1), the millennium shift of the Gregorian calendar. At this time, a discussion began as to the nature of calendars and the merits of the various alternatives. Such a discussion seems natural at a millennium shift, and, one might like to add, particularly this one. The great changes that took place during the first DAY of the Galactic Cycle made many people wonder what is actually going on on the planet. Yet, at the time of the millennium shift most people, in their absolute majority lacking meta-consciousness, still referred to the changes as the results of a 'millennium hype.' Materialism, in fact, may well be strengthened because of the prevailing lack of understanding of the true nature of the Mayan calendar as a calendar of the invisible universe.

As with all NIGHTS, the one that began on December 31, 1999 will serve to integrate the advances of the previous DAY and create the conditions for the one coming. Hence, the opportunities will be great for rethinking our lives and outlining the creation of a society based on compassion.

The second DAY of the Galactic Cycle will then begin on a very noteworthy day, December 25, 2000 (2.0.1), what the millennium change is meant to be all about, the birthday of Christ. The Vatican, for one, anticipated that throughout the year 2000 some thirty million people will visit Rome to celebrate the bimillennium of the birth of Jesus, since it now considers Rome rather than Bethlehem to be the center of Christianity. And generally, we can be certain that the attention of all human beings on the day 2.0.1, regardless of our whereabouts, will be on the fact that it will then be two thousand years since Jesus of Nazareth was born. Several groups of Christians in the United States also expected Jesus to return to earth in the year 2000.

From the perspective developed here it is interesting that the actual day of celebration of the bimillennium of the birth of Christ coincides with the beginning of the second DAY, that is, with a new pulse of divine LIGHT of the galactic creation cycle. We may be certain that many people, perhaps especially traditional Christians, at the beginning of the second DAY of the Galactic Cycle will be inspired to believe that the return of the Messiah is imminent. Jews and Muslims, also, whose religions similarly prophesy an Apocalypse, are likely to be strongly affected by this new LIGHT. Since a new pulse of spiritual phenomena will accompany the beginning of this DAY, events of a miraculous nature are not unlikely. Thus, through the course of this DAY an enthusiastic understanding that we are living the Apocalypse will dramatically increase until, at the beginning of NIGHT 2 (December 20, 2001; 3.0.1) a reaction will set in.

During this second NIGHT many will be exhausted by the great changes that have occurred and long for a return to the safe and comfortable life of the Planetary Underworld. This feeling will be especially widespread if already during the first two DAYS of the Galactic Cycle contacts with planetary civilizations other than our own have taken place. Some steps in this direction were taken already during the first DAY of the Galactic Cycle, as scientists early in 1999 were able to identify for the first time not only an earth-like planet around one foreign sun, but also a planetary system around another. In the new frame of consciousness we are thus beginning to see new things in the galactic context. It is likely, therefore, that the truth about extraterrestrial civilizations will come to be revealed during this cycle, since our frames of consciousness then will be expanded to eventually include the entire galaxy. Especially during its DAYS means of communications, using fields that we probably are only partially aware of today, will be developed. Considering that DAY 2 corresponded only to the optical telegraph in the Planetary Cycle, however, we should not expect communications with other planetary civilizations in the galaxy to have reached an advanced stage in the years 2001-2002. But possibly, proofs that other civilizations are out there will then be generated.

In this process of contacting civilizations of other planets it seems likely that the current discussions about the UFO phenomenon will be dissolved resolved. A major part of the explanation of the UFO phenomenon may be that the LIGHT phenomena observed are not vehicles at all, but holographic resonance projections

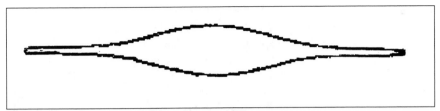

Fig. 80 Holographic projection of the galaxy as a UFO.

of the galaxy (see Figure 80). What above all speaks in favor of such an interpretation is the timing of appearance of UFOs, where the first real wave was reported in the year 1947 (the last 65 tuns of the Planetary Cycle began on October 4, 1947; see Appendix I). If this explanation to the UFO phenomenon is correct, UFOs would really be emanations from the World Tree, or rather the midplane of its trunk. At the risk of being speculative, the UFO pulses of LIGHT may be sorts of 'soul ships' reaching earth (and the rest of the galaxy), where each ship (in fact then a pulse of galactic LIGHT) harbors information from the World Tree and 'transports' the new individual souls that are to incarnate on earth on a given day. Currently popular ideas of extraterrestrials living among us are consistent with this view. The origin of the human being in the World Tree can also be seen from a new angle through this.

After the nostalgic reaction of NIGHT 2, the consciousness of the Galactic Underworld will, as DAY 3 begins, definitely be anchored on this planet. At this point it will be impossible to deny that a divine plan is operating, or that it follows a tun-based rhythm. No longer will it be possible to defer the vast changes taking place to psychological effects of the millennium shift or something else, and a noticeable number of people will start to use the Mayan calendar as a complement to the Gregorian. The pioneers will start to prepare for receiving the imprint of the True Cross and for the advent of Quetzalcoatl during the Venus passage, which is to occur at the midpoint of NIGHT 3.

Following this, as we reach the top of the seven-storied pyramid in the year 2005, the most significant truth of this Underworld will be formulated. At the next step, at the beginning of DAY 5 in the year 2007 of the Galactic Cycle, the Christ consciousness, the consciousness of the Cross, will definitely break through and be dissipated on a larger scale. This, then, is what may truly be referred to as the return of Christ, although the LIGHT of Christ, or the Cross, will now return within a Galactic, rather than a National, context (as was previously the case). Thus, if we chose to regard the appearance of Jesus on this planet shortly before baktun 8, and the fact that his teaching came to attract such a large number of followers during that baktun, as a result of a particular pulse of LIGHT and a particular Heaven of the Great Cycle, rather than as something primarily caused by an individual, then it is only logical to expect a return, a second coming, of Christ. It is then also logical to expect that this return will be the result of a special pulse of LIGHT and a special Heaven, specifically that of the fifth DAY of the Galactic Cycle. Of course, the individual of Jesus must have been very important, very courageous and loving, to be able to generate the following he did, but the point to realize is that his mission could not have been carried out without the LIGHT of the fifth DAY at his back.

As I will discuss in the final chapter, during the Galactic Cycle as well, the Cross and the new LIGHT will incarnate in the lives and actions of many individuals, where some may turn out to have more prominent roles than others. Doubtless, in the time to come, many individuals will present themselves as the returning Christ and surely also the LIGHT of the fifth DAY will be manifested through human individuals. Whether any of the carriers of the emerging Christ consciousness will be actual returning incarnations of Jesus remains to be seen. This is, however, somewhat beside the point as long as the new Christ consciousness manifests in courageous and loving individuals, promoted by divine LIGHT.

Following the breakthrough of Christ consciousness during DAY 5, a very severe reaction and much destruction may be anticipated during NIGHT 5—approximately the year 2008, ruled by the Lord of Darkness. NIGHT 5 will probably be a most difficult time, when many aspects of life pertaining to the Planetary reality will be destroyed in a reaction to the energies of the Galactic Underworld. If there will be such a thing as the battle of Armageddon this will be it, essentially taking place during the Gregorian year 2008. After the destruction occurring during this NIGHT room will be given to the renaissance of galactic life during DAY 6 and finally to the attainment of its highest level of expression during DAY 7. During the seventh DAY of the Galactic Cycle the highest truth will be revealed and the galactic frame of consciousness established in its unlimited form.

In making such a prophetic progression through the Galactic Cycle we must, however, also consider something else. Since the frame of consciousness generated by this cycle is so much higher than the previous, the role of an active choice becomes considerably more important than in the lower dimensions of consciousness where free choice, on the part of the human individuals, has played a relatively minor role. The predetermining role of the divine process of Creation has in lower Underworlds been proportionately more important. Maybe then in fact the evolution of Christ consciousness is not something that will automatically manifest just because it is part of the divine plan. Maybe the evolution of the new frame of consciousness is something that will happen only to the extent that we choose to make it happen.

This is not to subscribe to the New Age notion that we may create anything we like (we still have no control over the frames of consciousness that we are provided with by the divine process of Creation), but it implies that the role of choice as to how to relate to these frames will increase. Thus, roads will still be created for us, but we will now need to make active choices to walk them. Unlike what was the case in the lower Underworlds, when humans were mere puppets, we can maybe no longer simply expect God to do the work for us. Maybe for Christ consciousness to manifest during the Galactic Cycle it is required that we actively chose to have this happen and practice love and compassion emanating from our hearts. The more that are actively seeking to open their hearts the better are the prospects for the future of everyone. *If indeed God has chosen to create a being in His/Her image then ultimately to act and be in the image of God will mean to exert the same level of free choice as He/She does.* The truer this is, the more difficult it will be to exactly predict the manifestations of the divine plan.

To summarize: there is much to learn about the future by making parallels with other major creation cycles. Two things stand out: our frame of consciousness will be recognized as primary to matter. Yet the Mayan calendar has more to say about when things will happen than exactly what will happen. When things will happen is determined by a cyclic pattern brought about by the yin/yang dualities favoring human creativity during the DAYS and integration during the NIGHTS. External change during the DAYS will alternate with internal change during the NIGHTS. Because of the increasing role of human choice the exact manifestations of choice will be increasingly less predictable.

CHAPTER 12
THE RETURN OF THE GODDESS
AND REVELATION

THE MANY NAMES OF THE GALACTIC CYCLE

Even if the role of free choice is now making predictions more difficult, there are some pitfalls that may be avoided when it comes to relating to the future. Thus, there are some who think that the end of the Mayan calendar will mean the end of the world, but there are also those at the other extreme who say that nothing is predetermined. In the latter view human beings would be free to create the future in whatever way they like, and only the thoughts of human beings would determine the future. Such an attitude also lacks realism and may lead to the same absence of a sense of responsibility as in those who say the world is predestined to end in a catastrophe. Hence, if it were true that there was no plan, no purpose, no God, then this would mean that there would be nothing wrong with exploiting the resources of this earth to the fullest, and nobody would be able to say that this is wrong. Only if there exists a higher purpose for Creation designed by a higher intelligence does any deeper meaning of ethics, of right and wrong, exist. Only if God exists are we responsible to fulfill the purpose designed by Him/Her. It has been the main purpose of this book to demonstrate that such a higher purpose of Creation, and hence also of the individual human life, indeed exists.

The existence of a plan for the evolution of consciousness does not, however, mean that we human beings would not be co-creators of the world. It is not as if everything has been planned in detail; it is more like if God, through the divine plan, has provided us with a canvas and colors to accomplish our own tasks in creation. Although we ourselves may still determine what will be painted, what kind of world we want to create, He/She is providing the frames for it. God provides a plan for the evolution of consciousness, but how this is manifested in the physical reality to a large extent depends on us.

To an increasing degree we are faced with becoming responsible co-creators with God. The more of a meta-consciousness we develop, the more we will be able to see Creation from the perspective of God, and the better equipped we will be to substitute for Him/Her as co-creators. Yet at this point we are only barely beginning to understand how Creation works, and the overwhelming majority of humanity does not believe that an exact time plan exists. Thus, it is only now that we may begin to realize our role in the larger scheme of things. There is now evidence of the existence of a Creator God. What else could have provided a design plan of seven DAYS and six NIGHTS like the one that has been outlined here? The question is no longer whether we believe in God, but rather what we are to do with the existence He/She has given to us. Although these insights have not been widely assimilated they will gradually be spread in the phase of the divine process of Creation that we are now about to enter.

I have here referred to this new phase of Creation as the Galactic Cycle, but it has many other names as well. One is the Photon Belt, an idea that has been promoted in American New Age circles. What has been said here lends support to the idea of a photon belt. This phenomenon, however, would be unrelated to photons (the physical, particle aspect of LIGHT) or with a belt involving only certain star systems. This would simply be another word for the creation of the Galactic Underworld which will be effected by divine LIGHT and affect the entire galaxy with all of its inhabitants synchronistically. The photon belt will then in fact have seven pulses of LIGHT adhering to the tun shifts of the Mayan calendar (Figure 79).

The most well-known name for the Galactic Cycle, however, is the Apocalypse (or Revelation), used in Christian theology when referring to the scenario playing out at the end of time. Several of the most important ingredients in Mayan calendrics are in fact noticeable in the *Book of Revelation*, the last, and probably most important, book of the Bible. There we have, for instance, a reference to the number 144,000, whose background we have now identified in the number of days in a baktun. At the time the *Book of Revelation* was written, about AD 90, 144,000 was in fact the number of days in the period that most affected people, a DAY. Although several other explanations for the number 144,000 have been suggested, this one has the merit of being empirically verifiable.

Prophets and seers, such as John the Divine, who wrote the *Book of Revelation*, seem in visionary states often to access information about the divine plan, including numbers, that almost seem to have been taken from the Mayan calendar. But this is not really very surprising given that holy numbers such as 4, 7, 9 and 13 play a paramount role in the evolution of the divine plan, which is the very basis of prophecy, the ability of human beings to foresee the future. Nonetheless, the information from prophets is often scrambled and, unless there is some empirical verification, should probably be approached carefully. Prophets also often color their prophecies with their own individual points of view. The *Book of Revelation*, for instance, may well have been written in response to the persecutions that the Christians at the time were the victims of. Thus, it may have been written partly with the purpose of providing consolation for the Christians and creating respect for them from their opponents. Despite this coloring it seems clear that its author had attained a state of awareness where some authentic knowledge of the divine plan was available.

In addition to the number 144,000 there is also a cryptic reference in this book (12:6 and 12:14) to the tun, the 360-day period, as a 'time.' And, we may add, it is only in our own time, only as the Galactic Cycle and Revelation actually begins, that the tun is becoming the predominating 'time' of creation. Third and most importantly, the *Book of Revelation* in all possible contexts mentions the number 7. Typically it describes progressions through seven phases: 'in the days of the voice of the seventh angel, when he shall begin to sound, the mystery of God shall be revealed,' 'Seven spirits of God sent forth into the earth,' 'the seventh seal,' etc. The conclusion is thus almost inescapable that these phases refer to the progressions through the seven DAYS of the different Underworlds. Maybe, in fact, the central message of the *Book of Revelation* is the number 7. Through this number the alpha and the omega (*Revelation* 1:8 and 22:13)—the *Book of Genesis* and the *Book of Revelation*—the first and the last book of the Bible, are unified since they both describe the rhythm of the seven DAYS and six NIGHTS of God's Creation. In the end scenario described in the *Book of Revelation* these sequences all reach their seventh DAYS and today, as the creations of all the Nine Underworlds are drawing to their completion, this is what we see happening.

THE PLANETARY ROUND OF LIGHT
AND THE RETURN OF THE GODDESS

We shall now from the perspective provided by the Planetary Round of LIGHT briefly compare the National, Planetary and Galactic Cycles and describe the insights this might give us as to the nature of human consciousness in the corresponding Underworlds. The National Cycle, as we mentioned, was characterized by a concentration of divine LIGHT on the Western Hemisphere (Figures 15 and 29), a fact that had a number of significant consequences. First, it meant that the human beings in resonance with this particular global distribution of LIGHT see divine LIGHT through at least one of their eyes. Because of this fallout of divine LIGHT human beings throughout this cycle have, at least in the Western Hemisphere, fairly consistently believed in the existence of God. Another highly noteworthy thing is that the LIGHT/DARKNESS polarity of the Western and Eastern Hemispheres during this cycle allowed people to 'see' and, at least subconsciously, be aware of the presence of the Cross. The specific effects of this were discussed in Chapter 5.

A second aspect of the LIGHT shining on the 'male' Western Hemisphere throughout the National Cycle is that women were consistently diverted from public life and relegated to the role of side figures in that arena. The only exceptions were the few, such as for instance the queens Elizabeth of England and Kristina of Sweden, who happened to have kings as their fathers.

Also some of the manifestations of the Planetary Cycle may be understandable if we consider how the LIGHT was distributed during this. First of all, as mentioned, this cycle was the one when atheism first emerged, and as the cycle has progressed, materialism has gradually come to dominate the planet both philosophically and as a life-style. This we can understand if we consider that this cycle creates a resonance with a planetary creation field where no LIGHT falls on the Pacific side, the 'eyes.' Hence, in this Underworld human beings are blindfolded and do not clearly see the divine LIGHT and the existence of God, and concern for the earth and creation in all of its aspects has decreased. Atheism and materialism have spread to become dominant, at least among the official, publicly voiced ideologies.

Moreover, the consciousness of the Planetary Cycle is a non-dualistic consciousness without a left/right distinction between LIGHT and DARKNESS. This has led many now to believe that there is no such thing as truth in an absolute, objective sense. In this Underworld literary and movie heroes have often been presented in a gray zone between right and wrong. Thus, the absence of a divine guiding LIGHT, and the absence of a Cross creating distinctions during this cycle, has led people to think that there is no right or wrong, no true or false, no good or evil.

An aspect of the consciousness reigning during this cycle is that it has led to a much increased role for women in public life, thus beginning a process of generating balance between the genders compared to the imbalance of the National Underworld. The beginning of the creation of this Underworld saw the first instances, in the Boston Tea Party of the American Revolution and the Women's March on Versailles in the French, of women making their interests known as women. Throughout the Planetary Cycle the role of women in public life has then gradually increased in importance until today it has only a vague semblance to what it was like during the patriarchal National Cycle. This is because the LIGHT no longer falls exclusively on the Western Hemisphere as it did during the National Cycle. Instead, it is evenly distributed between the Western and Eastern Hemispheres, which represents a step in the direction of balance between yin and yang and hence between the genders.

Another aspect of the non-dualism of the Planetary Cycle is that it has led to a surge of interest in peoples of the Fourth World, such as Native Americans and other aboriginal peoples of the earth. These have been, at least until recently, relatively untouched by the patriarchal dualistic consciousness of the National Cycle and express today's version of the consciousness of the Regional Cycle. Since the consciousness of the Regional Cycle is unitary it has found ways of expressing itself through the similarly unitary frame of consciousness of the Planetary Cycle, especially after the beginning of its seventh DAY.

If we assume that the distribution of LIGHT also rotates 90° as the Galactic Cycle begins (Figure 29), we can base a few predictions on this. The first is that one of the effects of the Galactic Cycle will be to, pulse by pulse, DAY by DAY, contribute to an increased balance between the genders. This is because the divine LIGHT will fall on the Eastern Hemisphere, thus favoring holistic perspectives and qualities that women resonate with more strongly. It is, however, only as we reach the seventh DAY of the Galactic Cycle that the seven DAYS of the National Underworld, which have favored the Western Hemisphere, will be completely counterbalanced. Thus, there is a real foundation to the idea of a return of the Goddess. As a result of this change in consciousness, holistic, female perspectives will become increasingly dominant toward the later DAYS of the cycle. Holistic perspectives will also be favored by the very fact that reality will be seen from a higher, galactic perspective.

The second prediction we may make is that the Galactic Underworld will be a cycle when a belief in God, and maybe even more so in a higher spiritual ethics, will return. In the time to come, a new spirituality and a new belief in God and His/Her goodness will find much more evident manifestations. This is because our individual minds will again be in resonance with one of the Pacific eyes (this time on the eastern side) upon which the divine LIGHT will fall. This LIGHT/DARKNESS polarity means that people—at least those who have not become permanently blindfolded by the materialist consciousness of the Planetary Cycle—will during the later DAYS of the cycle be able to see the Cross creating the duality. Pulse by pulse the Cross will play an increasing role in dominating human consciousness. This process is what results in the Return of the True Cross. The poles of the Cross, however, will shift signs so that the LIGHT will fall on the Eastern Hemisphere. This is then the much heralded pole shift, which is really a polarity shift in consciousness and has nothing to do with the earth's axis or any other geophysical phenomenon. Already during the preceding era we have seen the initial signs of this shift in polarity, whose most immediately evident effect will be the end to the dominance of the Eastern Hemisphere by the Western. Since the upcoming cycle is dualistic, we may also expect a new quest for the objective Truth in a higher sense of the word than is currently the case. Through our enhanced resonance with the yin/yang duality maintained by the Cross we will increasingly be able to distinguish between good and evil, and to see the world through the eyes of God. We will eat more from the fruit of the Tree of Life.

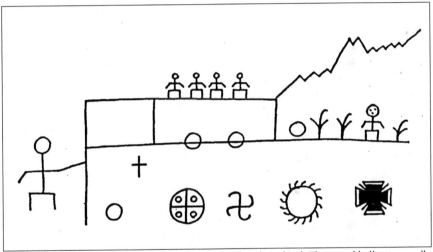

Fig. 81 The Hopi Prophecy with the two possible paths of mankind. The round balls supposedly refer to the occasions when God has shaken the world. A possible interpretation of this is that if humanity chooses the right path, the Eight-Partition star will appear and a more feminine era inaugurated.

It is also likely that during the Galactic Cycle our inner visions will be able to see the True Cross. Moreover, in the celestial location of the Eight-Partition-Place, we may literally again be able to see 'LIGHTNING' and a phenomenon reminiscent of the twinkling of a star. This prediction seems to be supported by the Hopi Prophecy (see Figure 81), where it is said that a new 'star,' depicted as an Eight-Partition-Maltese Cross, will appear to herald a more feminine era of mankind. This is supposed to happen after the world has been shaken twice by God, events usually believed to refer to World Wars I and II. Given that our consciousness will be governed by a new frequency during the Galactic Cycle, it is entirely possible that we will be able to see many different kinds of LIGHT phenomena that have been invisible to us during the Planetary Cycle. What this among other things would mean is a return of the star of Bethlehem, once again becoming visible to human eyes as the galactic Christ consciousness breaks through. Whether it will be as a guiding light for our inner vision or as a twinkling place in the sky, the duat, the abode of Anu, will return.

Third, the polarity shift will have significant political consequences in that the LIGHT in the Galactic Underworld will primarily fall on the Eastern rather than on the Western Hemisphere. The initial effect of the onset of this new dualistic cycle has been an exacerbation of the conflicts between the East and the West, expressed, for instance, in the wars between Western nations and Iraq in early 1999 and Serbia later the same spring. Toward the latter half of the Galactic Cycle, however, we may expect that the Western Hemisphere will no longer be able to dominate the rest of the world. As the spiritual wind starts to blow toward the East from the vertical arm of the Cross in Europe, the new energies that it will transport will with every DAY move farther east to include not only Belarus and Ukraine, but eventually also Russia and China. Thus, during the Galactic Cycle the Cross will be perceived as extending the LIGHT toward the East, in contrast to the National Cycle, when the LIGHT was extended in the western direction. This should mean that Asia will become a continent in turmoil. Conflicts between adherents of different religions, such as Islam, Christianity and Judaism, may also come to be exacerbated in the East, partly with a focus on Jerusalem.

The most immediate effect may be that the West will lose its control of the Middle East. As the cycle progresses, however, as the True Cross becomes more dominating, and the earthly reality will be seen by humanity from a higher galactic perspective, it is likely that a new universalism will bring about an inclusive transcendence of the differences between the religions of the world. To arrive at this new truth it seems that all religions will have to give and take. Yet it can probably be said that the better our understanding of the process of creation, and the better calendar that a religion is equipped with, the better will it be prepared to face the challenges of the Galactic Underworld.

Because of its place in the Planetary Round of LIGHT the Galactic Cycle may thus be regarded as the National Cycle in reverse, or, maybe better said, a cycle whose effects will serve to balance and compensate for those of the National Cycle. The Galactic Cycle reintroduces expressions of duality, and from DAY 4 and onwards these new expressions will develop into mature forms as the True Cross is reintroduced as the dominating factor determining human consciousness. The distinctions generated by the True Cross may turn out to be between physical and spiritual, as was the case during the Great Cycle, but because of the polarity shift these distinctions, or at least our interpretations of them, will now be reversed. Many of our most cherished ideas may thus be turned upside down as yin and yang switch places and the wholeness-oriented Eastern Hemisphere step by step increases its role in our thinking.

Among these things turning our cherished notions upside down may be what can be referred to as holistic technology or 'energy' technology. As we are entering a cycle giving us a new frame of consciousness, technology of a new kind is beginning to emerge. What I am thinking about, just as an example, is a range of people who are now working with energizing and purifying water according to techniques that cannot be understood from a traditional scientific background. And, in fact, since the presently emerging Underworld is at a higher level in the cosmic hierarchy we should not expect all of its emanations, such as new technology, to be understandable with the analytical tools developed by lower levels of consciousness.

A new relationship between spirit and matter is also developing as a result of the new frame of consciousness, and because of this we may expect to see how the human mind to a previously unseen degree is able to control matter. An example of this, which seems to have a strong wind at the back as the Galactic Cycle begins, is Breatharianism, the choice for human beings to live only on Prana, LIGHT energy without food intake. Many things will now begin to be developed from a higher perspective than previously, and in this we are only in the beginning.

This trend toward an increasing recognition of the role of consciousness is most evidently seen in medicine, where a change in people's attitudes has been going on for some time now. This change is linked to the change from the planetary to the galactic frame of consciousness. The bottom line is: people no longer want to be treated as pieces of matter, but as beings where the spiritual aspects play the predominant role. From this it follows that treatments of ailments and diseases may be based not only on medications and surgery, but on spiritual healing as well.

THE ETHICS OF THE NEW DISTRIBUTION OF LIGHT

Judging from the ancient prophetic scriptures, the Bible and the Qur'an, a distinction will again come to be introduced between good and evil, right and wrong. Given that we will now see the world in a new LIGHT, provided by a new polarity in consciousness, this seems reasonable. This new LIGHT will generate new criteria for judging the actions of others and ourselves. If we have not acted as we should have, or as the divine guidance has told us, we may become unfavorably judged according to this new duality of LIGHT. What might have seemed okay in the ethical gray zone of the Planetary Cycle may no longer do so in the LIGHT/DARKNESS polarity of the Galactic Cycle. These are, however, not issues to be resolved between ourselves and the churches or other human interpreters of religions. The ethical questions are only to be resolved in a discussion between ourselves and the new LIGHT or with God.

The new polarity of LIGHT in which things will be seen, however, does not necessarily mean that our actions in the past will be condemned. It could also mean that we will be forgiven and be able to forgive ourselves. Due to the emerging insight that the process of Creation itself has propelled many human deeds, these may come to be seen in a more forgiving LIGHT. For instance, maybe a present-day reincarnation of a Mongol warrior would not be responsible for having been part of Genghis Khan's army, creating pyramids of skulls of innocent people, considering that this happened as a result of the shift in the Heavens that occurred between baktuns 10 and 11? Was this subjugation of the world in fact not meant to happen in order to create the foundation for global contacts in the future? Were his actions not propelled by a cycle shift of divine origin? Many questions like these may come to be asked, given that the actions of human beings will have to be judged against the background of the particular consciousness reigning at the time they were carried out. Could, for instance, human sacrifice performed by Vikings in pre-Christian times be judged by the same standard as if it was performed today? Only as the Galactic Cycle progresses will we know what will be the standard against which our actions will be measured. Much seems to indicate, however, that we ourselves will agree with the judgment placed on us as the Galactic Cross continues to create distinction between good and bad, true and false, right and wrong, LIGHT and DARKNESS. Since our own consciousness will be in resonance with this new higher Cross, deep inside we will all know what the truth is.

The fact that the LIGHT of the Galactic Cycle will fall on the Eastern Hemisphere should, however, also logically mean that our actions will increasingly be judged in the LIGHT of a holistic perspective. This should mean that our actions should be judged according to what extent we have sought, through our actions, to serve the larger whole. It should mean that we would not be positively judged by the amount of money we have been able to accumulate or by how successful we have been in our careers. What will matter is to what extent we have through our actions served our fellow men, the planet as a whole and ultimately God and His/Her Creation. As the divine LIGHT starts to fall on the Eastern Hemisphere, what we have done for the larger whole is likely to be what will be favorably judged. This is the logical conclusion to draw about Judgment Day from the Planetary Round of LIGHT.

Some people like to make it easy on themselves by passing judgment on others based on the morality encoded in ancient, partly divinely inspired scriptures. We should bear in mind, however, that most of the holy scriptures of mankind were filtered through the patriarchal consciousness of the National Cycle. Issues of a private nature, such as infidelity, abortion or homosexuality, have thus been the moral focus of many of today's professed Christians. These views of many traditional Christians originate in the fact that during the cycle when the Bible was written the LIGHT fell on the Western Hemisphere. This, then, is what has led organized expressions of many religions to judge morality from a patriarchal point of view, focusing on individual conduct rather than on the effects that human actions have on the larger whole. Thus, it is likely that as we enter an era of a more wholeness-oriented morality, matters of a private nature will be judged in the new LIGHT based not on simplistic right/wrong formulas, but on what consequences our actions have had for the larger whole.

Maybe self-proclaimed judges of others will then in fact be those who will be the most severely judged in the new LIGHT, and maybe what will ultimately determine how we will be judged in this is what our primary motivation has been. Was our primary purpose to serve humanity and God in the development of His/Her plan, or was it to further our own interests? Maybe, if to serve the larger whole has been our primary motivation, wrongful acts of the past will be forgiven in the new Eastern LIGHT of the Galactic Cycle.

The True Cross does not, however, only have the planetary connotation as the Cross between the equator and the 12th longitude East. As we have seen, this earthly Cross of consciousness boundaries is really nothing but a resonance phenomenon of the Galactic World Tree, which exerts its effects through holographic resonance with that of our planet. As we enter the Galactic Cycle, we will thus become considerably more aware of spiritual phenomena being galactic phenomena. Although during the creation of the National Underworld a Cross was also dominating, a difference is that our frames of consciousness now will be expanded so that we will become aware of a Cross and a Heaven existing on a galactic level. What this will mean is that not only our own actions, but also all the religions of the planet, which emerged from the much more limited perspective of the National Underworld, will be seen and judged from such a higher perspective.

This entry into the Galactic Underworld will occur simultaneously on three levels—on the level of the human individual, on the level of the planet and on that of the galaxy, and changes in the polarity of consciousness ('pole shifts') will occur on all of these levels concurrently. We have already discussed the effects of the polarity shift on the individual and planetary levels, but ultimately both of these are resonance phenomena of a Galactic Round of LIGHT. Hence, we may expect a shift in the distribution of LIGHT on a galactic level also. As the earth enters the Galactic Underworld its future course will thus also depend on what hemisphere of the galaxy it is located in. Will it be in the BRIGHT hemisphere of the galaxy or in its SHADOWY counterpart? As I already mentioned, the indications from Sumerian, Mayan and Egyptian myth are that in the National Underworld we were in the DARK hemisphere of the galaxy. This would mean that in the Galactic Underworld the earth will be in its BRIGHT hemisphere, now coinciding with the wholeness-oriented galactic hemisphere.

Maybe from a galactic perspective the earth itself can also be said to be judged, albeit not in the same sense as the human individuals will be. Although the earth is alive in the sense of being the stage of a pulsating creation field on a distinct hierarchical level, it is not a living organism that has a free will and makes choices. It is thus innocent. Yet the entire eco-geological system will be judged as to its ability to sustain human and other life in the Galactic Underworld that we are now entering. To a large extent this future sustainability of the planet will be a result of the accumulated actions of all human beings up until now. It is thus timely to ask to what extent the climate of the planet will hold up despite the level of consumption of fossil fuels, deforestation, etc. Has the greed, at least of some, pulled the rug out from under us? Are we using the resources of the earth for pointless things that they were not meant for according to the divine plan? Have we become too many for this planet to support? It is not at all impossible that the ecosystem of this planet will experience serious strains as it enters the Galactic Underworld. Also the earth will need to undergo change to adapt to the larger galactic context, and the question is how well prepared it is for this. In astronomical, geological and biological respects there may be physical repercussions of the polarity shift in consciousness, repercussions that may undermine the coherence of the ecosystem of the earth. This will be especially true if, through our own way of stewarding the earth, and by continuing to run the engines at too high a speed, the whole earth has become more sensitive to climatological disturbances. Although they need not be reiterated here, many kinds of catastrophes may thus come to occur. When it comes to preparing ourselves for the future we thus have all the reasons in the world to consider also how our mother ship is faring, and seek to slow down the engines by lowering population and economic growth.

THE UNIVERSAL CYCLE

Then I saw a great white throne
and Him who was seated on it...
Revelation 20:11

The short Universal Cycle of 2011, probably totaling only $13 \times 18 = 234$ days, but possibly 260 days, is likely to be easier than the Galactic roller coaster, mostly because it is a cycle generating a unitary consciousness. At the end—or rather at the top—of this Underworld we may expect ascension to Heaven, or, more precisely, the descent of Heaven to earth. This will mean the final transcendence of the dualities generated by the Galactic Underworld, the return to the Source, and the meeting with God beyond even the dualities generated by the True Cross, which also has a Creator, the One God beyond all dualities. Because of the very limited frames of consciousness that we have had until now, it seems that it is our notions and visions of God that have suffered the most. Only as we draw to the close of the Universal Cycle will we gain a true picture of Creation and perhaps from this understand more of who God really is. Our current views will then likely be seen as a fathoming in the dark (although they may be improving; see, e.g., Donald Walsh, *Conversations with God*).

A thought that now seems to be emerging is that the evolution of the universe is all about God manifesting himself as human beings, meaning that collectively speaking we are God. There is probably a lot of truth to such suggestions, but we should recall that the universe evolved according to a divine plan long before there were any human beings around. Thus, while indeed the purpose of Creation may be for God to manifest himself as a human being, the Universal Human Being, it nonetheless remains true that there exists an intelligence above all manifestations of the divine plan, an architect of the divine plan in the beyond, God. God is more than the universe in all of its aspects. He/She is a spirit distinct from us, and as the Universal Cycle comes to a close, although we are increasingly, with each new Underworld, created in His/Her image, we will approach the greatest meeting of our lives.

And soon, as we will be endowed not only with a Galactic but also with a non-dualistic Universal frame of consciousness, these will make it possible for us to see the events of the past from a higher perspective than previously. Surely the perspective from the Universal Underworld, and the meta-consciousness creating an awareness of how events in the past have been conditioned by the divine process of Creation itself, will allow for true forgiveness. This then, maybe is what the *Book of Revelation* refers to in its verse 21:4: 'And God shall wipe away all tears from their eyes; and there shall be no more death, neither sorrow, nor crying, neither shall there be any more pain; for the former things are passed away.' From the perspective of the Universal Underworld the former things will have passed away. They will no longer be real.

All of Creation will thus be completed in the year 2011 with the particular LIGHT distribution of the Universal Cycle. This is when the divine LIGHT, for the first time since the paradise of the Regional Cycle, will fall on both eyes. Then, as we will see the whole Truth clearly, human beings will ascend. This ascension may be seen as the end of a spiral movement of the soul, where the climb of the Pyramid of the Underworlds combines with the circular movement of the Planetary Round of LIGHT to produce a spiral-formed movement toward higher consciousness. We will then come to live in the Tent of God, the Kingdom of Heaven, having reached enlightenment, a time-less cosmic consciousness, after completing the 108 movements of Shiva and climbing the Nine Underworlds.

In the near future to come—the upcoming 13 tuns—human beings will be endowed with not only one, but in fact two, new frames of consciousness, the Galactic and the Universal. To speculate about what life will be like in the Universal Underworld and beyond seems almost pointless. All that can be said in this regard is in very, very general terms, and judging from several ancient scriptures the end of Creation will mean the end of death, and hence the entry into an eternal life. Thus, the reason the Mayan calendar comes to an end may simply be that from that point and onwards there will no longer be a need for calendars. There is no need to keep track of time in an eternal reality. Another, and possibly better, way of seeking to come to terms with the end of time is to regard it as the attainment of a time-less cosmic consciousness, and an experience of unity with All-That-Is in its fullest sense, a disappearance of the line dividing life from death. Although many that live today have had temporary experiences of such a cosmic consciousness, these have only been temporary, due to our limiting frame of consciousness. At the end of Creation this may no longer be so and the eternal life may in fact manifest as a time-less cosmic consciousness.

To my knowledge there is only one Mayan prophecy that explicitly addresses the end of Creation, a prophecy that is from the *Book of Chilam Balam of Tizimin*, which reads: 'Presently Baktun 13 shall come sailing, figuratively speaking, bringing the ornaments of which I have spoken, from your ancestors. Then the god will come to visit his little cones. Perhaps "After Death" will be the subject of his discourse.' Although cryptic, as are most prophecies, it seems this one has the same message as many others regarding the end of time: God will initiate the human beings in a life without death. We will return to the Garden of Eden after having eaten more of the fruits of the Tree of Life.

CHAPTER 13

THE VENUS PASSAGES
AND THE RETURN OF QUETZALCOATL

THE TUN-BASED CALENDAR AS
A SCHEDULE FOR GALACTIC MEDITATIONS

Today many people react to prophecies as the previous with a resigned attitude that it will take several hundred years for such dramatic changes to take place. This is essentially because they are stuck in a materialist world view where matter is seen as primary to consciousness. 'Why would the earth need to revolve three hundred times around the sun for this change in consciousness to take place?' we may rightly ask. In fact, the number of times the earth revolves around the sun or the moon around the earth has nothing to do with the evolution of consciousness. Consciousness evolves according to a divine plan whether we like it or not, and all we need to do to recognize this is to replace the calendars of matter with the tun-based Mayan calendars of spirit. And surely we are now to reach a more spiritual era, the Galactic Cycle, during which the tun-based calendrical system will be revived. We may then ask if it would also be appropriate to follow in the footsteps of the ahauob and perform ceremonies or gatherings to prepare spiritually for the coming tun. If so, what would such preparations be like? What ceremonies would serve humanity in becoming aware of the divine process of Creation and in honoring the vibrations of the World Tree?

In recent years global meditations—some more limited in participation and some widespread—have become commonplace, usually with an aim to 'heal the earth' or tune in to new energies. Such meditations may have considerable value, since the alpha brain state of meditation creates an improved resonance with the creation field of the earth. However, an important aspect to discuss regarding such meditations is not only how they are to be performed, but also when. If global meditations are performed at tun or half-tun shifts they could develop into a means of 'tuning up' or updating one's awareness to the new Heavens that are now rapidly going to replace one another. Meditating at tun shifts could become a means to follow the evolution of the divine plan in a conscious way. This would mean that meditations, or other types of ceremonies, should have as their intended aim creating resonance between the human being and the highest Heaven and Underworld possible.

While prayer is talking to God, meditation is listening to Him/Her. Such listening may provide guidance for the future, as it once did for the ahauob. The higher the Heavens and Underworlds that we are able to be in resonance with through meditation, the more beneficial, because the closer to God will the source of our guidance be. Special techniques of meditation, however, may still need to be developed for this purpose. Since the frequency of the divine process of Creation is now speeding up—with the LIGHT being switched on and off every tun—most people will spontaneously tend to lag behind this rapid evolution. It may thus serve God's creation and ourselves if such meditations ould be carried out on a regular basis according to the rhythm provided by the Galactic Cycle (see Table 15).

Because of their purpose, the techniques to be used for such meditations should be passive and receptive rather than active and giving. The idea of these meditations would not be to seek to heal the earth by sending light or positive thinking. It would be to support human beings in receiving imprints of the higher Heavens, the new truths that become evident at tun or half-tun shifts, and then letting these guide our actions. When it comes to saving the earth what will really matter is not what we think or what we dream, but how we act, and through resonance with the true, invisible reality we may be guided to the right course of action. In this, meditative resonance with the new Heavens may turn out to be crucial for our evolution and how to relate to our planet and galaxy. It may not save the planet to meditate, but what may save the planet and ourselves is to what extent the new Heavens guide us to use less gasoline, less paper, etc., as well as to curbing population growth. It is these tangible things that will have an impact on our survival, not the meditations as such. It is thus possible that in the era to come, the Galactic Underworld, we will either repeatedly update ourselves with the new Heavens through meditation/conscious resonance or lag behind the divine process of Creation. It will probably not be wise a few Heavens into the Galactic Underworld to live as if we were still in the National or Planetary Underworld. Of course, we may meditate at any time when we are called to do so, but what is suggested here is to conduct meditations on a regular basis at the occasions of the tun and half-tun shifts when new Heavens are actually introduced into the Cosmic Projector. Such an arrangement would allow us to keep pace with the divine rhythm of Creation and act based on the new imprints we receive at half-tun shifts. Maybe such meditations provide the best way of ensuring that our own ways of being are continually updated to the divine process of Creation. Most likely the rhythm provided by the half-tun or tun shifts is the one that we will all eventually fall into to accomplish this goal, although some will do so before others.

The creation of an Underworld is in a very real sense like implementing a computer program, where each new Heaven provides an updated version of the program. We may thus regard the creation day (13 Ahau) of the Galactic Underworld, the Gregorian date January 4, 1999, as the time for the introduction of its first version, 0.0.0. The program for this Underworld is then continually updated day by day until its final version is implemented on the day 13.0.0 (October 28, 2011). Curiously enough, to denote a day by numbers and points in this way, e.g., as 1.3.1, is the commonly accepted way of writing dates in the tun-based system, the same format that is used for updating versions of computer programs.

In this terminology the divine program called the Galactic Underworld will be updated on an ongoing basis, although significant new innovations to the program will only be introduced every half-tun. An example of such an occasion is the day labeled 1.0.1 (1 tun, 0 uinals, 1 kin after the beginning of the Galactic Cycle; Gregorian date December 31, 1999). This day was incidentally marked by celebrations and meditations all across the world, not because of the knowledge people may then have acquired of Mayan calendrics, but for the simple reason that it 'accidentally' coincided with the Gregorian millennium shift.

We may thus regard the replacements of Heavens in the Creation of the Galactic Underworld as parallels to the updating of computer programs, and those of us who desire to acquire the most recent versions immediately had better meditate on the very days that they are introduced. In line with this, global meditations may be organized at every tun and half-tun shift of the Galactic Creation Cycle to aid and encourage people to keep pace with the rapidly changing reality that is now emerging. The proposed rhythm would step by step allow human beings to tune up their consciousness by developing resonance with the new Heavens, and from this a meta-consciousness will eventually come forth. Thus, a direct relationship between the human being and the Source, generating authentic guidance from the divine process of Creation, may come to be developed through meditation.

VENUS PASSAGES

Venus was the planet of greatest interest to the Maya. The Maya very closely studied the orbit and phases of this planet. Venus is the sister planet of the earth, and, indeed, we now know Venus to be of almost exactly the same diameter as our own planet. The Maya also knew that five synodical Venus cycles of 584 days equal eight years on earth (minus two days). In various ways they sought to understand how the movement of Venus was linked to the tzolkin, and in the *Dresden Codex*, the finest of the Mayan Codices, the Venus Tables play a prominent role. Much of the Mayan interest in Venus was linked to the fact that its phases were seen as symbolic of the processes of death and rebirth. Hence it was thought that in the eight days between the disappearance of the evening star and the emergence of the morning star Quetzalcoatl would return to the Underworld.

A peculiar thing about this sibling relationship between the earth and Venus is that, because of its particular rate of retrograde (meaning opposite spin) rotation around its own axis, Venus always presents the same face, or mirror, to the earth at conjunctions. This means that the rotational movements of the two planets are linked, by accident or not.

At most inferior conjunctions, that is, when Venus passes between the earth and the sun, its orbit does not intersect the disc of the sun since Venus moves in an orbit whose plane lies at a certain angle with that of the orbit of the earth. This means that it is fairly rarely, only about once a century, that Venus conjuncts the sun at the particular time when the planes of revolution of Venus and the earth intersect. It is only at conjunctions of this kind that Venus actually intersects the disc of the sun, although such an eclipse is hardly visible to the naked eye. Such an eclipse of the sun, lasting for about seven hours, is called a Venus passage, or Venus transit, an occasion when Venus may serve as the best of all possible Cosmic Mirrors. Such Venus passages occur pair-wise, separated by eight years (minus two days), and the most recent pairs of Venus passages appeared in the years 1761/1769 (Figure 82) and 1874/1882. As all of creation is now going toward its completion, a pair of Venus passages will appear on the days June 8, 2004 and June 6, 2012 (Greenwich Mean Time).

In Table 15 the creation dates of the half-tun shifts and tun shifts of the Galactic Cycle were summarized. These dates all fall on days that in the tzolkin count have the day sign

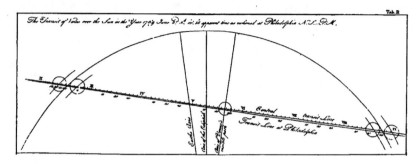

Fig. 82 The Venus passage in 1769 as projected by J. Ewing for the American Philosophical Society of Philadelphia.

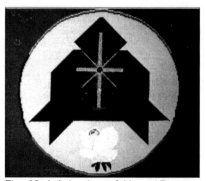

Fig. 83 Artist's view of Venus Passage (Courtesy of Anna-Maria Ljungberg).

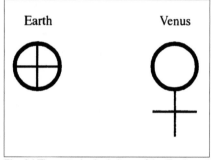

Fig. 84 The astrological signs of the Earth and Venus.

Ahau, and such days were those that the Classical Maya considered as days of creation, when ceremonies to mark the tun shifts were performed. Nonetheless, it is probably days that fall on the glyph Imix in the tzolkin count (see Appendix I) that should be considered as the beginnings of the new half-tuns or tuns. One of these beginning dates, 5.9.1, corresponding to the Gregorian date June 7, 2004, coincides very closely with the first in the pair of Venus passages, which will occur on June 8, 2004 (5.9.2). The occasion of this first Venus passage of June 8 may come to be the most important meditation of all time, given that it will be a meditation focusing on receiving the imprint of the returning True Cross. I will now discuss why.

Mythologically, the Maya would sometimes refer to the beginning of the Great Cycle as to the birth of Venus, and indeed a Venus passage in the year 3099 BC occurred in the very first katun of the Great Cycle. We shall keep in mind here that for the Maya and the Aztecs Venus was above all a manifestation of Quetzalcoatl. Thus, the birth of Venus here really translates into the birth of Quetzalcoatl, whom we have understood to be a symbol of the process of divine Creation with its seven DAYS and six NIGHTS. In this sense the onset of the Great Cycle, which follows this pattern of LIGHT, may indeed be described as the birth of Venus/Quetzalcoatl. If a Venus passage occurred during the first

The Mayan Calendar

katun of the National Cycle, it is interesting that another such astronomical event will occur in the final katun which completes this same cycle. Moreover, Venus passages also occurred pair-wise during the first, seventh and thirteenth (first, middle and last) katuns of the Planetary Cycle. This seems to indicate that both the National and Planetary Cycles began with the birth of Venus, marking the onset of processes that in a sense will be completed at the Venus passages in the years 2004 and 2012.

It is then interesting to look at what role the first pair of Venus passages in the Planetary Cycle played. This pair of Venus passages, occurring in 1761/1769 in the first DAY of the Planetary Cycle, was the first ever to have been studied by optical instruments. These Venus passages represented events that received considerable attention in ways that were very typical of the Underworld that was simultaneously beginning to be created. The Venus passage in 1769 was studied in 77 locations by 151 observers all around the world in a collective effort aimed at correctly estimating the distance to the sun. The effort failed in its immediate scientific aim, but was a success in another regard; it represented the first international collaborative project within science. Thus, not only did this event exemplify the new era of interest in the scientific study of nature, rapidly expanding at the beginning of the Planetary Cycle, but it also exemplified the transfer to a planetary consciousness, as for the first time the different nations of this planet collaborated around a scientific goal. Maybe, in fact, it was the first time ever that different nations collaborated around any higher goal whatsoever. Typically, the study of these Venus passages also meant the birth of American science, whose quality was then for the first time acknowledged by the European nations. The most important items of the first issue of the *Transactions of the American Philosophical Society* were the descriptions and calculations of the Venus transit in 1769.

Taken together this means that some of the phenomena that have characterized the evolution of the Planetary Cycle—science, international collaboration and America's leading role—found very typical expressions at the occasions of the Venus passages in the initial katun of this cycle. There are thus reasons to believe that the upcoming Venus passages in the years 2004 and 2012 will mark the completion of these very phenomena. In the previous chapter I hinted at what this completion of processes carried by both the National and Planetary Cycles may mean. Those things that previously have given people a sense of security—royal authority, written laws and national communities in the National Underworld and international collaboration, science and American dominance in the Planetary—will come to be replaced by the rule of the returning True Cross and the new, higher truth that this will carry. At the occasion of the first Venus passage on June 8, 2004, the past will begin to yield to the dominance of the galactic LIGHT.

All of the above and the fact that Venus is the sister planet of Earth and a manifestation of Quetzalcoatl means that the Venus passage of June 8, 2004 is designed as a perfect Cosmic Mirror to prepare us for the new reality that will then begin to dominate. Yet this physical reflectory event would be of only limited significance if it did not synchronize with the vibrations of the invisible universe, with the tun-based vibrations of the True Cross. So the really important facet of this occasion is that it will be perfectly scheduled for the celebration of the midpoint of the third NIGHT of the Galactic Cycle, a time when a new Qur'anic Heaven with a Cross will again be introduced. Earlier in this Chapter I suggested that such tun and half-tun shifts may be significant times for humanity to meditate. That such a half-tun shift concurs with this Venus passage is by itself a remarkable event and we will soon see what it means. The Venus passage of June

8, 2004 represents one of those remarkable events when not only two, but even three, four, five, six or seven, remarkable coincidences concur at one particular time, producing what we may call a multidimensional synchronicity.

The first Venus passage will thus occur on day number 182 of the third NIGHT of the Galactic Cycle. This, in other words, is the second day after the half-tun of the Sixth Heaven of this cycle (5.9.2) (in Yucatan the Venus passage of 2004 will begin exactly as the new day begins at 18 minutes past midnight on June 8). Thus, this Venus passage, which will take place during about seven hours, will be a natural rallying point for those seeking to synchronize meditations globally in the rhythm of the tun-based vibrations of the World Tree. But unlike at other such points in time, the Venus passage will bestow us with a Cosmic Mirror; it will provide an exceptional opportunity for all of humanity to join in meditation, since our attention will then just naturally be going outwards toward the Cosmos. Since it also occurs during the light season of the Northern Hemisphere, where the vast majority of the population of this planet is living, the Venus passage will at least for part of its duration be visible to almost everyone properly equipped for this. Certainly, the seven-hour-long Venus passage will present a unique support and opportunity for anyone desiring to receive an imprint of the new Heaven to guide his or her actions. No similar event is likely to recur.

THE RETURN OF CHRIST CONSCIOUSNESS
AND OF QUETZALCOATL

The half-tun celebration at which the Cosmic Mirror of this Venus passage is presented to us (5.9.2) is, however, no regular celebration. This is a very special half-tun celebration—that of the Return of the Cross. As we saw earlier when we studied the Great Cycle, the Cross had first begun to make itself known in the seventh baktun, baktun 6, but I also later argued that a new Qur'anic Heaven with this Cross had already been put in place during the midpoint of the previous Heaven. The first Venus passage will then in fact occur at the midpoint of the Sixth Heaven—this time of the Galactic Cycle—meaning that this will be shortly before the time when the balance will tip over in favor of the Cross. Yet at this special occasion it will not yet be dawn, since no LIGHT will then be enhancing the visibility of the Cross. So the Cosmic Mirror of the Venus passage merely brings the foreboding of the Return of the True Cross. But soon after this, at the beginning of the next DAY, DAY 4, the new galactic consciousness will start to balance that of the Planetary Underworld, and at the beginning of the fifth DAY, November 24, 2006, it will come to dominate. Thus, at the occasion of the first Venus passage it will still be DARK (in the middle of the NIGHT), the Beast may still rule, and it is unknown how many will go out to experience the return of the True Cross. The *Book of Revelation* spoke about the ones that do, in its verse 20:04: 'And I saw thrones and they sat upon them and judgement was given unto them: and I saw the souls of them that were beheaded for the witness of Jesus and for the word of God, and which had not worshiped the beast, neither his image, neither had received his mark upon their foreheads or in their hands and they lived and reigned with Christ a thousand years. . .'

To be a judge in this sense does not mean passing judgment or, even less so, punishing others. What it means is to be an example and an incarnation of the new truth carried by the True Cross, and the first that will be judged by this new measure are the participants themselves. Hence, since it entails judging oneself, a certain amount of courage may be required to receive the imprint of the new Cross through meditating at the Venus passage in 2004. Being a judge here probably means giving the Cross of God a chance to incarnate and for this to live among the human beings in the same way as it once did through the incarnation of Jesus.

Maybe then the meditation on the occasion of the first Venus passage is not for everyone. It will not be for those waiting to see who will turn out to be the winners in the struggles later to come. The Venus passage is for the early risers, ready to go out into the darkness to defy the Beast, and willing to rise in the middle of the night to see the first signs of the Cross. They will be greatly rewarded in having the Cosmic Mirror available as support for receiving the imprint of the Cross, and maybe a seven-hour-long meditation will be necessary to receive this powerfully enough to last through tumultuous times to come. This may be only for those who are spiritual enough to see through the materialist illusions and the materialist concept of time, and galactic enough to rise above the limited perspectives linked to particular spiritual and religious traditions. It may only be for those willing to transcend the limited frames of consciousness of the past. Nonetheless, participation is likely to benefit everyone. Yet it will be a choice, a choice that it is now time to make widely available.

How then are these meditations to be carried out technically and what are the best locations to receive the imprint of the True Cross? One possible technique of updating one's consciousness to the New Heaven is through a Gaia meditation. What this means is to imagine your own head inside of, or actually becoming, the earth. In such a meditation we may imagine positioning our eyes at the Hawaiian Islands so that our left brain halves correspond to the Western Hemisphere and our right brain halves to the Eastern. In this way we will be fully exposed to the global creation field of the New Heaven and remain in resonance with it. In the alpha state of meditation we will directly access the relaying creation field of the earth vibrating with a frequency of 10.2 Hz.

Very likely this technique should also be taken one step further by visualizing our heads surrounded by the galaxy with the galactic midplane separating our two brain halves, meaning that the World Tree, or the True Cross, will be recreated on our foreheads at the location of the third eye. On this occasion we may then in a meditative state of awareness focus intensely on the passage of Venus across the disc of the sun, while letting go of attempts to directly see the True Cross. If we identify strongly with planet earth and the galaxy and through meditation receive its new Heaven we will receive the imprint of the Cross whether we can see this directly or not. By holographic resonance anyone anywhere should be able to receive an imprint, but quite possibly the Hawaiian Islands, the eyes of the planet, will be an ideal spot to be on June 8, 2004, with northern Europe as a possible second choice.

While this Venus passage represents an extraordinary multidimensional synchronicity when many ancient prophecies seem to be converging, it is in its place to consider the changing nature of time as we pass into the vastly expanded framework of the Galactic Underworld. In the lives of many people synchronicities have become a common experience in recent years. As a continuation of this process, our linear consciousness of time will gradually be lost as we enter the Galactic Underworld, partly because of the expanded framework of our lives and partly because our new frame of consciousness will allow us to see through the materialist illusions. This will be especially true as we enter the second half of the Galactic Cycle, the era that the first of the two Venus passages heralds, and the linear/cyclical consciousness of time linked to our current planetary consciousness will definitely be transcended. What this will most likely mean is that not only single synchronicities, i.e., two different things coinciding in a meaningful way—which are really linked to a linear view of our life as a journey from the cradle to the grave—but also multiple synchronicities, several meaningful things coinciding simultaneously, will become commonplace. Time will come to be experienced as a sequence of galactic energies where each day will be like a multidimensional synchronicity generated by these. The Venus passage in 2004 is an example of such a multidimensional synchronicity that we can already now foretell.

The divine vibrations of the Cross or the various phases of Creation called Heavens and Underworlds are very precise. They are governed by a preordained rhythm that it is beyond our control to alter. We have every reason to believe that these rhythms are perfectly set for the purpose of the evolution of this universe. To imply something else would be to imply that God was not be omnipotent or that we ourselves knew better than Him/Her how this universe is to be created. This also means that the universe will not and cannot wait for us to do what we are supposed to do. The time schedule can not be altered, meaning that if we fail, we fail, and there can be no intervention of divine forces to change the course of events. Why? Because the plan is already perfect from the perspective of the evolution of the universe in its entirety, and to change this plan would make the universe imperfect. In fact, there is no indication, no empirical evidence, that the large-scale plan for the evolution of the universe has ever been altered through some kind of divine intervention. Everything points to changes in consciousness being initiated at precise moments in time, moments that are unalterable, and the best we can do is to adapt to them. There is no point in arguing with the Cosmos. Hence, for those that miss the first Venus passage with its opportunity of becoming a carrier of the True Cross, there are no guarantees that there will be a second chance. The second Venus passage of June 6, 2012 is probably of less importance, occurring as it does after the completion of the creation of the Nine Underworlds.

In this context it might be said that it would probably be fallacious to believe that it is the very astronomical event of the Venus passage that causes an alteration in the human consciousness to occur. Rather, the change in human consciousness takes place because a new Qur'anic Heaven dominated by the Cross, which our brains are in resonance with, is put in place at the same time. The purpose of the meditation is to make us conscious of the change in consciousness—to develop meta-consciousness. All that Venus really does at this super-synchronistic moment is to provide a mirror for us to focus our attention on while we meditate on the Cross. The Venus passage is an opportunity that means nothing unless it is taken. Thus, at this particular half-tun shift, when the True Cross will favorably begin to tip the balance against the materialist consciousness of the Planetary Underworld, we will receive some extra, remarkably timed help from the Cosmos to create resonance with the new Heaven. It may thus be advisable to meditate for the full duration of the seven-hour-long Venus passage to receive a strong imprint of the Cross, at least on a subconscious level.

We should also notice that the relationship that is established in this meditation is really one directly between the meditator and the Cross. Participation does not imply adherence to any specific religion or doctrine that any other human being may promote. The True Cross is not a manmade cross, but part of an invisible holy reality which is pure and immaculate. It is for this very reason that meditations on this occasion may guide us in taking the right course of action and becoming a 'judge' in the sense of *Revelation*

20:04. This meditation will help those participating to generate a frame of consciousness ruled by the True Cross, thus allowing them to distinguish between right and wrong from a higher perspective than our present one. It is our own individual choice to be a servant of the True Cross or not. If we are in resonance with the True Cross then at least we will have some idea as to what is right and what is wrong, and with this divine guidance it will thus become easier to open our hearts and choose the best course of action. The consciousness carried by the True Cross, the reinvigorated distinctions of right and wrong, is the Christ consciousness, which this time all of us may choose to embody. For this to happen, for true judgment to be spread, it seems we should spread the word about the Venus passage and other meditations at tun and mid-tun shifts.

Those who integrate the Cross through meditations on the occasion of the first Venus passage will indeed be judges, carrying judgment between right and wrong according to a higher ethic. They will show good judgment and be provided with the distinctions by means of which their own actions and those of others may be judged from their own example. Judgment is not punishment. To be able to judge actions and thus become an example for others through having integrated the Truth of the Cross is not something that allows you to punish others. The Qur'an Surah 82:18 says: 'Again, what will make you realize what the day of judgement is? The day on which no soul shall control anything for (another) soul; and the command on that day shall be entirely Allah's.' What the Qur'an says here is that trying to control another soul, presumably including through judging or punishing it, means intruding on the command of Allah, and thus doing the very opposite of what may be expected from you.

Incidentally, as a remarkable coincidence June 8 is the day of death of Mohammed, something that points toward the rebirth of Islam and the inclusive transcendence on this occasion of all the dualities that have generated the historical religions of humanity. Such transcendence is a logical consequence of the new galactic consciousness. The Venus

Ik

passage of June 8, 2004 thus seems to allow us to close the circle of the entire evolution of the National Underworld, with its conflicts between the historical religions of the Old World.

It will also allow us to close the circle of the religious drama of Mesoamerica: According to the legend, Quetzalcoatl had sacrificed himself to become the planet Venus but had vowed to return. We may thus note that in the Mayan/Aztec tzolkin count the days of the two Venus passages are 6 Ik/Ehecatl and 1 Ik/Ehecatl, respectively, where Ik in Mayan signifies 'spirit,' 'wind,' and Ehecatl is the Aztec name of the wind god, one of the manifestations of Quetzalcoatl. Thus, at this Venus passage, Quetzalcoatl will return to the Galactic Underworld. Being a symbol of the divine process of Creation, and carrying the new LIGHT, Quetzalcoatl will at this passage return from his guise of Venus, heralding the return of the True Cross, Vera Cruz. Quetzalcoatl is again transformed, but this time—at a multidimensional synchronicity of sorts—returns from Venus to the Underworld of its sister planet on a day marked by his very own sign, Ik/Ehecatl. Not surprisingly then, in the katun round of the Mayan *Books of Chilam Balam* (Jaguar Prophet) the present katun is described as one of spiritual regeneration and Messianic expectations. In fact, for this katun the *Books of Chilam Balam* declare the return of Quetzalcoatl.

The symbol used by the ancient Maya for the day Ik/Ehecatl is a 'T' (Figure 85)—a symbol that generally is believed to refer to the World Tree—thus again creating a link between Quetzalcoatl and the True Cross. Hence, a day that in the Classical calendar is dominated by Ehecatl/Quetzalcoatl and a 'T'/ World Tree is also a day when a new Qur'anic Heaven projecting a World Tree is introduced, a day when we may come to receive an imprint of this. As Venus passes across the sun disc Quetzalcoatl will return to incarnate among us as an expression of the True Cross.

The 'T' was, however, known also among the ancient Jews as a holy symbol, a symbol that has come to be known under the name of the 'Tau' Cross. In a verse in the Book of the prophet Ezekiel (9:4) it is said that the Lord would spare those in Jerusalem who carried the Tau Cross, i.e., the World Tree, on their foreheads. Everything is thus now brought together, with the focus on the occasion of the Venus passage in the year 2004, when through meditation we may as a sign of God's protection receive the Tau Cross on our foreheads.

Fig. 85 The Jewish Tau Cross (upper left), the tzolkin day sign Ik/Ehecatl (the wind god, Quetzalcoatl) (upper right) and a 'T'-shaped World Tree, showing the death of a human being at the roots and his rebirth at its branches (compare Fig. 44).

We are all personifications of the World Tree and of the Cross, and the purpose of the Galactic Cycle is only to make us conscious of this. All we need to recognize then is that none of us is the only one who is such an incarnation of the True Cross. Today, in 2000, we may not yet be able to see Quetzalcoatl, as little as we are able to see the Cross, because we are still blindfolded by the consciousness of the Planetary Cycle. But at the first Venus passage the early birds will be able to see Quetzalcoatl in the sky. Maybe in the Americas he will then be seen as returning from the East, carrying a balanced Cross, as the legend would have it. For the spiritual, however, it may not be so much a matter of seeing Quetzalcoatl or the Cross, but of being him or it, incarnations of the LIGHT of Christ and Quetzalcoatl. If so, we will truly be able to talk about a Mayan return, and a return of the Mayan calendar, as again we will be able to follow true time from the wriggling of Quetzalcoatl.

Recently, there has been much discussion about the possibility that the Bible holds a secret code that can be read by those with knowledge of archaic Hebrew and access to sophisticated computer programs. In the preceding we have, however, seen that there exists another Bible code that is easy to read, only requiring knowledge of the Mayan calendar. What has become evident here is the existence of a Cross where the Mayan calendar and Biblical prophecy meet, whose cross hairs are focused on the Venus passage in the year 2004. The Return of the True Cross, the return of the righteous and of Christ then is also the return of Quetzalcoatl. Quetzalcoatl is the True Cross and the True Cross is Quetzalcoatl, both of which will provide guidance from God. This is what there will be for us to seek in the years to come, and, for the sincere seekers, the star of Bethlehem will appear as a guiding LIGHT.

Fig. 86 Artist's view of the return of female Quetzalcoatl (Courtesy of Anna-Maria Ljungberg).

Appendix I
The Tzolkin
and the Aztec Day Gods

Mayan calendrics is much more complicated than has been discussed here and the serious student may desire to study it at any degree of complexity. The seven DAYS and six NIGHTS are just the most easily demonstrable reality basis of this calendrical system and thus a good starting point for understanding it. Nonetheless, it would be a grave error to say that this is all there is to it. No book about Mayan calendrics can ignore the discussion of the tzolkin, and of all the various parts of the Mayan calendrical system the 260-day tzolkin has been considered the most mysterious and enigmatic. The meaning of the tzolkin is mostly given as the 'count of days.' It may, however, also be translated into 'pieces of the sun,' and by inference to 'pieces of divine creation,' which may come closest to its true meaning given that among the Maya the sun has often been identified with God. In the tzolkin calendar the 260 days are followed through repeating a specific sequence of twenty glyphs (Figure 87) thirteen times (13 × 20), or by repeating the numbers 1 through 13 twenty times (20 × 13) according to a cog-wheel model (Figure 88) to produce 260 different combinations of the twenty glyphs and the thirteen numbers in a specific order beginning with 1 Imix and ending with 13 Ahau (Table 16).

Fig. 87 The twenty day signs of the tzolkin with their Yucatec names.

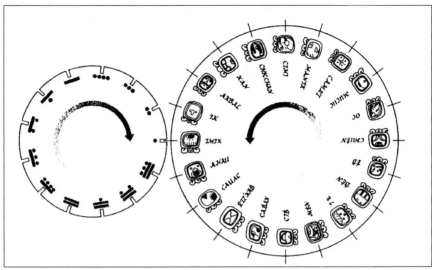

Fig. 88 Cog-wheel model of the twenty glyphs intermeshing with the thirteen numbers to produce the 260 combinations of the tzolkin.

Table 16
The 260 Combinations of 13 Numbers and
20 Glyphs of the Tzolkin in their Correct Order

1	1	Imix	22	9	Ik	43	4	Akbal
2	2	Ik	23	10	Akbal	44	5	Kan
3	3	Akbal	24	11	Kan	45	6	Chicchan
4	4	Kan	25	12	Chicchan	46	7	Cimi
5	5	Chicchan	26	13	Cimi	47	8	Manik
6	6	Cimi	27	1	Manik	48	9	Lamat
7	7	Manik	28	2	Lamat	49	10	Muluc
8	8	Lamat	29	3	Muluc	50	11	Oc
9	9	Muluc	30	4	Oc	51	12	Chuen
10	10	Oc	31	5	Chuen	52	13	Eb
11	11	Chuen	32	6	Eb	53	1	Ben
12	12	Eb	33	7	Ben	54	2	Ix
13	13	Ben	34	8	Ix	55	3	Men
14	1	Ix	35	9	Men	56	4	Cib
15	2	Men	36	10	Cib	57	5	Caban
16	3	Cib	37	11	Caban	58	6	Edznab
17	4	Caban	38	12	Edznab	59	7	Cauac
18	5	Edznab	39	13	Cauac	60	8	Ahau
19	6	Cauac	40	1	Ahau	61	9	Imix
20	7	Ahau	41	2	Imix	62	10	Ik
21	8	Imix	42	3	Ik	63	11	Akbal

The Mayan Calendar

64	12	Kan	109	5	Muluc	154	11	Ix
65	13	Chicchan	110	6	Oc	155	12	Men
66	1	Cimi	111	7	Chuen	156	13	Cib
67	2	Manik	112	8	Eb	157	1	Caban
68	3	Lamat	113	9	Ben	158	2	Edznab
69	4	Muluc	114	10	Ix	159	3	Cauac
70	5	Oc	115	11	Men	160	4	Ahau
71	6	Chuen	116	12	Cib	161	5	Imix
72	7	Eb	117	13	Caban	162	6	Ik
73	8	Ben	118	1	Edznab	163	7	Akbal
74	9	Ix	119	2	Cauac	164	8	Kan
75	10	Men	120	3	Ahau	165	9	Chicchan
76	11	Cib	121	4	Imix	166	10	Cimi
77	12	Caban	122	5	Ik	167	11	Manik
78	13	Edznab	123	6	Akbal	168	12	Lamat
79	1	Cauac	124	7	Kan	169	13	Muluc
80	2	Ahau	125	8	Chicchan	170	1	Oc
81	3	Imix	126	9	Cimi	171	2	Chuen
82	4	Ik	127	10	Manik	172	3	Eb
83	5	Akbal	128	11	Lamat	173	4	Ben
84	6	Kan	129	12	Muluc	174	5	Ix
85	7	Chicchan	130	13	Oc	175	6	Men
86	8	Cimi	131	1	Chuen	176	7	Cib
87	9	Manik	132	2	Eb	177	8	Caban
88	10	Lamat	133	3	Ben	178	9	Edznab
89	11	Muluc	134	4	Ix	179	10	Cauac
90	12	Oc	135	5	Men	180	11	Ahau
91	13	Chuen	136	6	Cib	181	12	Imix
92	1	Eb	137	7	Caban	182	13	Ik
93	2	Ben	138	8	Edznab	183	1	Akbal
94	3	Ix	139	9	Cauac	184	2	Kan
95	4	Men	140	10	Ahau	185	3	Chicchan
96	5	Cib	141	11	Imix	186	4	Cimi
97	6	Caban	142	12	Ik	187	5	Manik
98	7	Edznab	143	13	Akbal	188	6	Lamat
99	8	Cauac	144	1	Kan	189	7	Muluc
100	9	Ahau	145	2	Chicchan	190	8	Oc
101	10	Imix	146	3	Cimi	191	9	Chuen
102	11	Ik	147	4	Manik	192	10	Eb
103	12	Akbal	148	5	Lamat	193	11	Ben
104	13	Kan	149	6	Muluc	194	12	Ix
105	1	Chicchan	150	7	Oc	195	13	Men
106	2	Cimi	151	8	Chuen	196	1	Cib
107	3	Manik	152	9	Eb	197	2	Caban
108	4	Lamat	153	10	Ben	198	3	Edznab

199	4	Cauac	220	12	Ahau	241	7	Imix
200	5	Ahau	221	13	Imix	242	8	Ik
201	6	Imix	222	1	Ik	243	9	Akbal
202	7	Ik	223	2	Akbal	244	10	Kan
203	8	Akbal	224	3	Kan	245	11	Chicchan
204	9	Kan	225	4	Chicchan	246	12	Cimi
205	10	Chicchan	226	5	Cimi	247	13	Manik
206	11	Cimi	227	6	Manik	248	1	Lamat
207	12	Manik	228	7	Lamat	249	2	Muluc
208	13	Lamat	229	8	Muluc	250	3	Oc
209	1	Muluc	230	9	Oc	251	4	Chuen
210	2	Oc	231	10	Chuen	252	5	Eb
211	3	Chuen	232	11	Eb	253	6	Ben
212	4	Eb	233	12	Ben	254	7	Ix
213	5	Ben	234	13	Ix	255	8	Men
214	6	Ix	235	1	Men	256	9	Cib
215	7	Men	236	2	Cib	257	10	Caban
216	8	Cib	237	3	Caban	258	11	Edznab
217	9	Caban	238	4	Edznab	259	12	Cauac
218	10	Edznab	239	5	Cauac	260	13	Ahau
219	11	Cauac	240	6	Ahau			

In addition to 13 × 20 and 20 × 13, these 260 combinations may also be subdivided in other ways, e.g., as 4 × 65 or 5 × 52, which in ancient times both were considered as important. Such fractionations and their effects represent the bulk of the content of the *Dresden Codex*, the finest and most thoroughly studied surviving Mayan book. The Classical tzolkin count has been followed, apparently without interruption, for the past twenty-five hundred years in the highlands of Guatemala, and until the time of the Spanish conquest this same count was apparently used all over Mesoamerica. Some beginning dates in this count are given in Table 17.

Table 17
Beginning Dates (1 Imix) for the
Upcoming Classical Tzolkin Counts

Jan. 5, 1999	Dec. 30, 2003	April 7, 2008
Sep. 22, 1999	April 14, 2003	Dec. 23, 2008
June 7, 2000	Sep. 15, 2004	Sep. 9, 2009
Feb. 23, 2001	June 2, 2005	May 27, 2010
Nov. 10, 2001	Feb. 17, 2006	Feb. 11, 2011
July 28, 2002	Nov. 4, 2006	Oct. 29, 2011
	July 22, 2007	

Why then have the Maya been using a calendar that is 260 days, a calendar that very obviously is not based on any astronomical or seasonal cycle? Many answers have been suggested to this question, most of which have sought an explanation in some material aspect of human existence. One, which is very prevalent, and is given also by some present-day Mayan shamans, is that the tzolkin is a reflection of the human gestation period, which by modern medicine has been estimated at 266 days. But if this was the whole truth, why would there have existed just one tzolkin count synchronized all over Mesoamerica in ancient times? Would it not have been more logical if every individual kept her or his own tzolkin count starting at birth? Also, why would this very special way of counting combinations of the twenty glyphs and the thirteen numbers have been retained? If the gestation period were the whole explanation, why would the 260 days of gestation not have been counted straight from 1 to 260 and why would various subdivisions of the tzolkin have been studied? Very likely then, the truth underlying the tzolkin goes deeper than the gestation period.

To seek this truth we should note that the Maya have always considered the numbers and the glyphs of the tzolkin as a basis for divination. In modern language we would say that the different days that make up the tzolkin are associated with different energies. In this respect there is in European culture really nothing that compares to the tzolkin, since the tzolkin divination was based on the energies of time itself, which would vary from day to day according to a special pattern. Thus, the particular tzolkin day on which someone was born was considered as very important for the future life theme of that individual, since he or she would be conditioned by its particular energy. This is somewhat in the same way as the day of birth is important to Western astrologers, with the marked difference that here it is the energy of time itself, regardless of any of its physical manifestations through planets or stars, that is playing the key role. The tzolkin thus belongs to the invisible universe.

What then is the origin of these different energies characterizing the 260 days of the tzolkin? Is there a basis in reality to these energies that would truly allow us to use them for divination? One of the crucial facts to know for understanding the tzolkin is that it did not always refer only to single days, but sometimes also to longer periods of time such as katuns. This is evident, for instance, in the *Books of Chilam Balam*, which describe events in the cosmic creation scheme occurring in a sequence of katuns, which are each linked to a combination of the tzolkin. But if the combinations of numbers and glyphs can be linked to katuns, then they could in principle be linked also to longer periods in the tun-based system, such as baktuns, pictuns, etc. We may conclude that the tzolkin is not necessarily only a count of days, but a specific sequence of different phases in creation.

Thus, the sacred calendar has sometimes been used as a description of creation, and consequently the thirteen uinals, periods of twenty days, of the tzolkin may be considered as an energetic description of the progression of a divine creation cycle of seven DAYS and six NIGHTS. The tzolkin of 13 × 20 combinations may thus be regarded as a filtration pattern of divine LIGHT that may be applied to thirteen hablatuns, thirteen alautuns, etc., constituting the progressions through different

Underworlds. Each DAY or NIGHT then energetically corresponds to a specific uinal, a sequence of the twenty different glyphs. The tzolkin, however, is a pattern of LIGHT that has a higher, 260-unit resolution than the simplified scheme of seven DAYS and six NIGHTS that has been described throughout this book. When the filtration pattern of the tzolkin, as is mostly the case, is applied to the condensed period of 13 × 20 = 260 days, it may thus be regarded as a temporal microcosm of creation. It is then a high overtone of the filtration pattern that also regulates all the major creation cycles generating the Nine Underworlds. The Hermetic principle of time reads: 'As in the Longer Creation Cycles, so also in the Shorter.' The regular 260-day tzolkin is thus a temporal microcosm reflecting the progression through 260 energies of the major creation cycles (the Great Cycle, for instance, is constituted by 260 katuns, each corresponding to an energetic combination of the tzolkin).

The particular sequence of the thirteen days, each characterized by a number in the sacred calendar, is then to be considered as a temporal microcosm of creation at an even lower level than the thirteen uinals. In the thirteen-day count it is instead each single day that energetically corresponds to one of the seven DAYS and six NIGHTS of the major creation cycles. In Table 18 the various deities believed by the Aztecs to rule the various days of the thirteen-day cycle have been presented. Here they have also been coupled with the seven DAYS and six NIGHTS, as we know these from the previous chapters.

Generally speaking, the Aztec deities ruling the various days in the thirteen-day cycle seem to correspond very well to the descriptions that we have made of the progressions through the DAYS and NIGHTS of the major creation cycles. The deities associated with the days are nurturing deities of light and birth, while those associated with the nights are associated with darkness and war.

Previously I showed that DAY 5 (corresponding to day 9 in the thirteen-day count), which was ruled by QUETZALCOATL, brought about a breakthrough to LIGHT and Christ consciousness. (Indeed, it was during a DAY ruled by this deity of Light that human beings started the use of fire some 800,000 years ago; see Table 8.) Since the tzolkin is one of our most important tools for understanding the changing energies during the upcoming Galactic Cycle, it may then also be in its place (Table 19) to compare the time periods of the various Underworlds ruled by the god of darkness (the fifth NIGHT of creation, corresponding to day 10 in the thirteen-day count).

Table 18
The Character of the Thirteen Numbers of the
Thirteen-day Cycle (Deities Ruling the Thirteen Heavens)

Nr	light	Character	Aztec name of deity
1	DAY 1	Initiation	*Xiuhtecuthli*, god of fire and time
2	NIGHT 1		*Tlaltecuthli*, god of the earth
3	DAY 2	Expansion	*Chalchiuhtlicue*, goddess of water and birth

4	NIGHT 2	Reaction	*Tonatiuh*, god of warriors and the sun
5	DAY 3	Anchoring	*Tlacolteotl*, goddess of love and childbirth
6	NIGHT 3		*Mictlantecuthli*, god of death
7	DAY 4	High point	*Cinteotl*, god of maize and sustenance
8	NIGHT 4		*Tlaloc*, god of rain and war
9	DAY 5	Breakthrough to Light	*Quetzalcoatl*, Lord of the Light
10	NIGHT 5	Destruction	*Tezcatlipoca*, Lord of Darkness
11	DAY 6	Renaissance	*Yohualticitl*, goddess of birth
12	NIGHT 6		*Tlahuizcalpantecuthli*, god ruling before dawn
13	DAY 7	Completion	*Ometeotl*, the supreme deity, the lord and lady of duality

Table 19
Major Catastrophes during the Fifth NIGHT (Ruled by the God of Darkness)
of the Different Creation Cycles

Cycle	Beginning	Catastrophic event
Planetary	AD 1932	Hitlerism (1933), Stalinism, World War II, Atomic weapons
National	AD 434	Collapse of Roman civilization, Huns (434), Dark Ages
Regional	32,000 YA	Extinction of the Neanderthals (32,000 YA)
Human	640,000 YA	Illinoisan Ice Age (600,000 YA)
Anthropoid	12.8 MYA	?
Mammalian	252 MYA	Perm-Triassic extinction (251 MYA) 97% of all species extinct
Cellular	5.0 BYA	Meteor bombardment of the earth (4.5-3.8 BYA)

(YA = years ago, MYA = millions of years ago, BYA billions of years ago.)

In all of these Underworlds NIGHT 5 marks very significant periods of destruction and catastrophes. The most recent fifth NIGHT, the katun 1932-1952, is, however, probably the one that to modern people most immediately comes to mind as having been ruled by dark forces. (Hitler assumed extraordinary powers in Germany following the Reichstag fire, which took place three weeks into the new katun, when the world economy was hit the most by the Great Depression. This was followed by the Moscow trials in 1934 when Stalin took absolute power in the Soviet Union, which was followed by World War II, the Holocaust and the atomic bombs, until the katun ends with the Korean War and the invention of the hydrogen bomb). What Table 19 means is that in all the Underworlds NIGHT 5 is a period of destruction, which in the thirteen-day count is reflected in day 10. Also, the other days in the microcosmic thirteen-day count of the tzolkin will be ruled by the energies ruling the respective DAYS and NIGHTS of Creation.

Table 20
Overview of the Pulse-wise Evolution
during the DAYS *of the Creation Cycles*

DAY	Cellular	Mammalian	Familial	Tribal	Regional	National	Planetary	Galactic
1	Big Bang	Cell clusters	Monkeys	Homo habilis	Musterian	Thinite Kingdom	Theor. Telegraph	(?)
2		Ediacaran	Aegyptopith			Middle Kingdom	Optical telegraph	(?)
3	Galactic Disk	Trilobits	Dryopith	Homo erectus	Neanderthal	New Kingdom	Telegraph	(?)
4	Siral arms	Fishes	Dryopith	Homo erectus	Neanderthal	Greece	Telephone	(?)
5	Solar system	Reptiles	Dryopith	Homo erectus	Neanderthal	Rome	Radio	(?)
6	Prokaryotes	Mammals	Austr. Afr.	Arch Homo sap.	Cave paint.	Proto-nations	Television	(?)
7	Eukaryotes	Plac. Mammals	Aust. Afr.	Homo sapies	Agriculture	Modern nation	Computer netw.	(?)

On the next higher level of the temporal hierarchy, the destructive character of NIGHT 5 is reflected, for instance, in the tenth uinal of the tzolkin (kin 181-200, 12 Imix to 5 Ahau), while an energy of rebirth is reflected in its eleventh uinal (kin 201-220, 6 Imix to 12 Ahau; see Table 16). The gods of the thirteen numbers in Table 18 may thus also be used to describe the general character of each of the thirteen uinals of the tzolkin. The sequence of twenty glyphs (Figure 87) in each uinal is then meant to express the energetic change that each DAY or NIGHT undergoes as it passes from its beginning to its end. For further perspective, Table 20 describes the general rhythm of evolution of the passage through the days of all of the major creation cycles, which may be paired with the descriptions of the general character of these DAYS in Table 18.

In this way we may understand that the common 260-day tzolkin reflects energy changes that are really overtones of the filtration pattern of divine Light characterizing all the major creation cycles operating on a much larger scale in the creation of the Nine Underworlds. The scheme in Table 20, the Periodic System of Evolution, is described in detail only in *The Theory of Everything*, but it may be clear already from this table that there are commonalties in the progressions from seed to mature fruit in all the Underworlds.

We may now, from this large-scale perspective, also understand why the day of birth in the tzolkin is characterized by a particular energy that will set its mark on an individual. This is because it is a microcosmic reflection of the energies of the

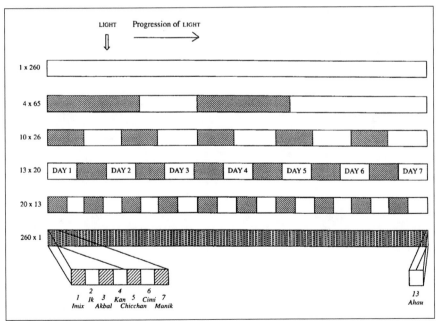

Fig. 89 Tzolkin as a filtration pattern of divine LIGHT. The Seven DAYS and Six NIGHTS produced by the division of tzolkin into 13 segments of equal size (20 units) is one of several filtration patterns that are layered upon one another in creation. The 260 combinations of glyphs and numbers of the tzolkin may be divided by all of the factors 2, 4, 5, 10, 13, 20, 26, 52, 65 and 130. Through the superimposition of the filtration patterns resulting from its division by these different factors each of the 260 units of the tzolkin will gain a unique energy.

major creation cycles. Since we have seen in the previous that these energies have a real existence, an outstanding consequence is that the energy dominating someone's day of birth is real. This also means that the tzolkin count is not arbitrary. There is only one in the 260 days that corresponds to the tzolkin energy of the major creation cycles, and thus in the cosmic perspective there can only be one true count.

At the bottom of Figure 89 the sequence of the 260 combinations of the tzolkin is presented, together with some of the subdivisions of the tzolkin. Included among these is the 13 × 20 subdivision, which produces the seven DAYS and six NIGHTS of a major creation cycle. Thus it becomes evident that the simple scheme of seven DAYS and six NIGHTS is just one, although probably the most important, aspect of the much richer and more complex filtration pattern of divine LIGHT that results from the combined action of all the subdivisions of the tzolkin and their alternations between LIGHT and DARKNESS.

Through this complex filtration pattern of divine LIGHT, each of the 260 combinations of numbers and glyphs of the tzolkin receives a unique energy that makes it distinct from all the others. Other than 13 × 20 and 20 × 13, 4 × 65 is the most important subdivision producing these effects. In principle, the resulting filtration pattern of 260 units is by itself time-less and may thus be applied to any

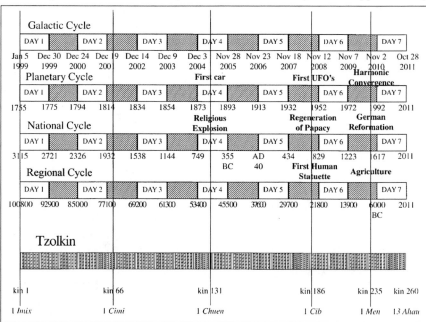

Fig. 90 The tzolkin with its specific filtration pattern of divine LIGHT in the lower row describes the evolution through the 260 sub-cycles of the different Underworlds. Thus, regardless of what Underworld is being created, significant events recur at certain tzolkin energies in all of the Creation Cycles. Thus, the impulses to both the German Reformation and the Harmonic Convergence were provided by 1 Men and manifested on 2 Cib. In this way there are specific piktuns, baktuns, katuns and tuns in the Major creation cycles that correspond to specific combinations in the tzolkin count. Thus, the day-by-day tzolkin count in the bottom row is a temporal microcosm of the longer tun based creation cycles above.

The Mayan Calendar

of the major tun-based creation cycles, since these can all be divided into 260 periods of equal duration. Thus, for instance, the National (Great) Cycle may be divided into 260 katuns and the Planetary Cycle into 260 tuns, either of which may be combined with the 260 combinations of the tzolkin. *Thus, at its core the tzolkin is time-less.* It is a filtration pattern of divine Light that may be combined with a range of different time periods—alautuns, baktuns, katuns, days, etc.—to produce creation cycles.

To exemplify this reasoning, the tzolkin combination 2 Cib corresponds to the katun 1519-1539 in the National Cycle and the tun 1986-1987 in the Planetary Cycle. The particular energy of 2 Cib was then what in the National Cycle brought about the German Reformation and in the Planetary the Harmonic Convergence, and in this way we may see that phenomena occurring at quite different times are energetically related. On a much lower level in the temporal hierarchy, the dates March 26 and December 11, 1998 also had the tzolkin energies of 2 Cib. This means that the same tzolkin energy is also expressed on singular dates, but this is only like ripples on the surface of the great waves of Creation.

To discuss how the filtration pattern in Figure 89 is playing out in all its complexity is beyond the scope of this book. We will only take a brief look in Figure 90 at what dividing the 260 units of the tzolkin into four segments of 65 units means, and how this subdivision manifests at different occasions in these major creation cycles. Applied to the Planetary Cycle this means that the years 1755, 1819, 1883 and 1947 would correspond to the beginning of such segments of 65 tuns each. These segments may be regarded as a filtration pattern that prepares for the upcoming Galactic Cycle, overlapping cycles that may be called pre-Galactic Cycles, which prepare us for the type of consciousness that this will bring. It is then especially noteworthy that 1947 was the year of the first UFO frenzy. This was very likely because at this time the holographic projections of the galactic disc, heralding the coming galactic consciousness, first became visible.

Two other things emerging at the same time also clearly show that during the last 65 tuns of the Planetary Cycle a galactic frame of consciousness comes into play. The first is the invention of computers in the years 1946-1948 and the other is the discovery by Oswald Avery through a transfection (genetic manipulation) experiment that DNA preserves the genetic information. At the time both these things were hardly noted by a wider public, but as the real Galactic Cycle began in 1999 the developments these initial occurrences had led to, the Internet and genetic manipulation, were topics of discussion in very many places.

The last 65-unit segment of the National Cycle—that starting to prepare for the Planetary Cycle—began in AD 730. It manifested in the defeat of the Muslims at Poitiers in AD 732. This was the first time the Papacy called its inhabitants to the defense of Europe against the Muslims and as a result of the outcome of this battle it gained some ground to stand on. Following this it rose to a power seen as standing above the various competing national interests in Europe. The fact that a power emerged that was seen as standing above the national interests attests to the fact that a pre-Planetary Cycle began. Considering that the pre-Planetary Cycles were ruled by the same distribution of LIGHT as the Planetary Cycle (Figure 29), it becomes logical that the Mayan seers keeping track of the movements of Quetzalcoatl at this point became confused. Although it was not until the mid eighteenth century that the tun-based Mayan calendars went completely out of use, their deterioration began much earlier, from AD 730 and onwards, in parallel with the general demise of their Classical culture.

Such segments of 65 tuns that we have here hinted at for the Planetary and National Cycles may in turn each also be divided into five segments of 13 tuns, corresponding in Figure 89 to the segments 20 × 13. The last of these periods began in 1986, which was about the time when the New Age movement turned more galactic in character, for instance at the Harmonic Convergence. These periods of 13 tuns may be seen as preparatory Galactic Cycles increasing in importance until the real Galactic Cycle began on January 5, 1999. Again, it is not the purpose here to present a time map of creation at this level of detail, only to indicate that it is indeed possible to construct one.

As a reflection of these processes in divine creation the Maya would also especially celebrate every 65 days of the tzolkin count. Curiously, as pointed out by Bruce Scofield, these so-called burner days do not coincide with the division of the tzolkin presented in Figure 90 beginning with 1 Imix (and yet there is very strong evidence from Classical times that this was indeed the beginning day of the tzolkin). Instead these celebrations had a rhythm of their own and were marked by the days 4 Ahau, 4 Chicchan, 4 Oc and 4 Men. A possible explanation of this rhythm is that the beginning of the rule of Quetzalcoatl (breakthrough to Christ consciousness) was considered so powerful that it created a rhythm of its own, prepared for on the day 4 Ahau.

As a final observation we may note in Figure 89 that as the tzolkin comes to its last unit, called 13 Ahau, no filters of DARKNESS are obstructing the passage of divine LIGHT. Thus, as we arrive at the completion of creation in the year 2011, when all the Nine Underworlds will have progressed to the unit 13 Ahau, the divine reality will be clearly visible, and our vision will be unobscured by darkening filters. At that point we will simply know the truth and there will be no need for explanations. This truth will be evident as we see the LIGHT of God. To the advanced reader studying the appendices it may therefore be suggested that what creation is all about is not really introducing Heavens in the Cosmic Projector, but rather about step by step removing darkening filters that are there to begin with.

APPENDIX II
THE CORRELATION OF THE TUN-BASED CALENDRICAL SYSTEM WITH THE DIVINE PROCESS OF CREATION— WHY THE DIVINE PROCESS OF CREATION IS COMPLETED ON OCTOBER 28, 2011

You corn kernels, you coral seeds, you days,
you lots, may you succeed, may you be accurate,
Popol-Vuh

In the *Popol-Vuh,* it is recounted how the gods would pray before the mouth and face of the Plumed Serpent for what had been created, the human beings. A few creations had failed before the present one because the human beings had not then kept the days of the gods. Why would it be so important to use a correct calendar, and why have the Quiché Maya, authors of the *Popol-Vuh,* kept an unbroken tzolkin count all the way from before the Classical era to the present time? Placing such an emphasis on a calendar is a fairly different approach from the one taken by us in modern society, who tend to regard the choice of calendar as an arbitrary one with little impact on life. But it may be that for us also keeping the days of the gods could be a way of saving life on earth. If so, we need to take a look at the nature of the true tzolkin count and the so-called correlation question of the Long Count.

For a long time, the question of how the Mayan Long Count was to be correlated with the Gregorian calendar seemed to be a hair-splitting issue that was of interest only to professional Mayanists, who would sometimes spend long nights in libraries or in hidden temples to find the crucial dates that would provide the keys to this correlation. The origin of this problem is that as the Spanish came to the land of the Maya the latter had already abandoned the use of the Long Count. Thus, there is no instance of a Long Count date that was written also as a Gregorian (or Julian) date, which means that this correlation problem has had to be solved by indirect methods. This is not the place to discuss how the problem was solved, but only to point out that these very technical questions about the correlation of different calendars have, relatively suddenly and unexpectedly, become an issue of critical importance to the future of humanity. If it is true, as the *Popol-Vuh* says, that a creation may fail because the human beings do not observe the days of the gods, then the use of the correct calibration between the ancient Mayan calendars and our present physical calendar becomes one of paramount importance. These questions then need to be brought out of the research libraries to the public at large, which in turn will have a responsibility to take an informed stand in the matter.

Throughout this book, I have been using the so-called 584,283 correlation, according to which the day 0.0.0.0.0 4 Ahau 8 Cumku, the beginning of the Long Count, is identical to the day August 11, 3114 BC in the Gregorian calendar. This, the GMT or Thompson correlation, is the correlation accepted by most researchers, and many groups of Maya still today follow a tzolkin count that conforms to it. The beginning days, 1 Imix, of this Classical tzolkin count in the years to come were given in Table 17.

A significant minority of researchers, however, adhere to the 584,285 correlation, which would identify the same creation day as August 13, 3114 BC. This would place the Classical tzolkin count two days out of phase with the one still in use among the Maya, but would have the advantage of placing the creation day on August 13. This would be attractive because there is evidence that the Classical Maya considered the day falling 52 days after summer solstice, i.e., August 13 in the Gregorian calendar, as the day of creation. Such evidence is provided by the many alignments of pyramids and buildings pointing to this particular day of the solar year described in Vincent Malmström's *Cycles of the Sun, Mysteries of the Moon*.

So there seems to be a discrepancy here. While most groups of Maya today follow a tzolkin count which would make the day August 11, 3114 BC the creation day 4 Ahau, there is considerable evidence that the Maya thought that the day (corresponding in the solar year to) August 13 was when creation took place. The likely resolution to this discrepancy is that the 584,283 count is the correct correlation between the Long Count and the Gregorian calendar, although the Maya who developed the Long Count some time prior to the birth of Christ had in fact aimed for it to begin on August 13, 3114 BC. The reason they missed the creation day they had aimed for, August 13, and instead hit on August 11, 3114 BC, may have been a slight error in their estimate of the duration of the solar year. This error was also magnified by an extrapolation to a point three thousand years into the past. An error of two days in three thousand years is, however, a very small error indeed and we should rather be amazed at the astronomical accuracy of a people living around the time of Christ than be surprised that their calculations show a small error. For this reason I will maintain, with the majority of researchers today, that the tzolkin count used by the majority of Maya living today is a straight unbroken continuation of that used by the Classical Maya.

But is the traditional tzolkin the true count? Is it, in other words, true in a deeper sense than mere tradition? Is the traditional tzolkin a true microcosm of the divine process of Creation, and hence an exact overtone of the 13 × 20 katuns of the Great Cycle? If the Great Cycle really reflects vibrations generated by the World Tree, then there can only be one true tzolkin count, the one which is an exact overtone of the Great Cycle, and the question is then whether the traditional count is that true count. Of course, we have reasons to believe that the Classical Maya were in a more advanced resonance with the Cosmos than we are today. Judging from this, and the fact that they were able to calibrate the wriggling movements of Quetzalcoatl in a way that has not been possible in recent centuries, we have reasons to take the traditional count seriously and propose that it indeed is the true count. In recent years, furthermore, there was one instance where the accuracy of the Classical count seems to have been verified, namely in the so-called Harmonic Convergence. This was an event that was widely celebrated by meditations and other spiritual ceremonies on the Gregorian days August 16-17,1987. The amount of convergence on exactly these dates may partly be explained by the fact that they concurred with the first two days, 1 Imix and 2 Ik, in the traditional tzolkin count (the other part is explained in Appendix I). Thus, according to the Classical count, those two days should have meant the beginning of a 260-day period of rebirth, and many would probably intuitively agree that it was. Although it was only known by a few at the time that the Harmonic Convergence fell on the two first days of a tzolkin round, this event may be seen as the first step in humanity's not always straight path toward recovering the true tzolkin count.

If we may thus identify the traditional tzolkin count as the true count, we have come a long way in having a basis for the calendar of the future. All Mayan day-keepers seem to agree that the tzolkin is the master calendar, the one that all the others revolve around and are correlated with, and from this we may understand their faithfulness in keeping the sacred calendar—the days of the gods. Using a true tzolkin count is thus crucial for us when developing a calendar for the future. However, when it comes to developing a true non-physical calendar the most important correlation problem still remains. This is whether the Mayan Long Count, going back to August 11, 3114 BC and ending on December 21, AD 2012, is an exact calibration of the seven DAYS and six NIGHTS of divine Creation. I have already previously hinted that there are very strong and compelling reasons to believe that it is not, and that instead the divine process of Creation is going toward its completion on October 28, 2011. I will summarize some of these arguments below.

First, the Long Count is believed to have been implemented in the pre-Classical site of Izapa on the Pacific coast of Mexico. The most likely explanation to why the date August 11 was chosen as the beginning of the Long Count is that this was the day of solar zenith in Izapa. It is known that the dates of solar zenith were of paramount importance to the Maya. The solar zenith would in fact be the most natural day to start counting time in a tropical region. The date of July 26, for instance, which in later times among the Maya seems to have been celebrated as a new year's day, goes back to a solar zenith, the one of the location of Edzna on the Yucatan peninsula. Since, however, Izapa was one of the oldest Mayan sites—where time was considered to have begun—the date August 11 may have come to be regarded as holy, and thus impossible to change because of the strong tradition backing it up. (We may consider that it would not be so easy for someone living today to change the day of celebrating Christmas even if it became known with certainty that Jesus was not born on this particular day.)

Of course, if the beginning date of the Long Count was set at the day corresponding to August 11 because this was the day of solar zenith in Izapa, then we know for certain that this could not be the correct beginning date for the Great Cycle. If, as the inscriptions in Palenque state, its beginning was set by the day that the First Father raised the World Tree, which is galactic in nature, we have to widen the perspective from Izapa. If the Great Cycle is a divine, non-physical creation cycle affecting the whole planet synchronistically, then there is no reason to believe that this should begin on the day that the sun is in zenith in Izapa, Edzna or anywhere else for that matter. We would then have to assume that the beginning date of the Long Count, August 11, was set on the basis of the particular location of the Izapans, who, like everyone else in these early days, lived under the illusion that they were living at the center of the world. This would then mean that the Long Count does not describe the Great Cycle exactly. Hence, we would have to conclude that both the date set for the beginning of the Long Count, and the date when as a consequence it happens to end, December 21, 2012, were based on this local perspective of the Izapans.

There is, however, another equally strong piece of evidence that the Great Cycle did not begin on August 11, 3114 BC and will not end on December 21, AD 2012. This is that these two dates fall on days that are 4 Ahau in the Classical tzolkin count. But if the traditional tzolkin is true and if it is a temporal microcosm of the Great Cycle, then the Great Cycle needs to end on a day that is 13 Ahau, not 4 Ahau. This is because there are exactly 7200 tzolkin rounds in this creation cycle. If the 260-day tzolkin count is a true temporal microcosm, a true overtone of the vibrations of the World Tree generating the Great Cycle, the Great Cycle would have to begin on the same day, 13 Ahau, as a tzolkin round does (there are $7200 \times 260 = 5200 \times 360 = 1,872,000$ days in the Great Cycle). This means that the Great Cycle has to begin (and end) on a day which is 13 Ahau and not 4 Ahau, as is the case with the Long Count. Taken together, the two arguments seem to imply that the Long Count is not an exact calibration of the Great Cycle. If, indeed, it is true as it is said by Mayan day-keepers that the purpose of the tzolkin is to serve as a hub for all calendar cycles, then the tzolkin must have the last say, and hence the true Great Cycle must begin on a day that is 13 Ahau in the tzolkin count.

While this discussion may seem very technical to the modern reader who may be unsure as to the value of using a spiritual calendar to begin with, it seems obvious that the ancient Maya were very much concerned with these types of questions. Is there then no indication from Classical times that the Maya had a sense that there might have been something wrong with the day that had been set as the beginning of the Long Count? Well, in the creation story of Palenque, written maybe a thousand years after the Long Count was devised, and when the Mayan day-keepers had accumulated considerable calendrical knowledge compared to the early days of Izapa, there is indeed such an indication. This is in the description of the birth of First Father, which is said to have taken place June 16, 3122 BC, that is, more than eight years before the beginning of the Long Count. Yet when the inscription states what the First Father did on the date of the beginning of the Long Count it uses a glyph that normally was used when indicating the celebration of the seventh birthday of a king. It is then interesting to note that if we add seven, instead of eight, years to the date of birth of the First Father we arrive at June 16, 3115 BC. Since the following day, June 17, 3115 BC, is 13 Ahau in the Classical tzolkin count, this would indeed qualify as a possible beginning of the Great Cycle. We may now wonder if the scribes and priest-astronomers of Palenque who built the Group of the Cross had become aware that there was something wrong with the

Long Count, based on their observations of the wrigglings of Quetzalcoatl, but chose to communicate this in a very subtle way so as not to upset the thousand-year-old tradition of the by then strongly ingrained Long Count. Thus, there is a possible alternative candidate for the beginning of the Great Cycle in the Gregorian date June 17, 3115 BC, which would place the completion of this cycle, and the completion of all of creation, on the day 13 Ahau, October 28, AD 2011.

In the era in which the Maya lived the need to know exactly when the Great Cycle began, however, may not have been as critically important an issue as it is today. In Classical times the evolution of the divine plan was predominantly determined by a baktun rhythm of approximately four hundred years, and an error of a year or so may then have been of less importance. Today, however, as creation is about to enter a tun-based rhythm, an error of more than a year makes a significant difference, and during the Galactic Cycle it would bring people completely out of phase with the divine process of Creation.

To finally resolve the issue and identify the day when the Great Cycle ends, however, we will need some kind of empirical evidence to back up the new correlation. Since Europe is the part of the world that is most immediately affected by the wave generator of the True Cross, it seems likely that this is where we should first look for evidence. Also, since the frequency of the process of creation is now speeding up, our best chances of finding crucial events that would correlate exactly with the divine process of Creation is in recent times. As European unification is one of the most important processes that have prepared for the Galactic Cycle, I have compared the dates of some important events in this process with the dates for some critical cycle shifts. These dates have been calculated on the assumption that the Great Cycle, and indeed all of creation, will be completed on the Gregorian day October 28, 2011:

Planetary Cycle	Beginning date	Historical event
katun 10	Sep. 5, 1952	Decision to create a European political union (Sep. 10, 1952)
katun 11	May 25, 1972	Beginning of monetary convergence (March 21, 1972)
katun 12	Feb. 10, 1992	Decision to create monetary union, Maastricht Treaty (Feb. 7, 1992)
Galactic Cycle		
tun 0	Jan. 4, 1999	Euro goes into effect (Jan. 4, 1999)

The last two dates—for the signing and then the implementation of the Maastricht Treaty—conform extremely well with the relevant cycle shift calculated on the assumption that the major creation cycles are going toward their completion on October 28, 2011. Similarly, a detailed study of Hitler's rise to power, leading to a perverted attempt at European unification, shows very clearly that the decisive shift took place right at the beginning of the fifth NIGHT of the Planetary Cycle, the one ruled by the god of darkness. Since during the National Cycle it was under the vertical arm of the True Cross that events most closely followed cycle shifts, there are reasons to take this information very seriously as a basis for calibrating the process of creation with the Gregorian calendar.

Fig. 91 Inscription of Long Count date (9.12.6. 5.8 3 Lamat) from the Classical era. At the top is the glyph signifying a Long Count date, and below follow the various number of baktuns, etc.

We may also notice another thing in this regard: Several people who lack a scholarly background in Mayanism, but have intuitively sensed the reality of the Mayan calendar, have placed the end of the Great Cycle in the year 2011 rather than in 2012. Thus, Frank Waters, although a scholar himself, inaccurately gave the ending date of the Great Cycle as December 24, 2011, and it seems that following his lead Peter Balin and Ken Carey both gave its date of ending as December 21, 2011. Solara placed it on December 31, 2011 (she also set the so-called 11:11 event on January 11, 1992, only one month short of the beginning of the seventh day of the Planetary Cycle). Although these dates may all go back to an error in calculation, our reasoning above seems to indicate that this error was reminiscent of a Freudian slip, an error that contained more of the truth than the formally correct version. As we progress more deeply into the Galactic Cycle and its inherent rhythm becomes more strongly experienced, this question is likely to be automatically resolved.

The Mayan Calendar

APPENDIX III
HOW TO CALCULATE YOUR
SPIRITUAL BIRTHDAY AND TZOLKIN DAY

Spiritual birthday example: Suppose you were born on the Gregorian date October 3, 1960. Then, from Tables 21a and 21b, add 21915 + 470 + 3 = 22,388. Dividing this by 360 gives 22,388/360 = 62.1888. Subtract the integer part and multiply the remaining decimal part by 360 to obtain 0.1888 × 360 = 68. To know on what date your spiritual birthday will fall in the year 1999, begin at the first day of the tun (January 5, 1999; see Table 15) and count until you come to day number 68, which happens on the day March 13, 1999. Of course, the Gregorian date of the spiritual birthday will vary from year to year, and you will have to repeat the calculation based on the different beginning dates in Table 15.

Remember to calculate Mayan birthdays on the basis of your time of birth in Central Standard Time. Thus, if you were born in England before 6 a.m. you should consider yourself as born the day before the date you were born in England.

Table 21a
Day Numbers Corresponding to the
Last Two Digits in the Gregorian Year

Year	Day #	Year	Day #	Year	Day #	Year	Day #
1900	0	1918	6574	1936	13149	1954	19723
1901	365	1919	6939	1937	13514	1955	20088
1902	730	1920	7305	1938	13879	1956	20454
1903	1095	1921	7670	1939	14244	1957	20819
1904	1461	1922	8035	1940	14610	1958	21184
1905	1826	1923	8400	1941	14975	1959	21549
1906	2191	1924	8766	1942	15340	1960	21915
1907	2556	1925	9131	1943	15705	1961	22280
1908	2922	1926	9496	1944	16071	1962	22645
1909	3287	1927	9861	1945	16436	1963	23010
1910	3652	1928	10227	1946	16801	1964	23376
1911	4017	1929	10592	1947	17166	1965	23741
1912	4383	1930	10957	1948	17532	1966	24106
1913	4748	1931	11322	1949	17897	1967	24471
1914	5113	1932	11688	1950	18262	1968	24837
1915	5478	1933	12053	1951	18627	1969	25202
1916	5844	1934	12418	1952	18993	1970	25567
1917	6209	1935	12783	1953	19358	1971	25932

1972	26298	1982	29950	1992	33603	2002	37255
1973	26663	1983	30315	1993	33968	2003	37620
1974	27028	1984	30681	1994	34333	2004	37986
1975	27393	1985	31046	1995	34698	2005	38351
1976	27759	1986	31411	1996	35064	2006	38716
1977	28124	1987	31776	1997	35429	2007	39081
1978	28489	1988	32142	1998	35794	2008	39477
1979	28854	1989	32507	1999	36159	2009	39812
1980	29220	1990	32872	2000	36525	2010	40177
1981	29585	1991	33237	2001	36890	2011	40542

Table 21b and c
Day Numbers for Calculating the Tun or Tzolkin Birthday
Corresponding to Different Months of the Gregorian Year

Month	21b Tun	21c Tzolkin
January	197	237
January (leap year)	196	236
February	228	268
February (leap year)	227	267
March	256	296
April	287	327
May	317	357
June	348	388
July	378	418
August	409	449
September	440	480
October	470	510
November	501	541
December	531	571

Tzolkin day example:
Suppose you were born on January 19, 1960 and want to know what day this corresponds to in the tzolkin. Then add 21,915 + 236 (1960 was a leap year) + 19 = 22,170 from Tables 21a and 21c. Divide this number by 260 to obtain 22,170/260 = 85.2692. Subtract the integer part and multiply by 260, giving: 0.2692 × 260 = 70. In Table 16 you will find that tzolkin unit number 70 corresponds to 5 Oc. If you count from the beginning of the tzolkin round starting on January 5, 1999 (Table 17) you will find that 5 Oc in the year 1999 falls on March 15. To find such Gregorian dates you may also consult a Classical Mayan calendar, computer programs, web sites or Conversion Codices. Again remember to make corrections if you were not born in Central Standard Time.

The Mayan Calendar

Note: Your spiritual birthday will always fall on a day that is dominated by the same glyph as your tzolkin day. Thus, the person born on January 19, 1960 will have her spiritual birthday on day number 170 in the tun, which is the day June 23, 1999 (0.8.10 in the Galactic Cycle). This day is 1 Oc in the tzolkin count, which means that it falls on a day that is governed by the same glyph, Oc, but not on the same number, as her tzolkin day of birth.

The spiritual birthday and the tzolkin day have fundamentally different meanings. While the tzolkin day represents the energy of the particular day we were born, which in one way or another sets the themes of our lives, the spiritual birthday marks the beginning of a new 360-day phase of life, which then may be either LIGHT or DARK, representing movement forward or rest, respectively.

The interpretation of the tzolkin day of birth is outside the scope of this book, and the interested reader is referred either to Bruce Scofield's or Kenneth Johnson's books in the bibliography. In daily life the tzolkin has served several different functions among the Maya, as 'astrology,' for the religious festivities, to follow the changing energies of the days and for divination. Those interested in consciously seeking to come in phase with the tzolkin may choose several different ways. Meditating on the day signs is one; listening to one of thirteen tones on a meditative tape or using aromatic essences on different days are others. The Aztecs used to have a diet that prescribed eating certain kinds of food on each of the day signs. It is a free-for-all!

THE CLASSICAL MAYAN TZOLKIN COUNT AND THE DREAMSPELL ARE LINKED TO DIFFERENT CONCEPTS OF TIME

In the past decade interest in the calendars of the Maya has increased worldwide. Ultimately, this is because a new consciousness of time is now emerging. A new age gives rise to a new consciousness of time, which in turn requires a new calendar for this to be expressed. Anyone who takes an interest in the ancient culture of the Maya will soon realize that this people had an understanding of time that was vastly different from our own. Many have come to use it for their own spiritual evolution, and so the Mayan calendar has again come into use in the modern world.

But what then is the Mayan calendar? It turns out this is not as unambiguous as one might think. The so-called day-keepers in Guatemala and Mexico use some twenty different calendars in parallel. Moreover, through the ages these have undergone significant change. For instance, no inscriptions of the chronology of the ancient Maya, the so-called Long Count starting on August 11, 3114 BC and ending on December 21, 2012, have been found that were made after the tenth century AD. The fact that they abandoned this calendar gives us reason to suspect that also the consciousness of time of the Maya underwent some significant change since the Classical culture reigned between AD 200 and 800. What this all means is that there hardly exists such a thing as a Mayan calendar cut in stone for us simply to assimilate. And even the Classical tzolkin count has been lost among some groups of Maya, giving the false impression that there is no True Count.

Regarding calendars used on a daily basis, it was the calendar—inspired by the Maya—launched by José Argüelles in 1990 that went by the name of Dreamspell that first came to be used in the modern world. José and his wife Lloydine asserted that the planet was threatened by an environmental catastrophe because of our use of the Gregorian calendar. As an alternative they suggested a calendar based on 13 moons each of 28 days plus an extra day, July 25, outside of time (13 × 28 + 1 = 365). In their system the leap day every fourth solar year was simply ignored, apparently to keep the ideal of 13 × 28 intact. These thirteen moons were then linked to a special tzolkin count (260 different combinations of thirteen numbers and twenty different glyphs) in which each individual could find his or her 'Galactic Signature.' The idea underlying the Dreamspell seems to have been that if human beings lived in phase with the natural cycles, in this case probably primarily the female cycle of about 28 days, we would treat the earth better and thus avoid an impending catastrophe. This idea may have attracted some, but certainly many more were attracted by the idea that the particular day on which they were born had an inherent energy described by their Galactic Signature, that is, tzolkin day. This latter idea certainly had support from the notions of the Maya, in principle.

There was, however, a very significant problem with the Dreamspell. The Maya had never used the particular tzolkin count that was linked to it. The Argüelles had simply invented their own tzolkin count, apparently thinking that this was an arbitrary matter. Yet many of the followers of Dreamspell, mostly for lack of knowledge, simply presented Dreamspell as the Mayan calendar. Many have thus been deluded into thinking that the Galactic Signature they had been assigned was the one the Maya would have used. This was highlighted as the so-called True Count debate raged on the Internet in 1995, where especially John Major Jenkins energetically asserted that Argüelles' count was false and that it had never been used by the Mayan people themselves. In addition, there still existed a tzolkin count, which in Classical times had been used throughout the entire Mesoamerican region and had survived until today in the highlands of Guatemala and elsewhere among the Mayan day-keepers. Jenkins stated, and I think rightly so, that Argüelles' followers had no right to present the Dreamspell count as the calendar of the Maya and that it was a kind of cultural imperialism to ignore the 'surviving' sacred calendar that was still in use.

The Council of Elders of the Quiché-Maya in Guatemala has also strongly spoken out against Argüelles' calendar being called the Mayan calendar. Argüelles' response to this criticism seems to have passed through two different phases. His initial response was to claim that he had received his calendar by divine revelation. Since he saw himself as an incarnation of Pacal Votan, everything he did was supposedly in accordance with the divine plan. To my knowledge he never responded in a direct way to the issues of authenticity raised. During this period Argüelles developed something of a cult around his own person, and this cult certainly did not encourage his followers to find out the truth for themselves.

As we discuss a new calendar for the future, however, I believe that it is most important to specify what the purpose of this calendar and chronology should be. Unless we do so we may either run into the kind of pie throwing that was typical of the True Count debate or become resigned to an attitude that has become common today, to claim that 'anything goes.' (But then, if there is no True Count, what value would there be in following any tzolkin count?)

I feel, however, that it is important to realize the predominant role of the tzolkin for developing a Mayan calendar for the future. It seems that without exception Mayan day-keepers maintain that the tzolkin count is the hub around which all other calendrical cycles turn. The tzolkin has been regarded as the master calendar around which all the others revolve. If it is true that the tzolkin count plays such a crucial role, then the consequence if we desert it would be that our calendrical system could end up anywhere. Unless we respect the sacred calendar—and its divine origin—there will be no hub keeping the various other calendars in phase with the cosmic energies.

A clear example can be given of this. Many people have become fascinated by the fact that the Mayan Long Count ends in the year 2012, sensing that this may be a time of fundamental importance to humanity. And, as we have seen, the

Mayan Long Count is a fairly exact calibration of the process of evolution of the human consciousness. This Long Count calendar is, however, directly linked to a certain tzolkin count, the Classical, meaning that it is only those that respect this hub of the calendars who will be in phase with the particular evolution of consciousness that the Long Count carries. If we instead choose to use another tzolkin count than the Classical, we will not be able to logically integrate the divine creation cycles in our thinking and we will thus miss the whole point of the spiritual calendars of the Maya—the possibility of being in phase with the ascension of humanity.

What then is the purpose of calendars? During the last five thousand years they have had an important purpose in aiding people in keeping track of the agricultural year. For this purpose a calendar based on astronomical observations, and an exact determination of the duration of the solar year, 365.2422 years, seems natural. A calendar that follows the astronomical year is useful for telling us when to sow and harvest, etc. The Gregorian calendar, for one, fulfills this purpose very well, and with the beginning of the last, twentieth century, it provided the basis for practical farmer's almanacs. The same may be said also about a frozen haab, which is a Mayan calendar that is made up of 18 uinals of 20 days plus the 5 extra days, the vayeb, when the gods rested (18 × 20 + 5 = 365). The thirteen moons of Dreamspell (13 × 28 + 1) fulfills the purpose of a calendar for the seasonal changes equally well. It is, however, questionable if either the haab or the thirteen moons has anything to offer that goes beyond the Gregorian calendar when it comes to following the seasons or in aiding agriculture. I would say they do not.

In contrast to physical calendars, the emphasis in this book has been on spiritual cycles based on the 360-day period followed in ancient times by many cultures in parallel with their agricultural calendars. The 360-day period of the tun is a key unit for the evolution of consciousness, and increasingly higher levels of human consciousness evolve according to rhythms given by different multiples of the tun. Thus, the frequency of creation increases step by step with each new level of consciousness in a pyramidal structure. Only calendars that are constructed in accordance with such a hierarchical structure of time cycles, however, can create an understanding of the evolution of consciousness. Calendars that are based on an endless repetition of, for instance, the 28-day period or the 365-day period, on the other hand, will always lead to a linear concept of time, and if such time periods are locked with the material reality, which they mostly are, they cannot reflect the frequency increase.

To return to the issue of the Dreamspell calendar, then, it is a highly telling detail that this simply omits the leap day every fourth year. What this would mean is that this particular day would lack a special tzolkin energy of its own. Or, in other words, since the tzolkin is a microcosm of the divine plan, this day would not be part of this plan. To a Mayan day-keeper it would be unthinkable to have a day without energy. While the leap day may seem like a small detail, it highlights that in the Dreamspell concept of time matter is considered as primary to consciousness rather than the other way around. In the Dreamspell calendar it is apparently more important to follow the physical cycles than the divine, and so it loses one day in relation to the True Mayan tzolkin count every four years. In reality, of course, the leap day is also part of the divine plan and of the energy sequence of the tzolkin. In this we may see the paramount importance of the tzolkin count as the hub of a cogwheel mechanism. If someone puts sticks in the hub, soon the whole mechanism will be out of order. Following calendars based on the material reality, such as the Gregorian, the haab or the thirteen moons, can only result in keeping us fettered to materialist concepts of time and thus remaining blind to the divine plan.

PRECESSION VS. DIVINE CREATION—WHAT IS DRIVING THE EVOLUTION OF CONSCIOUSNESS DESCRIBED BY THE MAYAN CALENDAR?

How is the Mayan Long Count to be explained? Why did this ancient people, who were the most mathematically advanced of their day, choose to use a chronology that consisted of thirteen different periods of 144,000 days each, starting on August 11, 3114 BC and ending on December 21, AD 2012? On a more fundamental level, three different types of answers have been given to this question, a materialist, a spiritual and what might be called a pseudo-spiritual, answers that are linked to different world views. In the materialist world view the astronomical, physical cycles are seen as primary to the spiritual, whereas in the spiritual world view they are seen as secondary.

The first type of answer is the standard anthropological explanation that says that the beginning date for the Long Count was chosen because of some myth that lacked a real meaning. The choice of baktuns, katuns, tuns, etc., for following time is then simply explained by the Mayan way of counting, which used twenty as a base. According to this line of reasoning they chose the number 20 as the basis for counting because it corresponds to the sum of fingers and toes on a human being. And in this view the celebration of katun shifts, etc., is in principle no different from our own celebrations of century and millennium shifts. The tzolkin, intimately linked to and synchronized with the Long Count, is seen as a reflection of the human gestation period rather than the other way around. This may be described as the standard academic view. It is also a materialist view, where the Long Count is seen as merely a way of keeping track of physical time, where the counting system is seen as based on material factors such as the number of toes, fingers, etc.

The first suggestions in modern times that the Mayan calendar was really a reflection of changing ages were probably those forwarded by Frank Waters in his *Mexico Mystique* of 1975 and by Peter Balin in his *Flight of the Feathered Serpent* in the same year. Balin saw the Venus passages at the end of the Cycle, while Waters sought explanations to the beginning and ending dates of the Long Count in their horoscopes. Nonetheless, Waters made the crucial observation that the beginning date of the Long Count was not all that different from the beginning of the Jewish calendar. He also pointed out that this was the time when the first higher civilizations emerged on this planet. These were very important steps toward finding the basis in reality of the Mayan calendar.

José Argüelles took the next major step in *The Mayan Factor*, where he outlined several crucial ideas for the future understanding of the Mayan calendar. There he emphasized the Mayan cycles of 260 and 360 days, and the fact that these lacked physical correspondents. He also suggested that human history was the result of a galactic beam of thirteen baktuns that created the seasons of human history, and made an initial description of how this manifested. In this, Argüelles took major steps away from the astrological perspective toward a spiritual explanation, where the archetypal influences of the tzolkin symbols were seen as playing a primary role. His explanation of why the Great Cycle had started at the point that it did was vague, however, and implied the existence of some kind of active seeding by a galactic federation, rather than an evolving divine plan. Argüelles was the first in modern times to systematically work on the deeper meaning of the Mayan calendar and presented an alternative interpretation to that of the academic by suggesting that the Great Cycle caused the spiritual evolution of humanity. This line of thinking may be called the spiritual interpretation of the Mayan calendar.

The present work essentially belongs to the same paradigm, but introduces three key facets that are crucial for our understanding of the Mayan calendar. First, it shows that the Great Cycle is just one of nine different major creation cycles, where the first goes all the way back to the Big Bang. Second, it identifies the holographic projections of the World Tree on the galactic, planetary and human levels. Third, it unifies the Mayan calendar with the Old World Creation story and so identifies the thirteen Heavens of the Maya with the seven DAYS and six NIGHTS of God's Creation.

In addition to the materialist and spiritual, there is an explanation of the Mayan calendar that may be called the pseudo-spiritual. This recognizes the existence of different qualities and energies linked to the various time cycles of the Maya, but seeks to base these upon the physical reality. This is fairly common today, when we are all still affected by the materialist planetary frame of consciousness and a more spiritual galactic consciousness is only beginning to emerge. An example of such a pseudo-spiritual interpretation is Argüelles' later work with the Dreamspell, where he departs from the Mayan tzolkin count and places more emphasis on the astronomical year than on the spiritual qualities of the days.

Another example is provided by John Major Jenkins' book *Maya Cosmogenesis 2012*, in which the author seeks to ground the Mayan Great Cycle, and its changing energies, in the 26,000-year astronomical cycle that the earth undergoes because of precession. Both writers thus seek to adapt the spiritual cycles to the astronomical rather than the other way around, something that I believe can only lead to a dead end. The Dreamspell calendar was discussed in Appendix IV and the present appendix will be devoted to Jenkins' theories and the astrological Doctrine of the World Ages generally. The three types of explanations, the materialist, the spiritual and the pseudo-spiritual, have widely different consequences, and for this reason this is not a question of merely an academic interest.

Before discussing precession, however, I would like to give some words of praise for some of Jenkins' work. First of all, Jenkins has made a significant contribution in clarifying the nature of the true tzolkin count, and he should to a large extent be credited with having exposed the nature of the Dreamspell as an invented count. His defense of the true 584,283 tzolkin count against academic aberrations is also impressive. Also, although he has developed his thinking outside of the beaten academic path, Jenkins knows the Maya and their myths and is very well versed in the literature about them.

Jenkins' idea in *Maya Cosmogenesis 2012* is essentially that the Maya had targeted the ending date of their Long Count, December 21, 2012, because a specific alignment between the midwinter solstice sun and the galactic center supposedly would occur then. Thus, they would have devised the Long Count calendar to describe the last in a series of five Great Cycles (together they have a duration of 25,626 years) that would reflect the precessional cycle of the earth, currently estimated at some 25,920 years. In his work, Jenkins then disregards the 5125-year-long Long Count actually used by the Maya and shifts his attention to the sum of five such cycles, amounting to a period of 25,625 years. The idea has caught on and many now seem to think that the Maya some twenty-five hundred years ago had determined the exact duration of the precessional cycle so that the Long Count ending date hit right at its end in the year 2012. To the many who believe in the astrological Doctrine of the World Ages this has had a strong appeal.

A discussion of precession and the astrological Doctrine of the World Ages is hence appropriate here. The phenomenon of the precession of the earth, resulting in the wobbling movement of its axis, was first described by the Babylonian Kidinnu in 315 BC and the Greek astronomer Hipparchus of Nicea in 130 BC. It seems likely, however, that a drift in the position of stars had been noted even earlier; very likely, as human beings gained a long-term consciousness of the passage of time around the beginning of baktun 6 (see Chapter 9), speculations about a possible link between the moving positions of the stars and the coming and going of ages began. There is no reason to believe that the Maya, who commonly aligned their buildings with the heliacal rising of stars, would be an exception to this awareness of the precession of the earth.

From the limited perspective of an inhabitant of this planet the precessional movement becomes apparent through the slow change in the points on the horizon where stars rise. This is generated by the slow wobbling movement of the earth's axis, which is similar to the circular movement of the axis of a spinning gyroscope (or bicycle wheel) that a force has been applied to. Our own situation on earth may then be likened to that of a flea living on a spinning gyroscope whose axis wobbles. Because of this wobbling movement, the outlook of the flea on the external world will gradually undergo change. Thus, the flea would experience a change in perspective when looking out, 'changing ages,' as the axis of the gyroscope would be pointing in different directions. This is a parallel to what the ancients did from their earth-centered perspective. The point to realize, however, is that these changing views of the ancients—or of the flea—do not bring about a change in consciousness. Precession only changes the external appearance of the sky.

There is thus nothing mystical about this movement, which is explained by Newton's law of gravitation. According to Newtonian mechanics the equation determining the precessional cycle of the earth is:

$$d(prec)sun/dt + d(prec)moon/dt = KPS \cos (eps)$$

where *eps* is the inclination of the earth's axis (23°) and *KPS* is an expression of the degree of bulging of the earth. What this equation means is that the duration of the precessional cycle is directly dependent on the masses and distances of the sun, moon and planets, the inclination of the earth's axis and its degree of bulging. (Mars, which is smaller than the earth and further from the sun, has a precessional cycle of some 170,000 years.) The duration of the precessional cycle is thus entirely based on physical factors, which may be calculated and explained by exactly the same equations that are used to place space probes on Mars, build skyscrapers, etc., and whose validity there is thus little reason to question. What this means is that if precession were behind the coming and going of ages, then inhabitants of a planet whose axis had another declination than our own would develop at a different rate than ourselves. On a planet with no inclination of the axis (and hence no precession) no evolution could take place. On a planet made from a non-bulging material (and hence no precession) no evolution could take place. A planet with no moon would have a considerably slower precessional movement and hence a much slower rate of evolution of the consciousness of its inhabitants. From a creationist perspective it seems extremely unlikely that the evolution of consciousness should directly and proportionately depend on such physical factors. Yet the astrological Doctrine of the World Ages has been based on this astronomical movement. This doctrine states that as the polar axis shifts direction as a result of the precessional movement, the vernal point will point toward the twelve different signs in the zodiac during eras each of 2,160 years. Each of these eras is then called an age, which carries certain qualities.

Three things stand out about this doctrine: (1) It is arbitrary. Thus, the vernal point at spring equinox determines the sign supposedly characterizing an age. But why spring equinox? If the autumn equinox was chosen another sign would rule the ages. Jenkins has chosen the midwinter solstice, which seemed to fit the Mayan ending date, but this is arbitrary too. Why not let the summer solstice determine the age? Similarly, the division of the zodiac into twelve signs is arbitrary in this context. The Maya divided the zodiac into thirteen different constellations, and the same is true for some recent astrologers who have introduced a thirteenth sign, Ophiucus. Thirteen signs would create different definitions of the ages. (2) The fact that ancient peoples may have speculated about a link between the earth's precession and the passing of ages does not prove that such a link exists. More likely, because the precessional cycle was the only physical evidence the ancients had of a time period of longer duration, and because of their belief system, according to which the changing positions of stars and planets in the sky influenced civilizational development, it seemed logical to them that the precessional movement causes the changing times. But this does not prove that this notion is true. It only explains why some ancient peoples might have thought so. And, really, no one has proved that precession has an effect on human consciousness. To provide such proof would mean to clearly show how the coming and going of ages is directly linked to the precessional cycle with an exactness on par with what has been shown here regarding the influence of the divine process of Creation on the different baktuns of the Great Cycle. Despite the lack of such evidence, the Doctrine of the World Ages has had a long history, and like a medieval papal doctrine the idea continues to live on. Since the early 1970s the notion of an approaching Age of Aquarius has been the very foundation of the New Age movement. (3) The astrological Doctrine of the World Ages is earth-centered rather than galactic. Thus, the coming and going of ages is believed to be determined by our own local solar system, since this is what determines the duration of the precessional cycle. In a galactic view, on the other hand, the earth is nothing but a holographic resonance projection of the entire galaxy, meaning that the spiritual cycles on earth have the same duration as the spiritual cycles in the galaxy and the universe at large. The spiritual cycles of the galaxy and the change in consciousness that they cause on earth is thus not dependent on the exact physical position of the earth in relation to the solar system or any other physical factor.

In *Maya Cosmogenesis 2012* Jenkins partly distances himself from the standard Old World Doctrine of the World Ages. Noting that the Maya divided the zodiac into thirteen rather than twelve constellations and that many astrological authorities place the advent of the Age of Aquarius several centuries into the future, Jenkins rejects this as the basis of the Mayan chronology. Following the lead of Terence McKenna, who wrote a foreword to his book, he instead comes to build almost his entire argument for the precessional theory on what he claims is a rare alignment of the midwinter solstice sun with the center of our galaxy at the ending date of the Long Count.

There are several serious problems with this interpretation. First, Jenkins argues that the Great Cycle was based on an event targeted at its ending date, rather than by its beginning date. The fact is, however, that the explanations we have from the ancient Maya, from the seventh century AD in the capital of Palenque, clearly do not describe events at the end of the Long Count but rather around its beginning in 3114 BC. And if we listen to what the Maya had to say about this creation date it makes sense from what we know actually happened in Sumer and Egypt at the time.

Already this highlights the strangest and most inexplicable omission in Jenkins' work—the total neglect of the Creation stories actually presented by the ancient Maya in Quirigua and Palenque. These describe Creation at the beginning of the Long Count, in 3114 BC, as it was viewed by the ancient Maya. Thus, if we want to understand the meaning of the Long Count I feel that one of the first places to go is to the accounts of the Maya themselves, which have been described in some detail by Schele and co-workers. But in Jenkins' hypothesis the beginning of the Long Count lacks meaning—it is nothing but the last fifth of a precessional cycle—and therefore he places the attention elsewhere. Nonetheless, I do not feel that the description of Creation in Palenque is something that serious research about the meaning of the Long Count can allow itself to overlook.

This omission is all the more serious because the evidence he presents to support his theses is his own interpretations of myths and steles. Interpretations of myths are, however, very shaky ground to build theories upon. In my own book I have presented very different interpretations of some of the myths that Jenkins uses. We can, however, never be certain as to the meaning the ancients placed on myths, and I do not claim that my interpretations of Mayan myths are exclusively correct.

Ancient myths often have several layers of meaning, and it may even be that the meaning of these has changed as the consciousness of human beings has evolved. A myth that meant a certain thing to the Maya of baktun 7 might have meant something entirely different to the Maya of baktun 10, not to mention Swedish scientists of baktun 12. Also, deep esoteric spiritual truths might have been popularized in materialist terms for broader layers of Mayan society to assimilate (something that, incidentally, also happens today as some seek astronomical explanations to spiritual cycles).

The ancients are not here to ask, so it would seem that we will never know exactly what their symbols and myths meant. What is unique about the ancient Maya, however, is that they have helped us understand their myths through the extensive use of dates. While an ancient myth may be ambiguous by itself a date is not, and a date means the same to us as it did to them. I would like to exemplify this with a myth discussed by Jenkins, the shooting of Seven-Macaw by the Hero Twins, Hunahpu and Xbalanque. While I interpret this as the seventh DAY of the Regional Cycle being brought to an end by the new yin/yang polarity initiating the beginning of the dualistic Great Cycle, Jenkins interprets Seven-Macaw as the Big Dipper, which begins to fall from its north pole location in the sky sometime around 1000 BC. Since anthropologists agree that the Maya identified SevenMacaw with the Big Dipper, it would at first seem that Jenkins has a strong case. But what if the fall of the Big Dipper from its polar position was just a way of popularizing the end of the seventh DAY of the Regional Cycle (I have already suggested that during NIGHTS the ancient Egyptians would be led into identifying the seven LIGHTS of a creation cycle with seven stars, and there is no reason why the ancient Maya would not have succumbed to the same type of illusion regarding the Big Dipper in the NIGHT of baktun 7). Thus, if Jenkins' interpretation were correct, we would expect that they would have dated the fall of Seven-Macaw to baktun 5, which is when the Big Dipper began to fall from its polar position. But in fact they do not. They date the fall of Seven-Macaw to May 26, 3149 BC, even before the present creation began with the First Father raising the World Tree, a date consistent with the seventh DAY of the Regional Cycle being brought to an end.

The neglect of the actual Mayan dates presented in the Creation stories is in my opinion very risky when it comes to interpreting them. To the Maya, time was holy, and they took adherence to date very seriously. To give another example of this, Jenkins interprets the rebirth of the First Father as a symbol of the midwinter sun being in the location of the galactic center at the end of the precessional cycle. In Palenque, however, it is described that this very rebirth took place on June 16, 3122 BC, which is before the beginning of the Long Count, and not at its end (nor does it fall on a midwinter solstice).

Instead of basing his work on the actual datings and descriptions presented by the Maya regarding the beginning of the Long Count, Jenkins devotes much space to arguing that the Maya knew about precession, and there is, at least in my own view, really no reason to doubt that they did. In the Mayan cities pyramids and other buildings were often aligned with the rising of certain stars, and as time went by they probably noted a precessional shift. But so what? Nowhere in the Mayan accounts from ancient times is a cycle of 26,000 years described. Nowhere! Is it then defendable to simply ignore their own accounts of Creation at the beginning of the Long Count? Moreover, if no one has ever demonstrated that precession has an influence on human consciousness, is it really meaningful to base a theory upon it?

Another Mayan mythological concept that is important to discuss is the World Tree. Jenkins suggests that this is formed by the cross of the ecliptic (local planetary component) and the equator of the Milky Way (galactic). But this interpretation is impossible. The ecliptic and the galactic midplane are at an angle of about 60° in relation to each other, and in *all* representations from the Maya the World Tree is formed by the perpendicular arms of a cross, which give rise to the four geographical directions on earth. I have seen no exception to representing the World Tree as a perpendicular cross, and if the World Tree were formed by the 60° angle of the ecliptic and the galactic midplane it could not be the source of the four perpendicular directions. Since our resonance with the World Tree is the very basis for our orientation in the world, a 60° World Tree would leave us very disoriented. The four perpendicular directions are part of a world view common to all Native American peoples, (see Gordon Brotherston, *Book of the Fourth World*) and Medicine Wheel ceremonies, for instance, are always based on the four perpendicular directions.

As Schele and co-workers point out, the ecliptic is, in the crosses of Palenque, instead symbolized by a snake twined around the perpendicular arms of the cross. The same symbolism, incidentally, is also present in ancient Nordic mythology, where Midgårdsormen (the middle area serpent) is symbolic of the ecliptic outside of the World Tree. It is not part of the World Tree. In reality, *the true Galactic Cross is invisible (it has no material manifestations) and is formed by the galactic midplane and a line perpendicular to it.* To realize this distinction between the double-headed serpent and the horizontal arm of the cross is crucial as it shifts the perspective away from our local planetary environment, of which the ecliptic forms part, to the true invisible Cross, which is a galactic phenomenon.

Here Jenkins' omission of the Mayan Creation story surfaces again. This describes that the First Father raised the World Tree in 3114 BC, and I have shown empirical evidence from human history that its holographic projection on earth (which has 90° angles) becomes evident in the even-numbered baktuns of the Great Cycle, one of which began in 3115 BC. But with Jenkins' interpretation of the World Tree as the 60° angle between the ecliptic and the galactic midplane the Creation story in Palenque completely lacks meaning, and, as far as we know, nothing happened with the 60° cross between the ecliptic and the galactic midplane in the year 3114 BC.

But if the Long Count is not based on its ending date, but on its beginning date, what is this latter date based upon? Well, *the beginning date of the Long Count is the day the sun stands in zenith in Izapa,* the location where the Long Count was most probably invented. It is well known that the day of solar zenith played an important role among the ancient Maya, judging from the many shafts serving to determine solar zenith dates that have been discovered. In a tropical region it is very understandable that this would be a candidate for a day 'when time began.' It is thus simply an accident that the ending date of the Long Count falls on a midwinter solstice, since this is where the ending date must fall if its beginning is set at the solar zenith in Izapa. Jenkins points out that the beginning date of the Long Count is the solar zenith in Izapa, but does not draw the natural conclusion that it is just an accident that the ending date of the Long Count falls on a midwinter solstice (where by necessity it will fall if it begins on the day of solar zenith in Izapa).

After all, to compute the day of solar zenith some three thousand years into the past is feasible. We may understand how it could have been done, given the level of exactness the Maya had attained in estimating the duration of the physical year. To project the galactic location of the midwinter solstice two thousand years into the future, on the other hand, simply would not have been feasible. It is one thing to be aware of the effects of precession and an entirely different thing to compute its cycle or to make projections about its course a few thousand years into the future, and Jenkins provides no explanation as to how it could have been done. Even if such a computation may seem easy for people with astronomical software on their home computers, the fact is that even today's scientists, using laser technology and satellite-based measurements of the earth's movement, are uncertain as to the duration of the precessional cycle by a few hundred years (notably because the earth's axis does not really describe a cycle and hence does not return to the same point) and would shun a task of pinpointing a precessional position a few thousand years into the future.

A key question, however, is whether the midwinter solstice sun actually eclipses the galactic center in the year 2012. The fact of the matter is that the midwinter solstice sun will be closest to the galactic center in the year 2219, long after the ending date of the Long Count, and this both McKenna and Jenkins acknowledge. But it is also true that the crossing by the midwinter solstice sun of the galactic equator, which Jenkins considers a more appropriate marker for the changing of the ages, occurred already in 1998. The logical conclusion from this would then be that we would already have passed into the new age, and, since the Mayan calendar was inaccurate, there would be no reason to use it. Jenkins recognizes in a passage and in the footnotes of his book that the alignment already occured in 1999, and has confirmed this in contacts with astronomers and with astrologers, who have noted this alignment. Yet throughout his book he keeps referring to 'the end-date alignment' as if this was a reality, when in fact *the midwinter solstice sun does not align with the galactic equator in the year 2012*. It is not easy to understand how this is to be interpreted. Are we to believe in something we now know to be wrong because Jenkins thinks the Maya believed in this? He rebuffs those with exaggerated demands for accuracy in this matter. Well, I do not think we can be accurate enough. The thing is that the Long Count is coordinated with the tzolkin count, and if Jenkins' precession hypothesis were true then this would mean not only that the Maya had made an error in calibrating the precessional cycle, but also by consequence that the tzolkin count used in Classical times would be wrong. Personally, I do not believe it is.

The theory presented in this book has, however, already disproved the precessional theory, in that it has shown that one of the major Mayan creation cycles, that of thirteen hablatuns, goes back all the way to the Big Bang, to a time when no planets and stars or even galaxies existed. Hence, the tun-based Mayan creation cycles, of which the Great Cycle is one, describe a creation that is primary to all physical phenomena, and this includes the sun, the moon and the earth, whose mechanistic relationship determines the precessional cycle. Thus, the precession of the earth is not the basis for the tun-based calendrical system. If anything, the tun-based system may explain the precessional cycle of the earth and it partly does, but this would be outside the scope of this book. Thus, divine creation is primary to matter.

Moreover, the theory presented here has demonstrated, to the extent that it is possible today, that biological evolution on earth is just an aspect of the evolution of consciousness in the entire galaxy. But if the evolution of the planet results from a holographic resonance projection of our galaxy, it cannot depend on factors such as the masses of the earth, moon and sun or the declination of the earth's axis, which are particular to our own planet. Emphasis on precession thus limits us to a local planetary perspective and stands in direct contrast to a holographic, galactic model where the periodicity of the evolution of consciousness on our own planet is determined by energy changes taking place on a galactic level.

There is a final point to discuss: As Jenkins himself points out, the tzolkin is older than the Long Count by some five hundred years. The Long Count, which was devised later, was then developed so as to be in synchrony with the tzolkin, meaning that, for instance, katun endings always take place on Ahau days, creation days. Jenkins presumably shares the view of most everyone engaged in the Mayan calendar that the tzolkin is a sequence of energies reflected in its various combinations of numbers and glyphs (he has in fact written extensive and interesting material on the subject). But if the Long Count was developed on top of, and after, the tzolkin in such a way as to be synchronized with it, then the Great Cycle, too, must reflect a sequence of energies. And, of course, the progression through thirteen cycles, such as thirteen days or thirteen baktuns, reflects a growth cycle from seed to fruit. But if the days of the Long Count are locked in their positions by the tzolkin, which itself reflects creation energies that are real, how can the Long Count at the same time reflect precession, which is a mechanical movement? The answer, as I have argued, is that the Long Count does not reflect the precessional cycle of the earth, which according to the definition used by Jenkins would have ended on December 21, 1998. Not surprisingly, this date falls on 12 Cimi and is not an Ahau day in the tzolkin count.

What then about Terence McKenna's time wave, which is sometimes also claimed to end on December 21, 2012? Well, Peter Meyer, who developed the mathematics of it, has pointed out in an article on his web site that this time wave has been anchored with human history by the choice of only one particular event, the Hiroshima atomic bomb explosion, and even so, even with the particular anchoring McKenna has chosen, the time wave ends on November 18 and not on December 21, 2012. The conclusion is that neither McKenna's time wave nor Jenkins' closest fix of the midwinter solstice to the galactic center actually fits with the December 21, 2012 date. So maybe it is time for some new thinking regarding the actual ending date of the Great Cycle.

Why then, we may ask, does the idea that the earth passes through an evolutionary 26,000-year cycle have such an appeal? Probably because there actually is some truth to it. The last 65 tzolkin units of the Regional Cycle began 26,000 tuns ago (see Appendix I). An important change in human consciousness was indeed the result of the beginning of these 65 last units of the 260-baktun Regional Cycle. In a sense, this was the time when the earth became whole, and as a resonance projection of this the human being became whole and attained a self-reflective consciousness. We see this manifested in parallel ways at different hierarchical levels of the universe. On the level of the earth, we may note that the oldest undisputed date for inhabitants in the Americas (on the Los Angeles river) is around 24,000-23,000 BC, meaning in practice that we have reasons to believe that from this time and onwards the whole earth was inhabited by carriers of a human consciousness. On the level of the human being, the oldest human statuette discovered (in Bohemia) is dated to the same time, reflecting the emergence of a self-reflective human consciousness. These are holographic resonance phenomena, so that at the same time as the whole earth would have been seen from the outside as covered by human beings, a statuette of a human being, thus also visible from all directions, was for the first time created by a human being. The beginning point of the 65 last baktuns of the Regional Cycle thus brought self-reflective consciousness, and this was a very important step. Similarly, the beginning points of the last 65 katuns of the Great Cycle in AD 730 and the last 65 tuns of the Planetary Cycle in AD 1947 brought changes in consciousness in line with the energy pattern of the tzolkin. It is only that this energy pattern and these points in time have nothing to do with precession.

The reader may wonder what is the purpose of such a lengthy critique of Jenkins' work and the precessional theory. Does it really matter what we believe is the underlying mechanism of the Mayan Long Count? I think it does. I feel it is important, and maybe crucial to the future of humanity, because the precession and divine creation theories have very different consequences. Thus, in the precession view, the end of the Great Cycle represents nothing but the beginning of a new 26,000-year cycle of the earth's movement, and the changing consciousness of mankind is then supposedly shaped by an endless line of such repeating cycles. In the precession view there is not necessarily a divine plan behind the evolution of human consciousness, since this seems explicable by the movements of matter. Thus, the precessional theory leads to a concept of time that is both linear and materialist.

In the creation view, on the other hand, the energy changes are not explained by any material changes, but directly through divine LIGHT, thus providing proof of the existence of God and the need for human beings to live up to such an origin. Because there is then a temporal hierarchy of creation cycles, the current acceleration of time becomes understandable. In the creation view the end of the Great Cycle means the completion of divine Creation, and the liberation from energy changes of a divine origin shaping our path. Mankind will come of age to shape its own path at the end of time as we know it. But to arrive at this we may value a correctly calibrated calendar to help us surf on the waves of creation.

BIBLIOGRAPHY

THE MAYAN CALENDAR AND MAYAN ASTROLOGY

- John Major Jenkins, *Tzolkin, Visionary Perspectives and Calendar Studies,* Borderline Sciences, Garberville, CA 1994.
- Kenneth Johnson, *Jaguar Wisdom—Mayan Calendar Magic,* Llewellyn Publications, St Paul, MN 1997.
- Vincent Malmström, *Cycles of the Sun, Mysteries of the Moon, The Calendar in Mesoamerican Civilization,* University of Texas Press, Austin, TX 1997.
- Bruce Scofield, *Signs of Time, An Introduction to Mesoamerican Astrology,* One Reed Publications, Amherst, MA 1994.
- Bruce Scofield, *Day-Signs—Native American Astrology from Ancient Mexico,* One Reed Publications, Amherst, MA 1991.
- Tony Shearer, *Beneath the Moon and Under the Sun,* Sun Books, Santa Fe, NM 1987.

NEW THOUGHT REGARDING THE CALENDAR

- José Argüelles, *The Mayan Factor, Path beyond Technology,* Bear & Co, Santa Fe, NM 1987.
- José Argüelles, *Surfers of the Zuvuya—Tales of Interdimensional Travel,* Bear & Co, Santa Fe, NM 1987.
- Peter Balin, *The Flight of Feathered Serpent,* Arcana Publishing Co, Wilmot, WI 1978.
- Carl Johan Calleman, *Maya-hypotesen—Svenskarnas roll för Gaias födelse år 2012,* Eget förlag 1994.
- Carl Johan Calleman, *The Theory of Everything—The Universal Evolution of Consciousness and the Existence of God Proved by the Time Science of the Maya,* Unpublished manuscript.
- Adrian G. Gilbert and Maurice Cotterell, *The Mayan Prophecies—Unlocking the Secrets of a Lost Civilization,* Element Books, Shaftesbury, UK, 1995.
- John Major Jenkins, *Maya Cosmogenesis 2012,* Bear & Co, Santa Fe, NM, 1998.
- Terence McKenna and Dennis McKenna, *The Invisible Landscape, Mind, Hallucinogens and the I Ching,* Harper, San Francisco, CA 1993.
- Hunbatz Men, *Mayan Science and Religion,* Bear and Co, Santa Fe, NM 1990.
- Frank Waters, *Mexico Mystique, The Coming Sixth World of Consciousness,* Swallow Press, Chicago, IL 1975.

MAYAN HISTORY

- Michael D. Coe, *Breaking the Maya Code,* Thames and Hudson, London, UK, 1992.
- Michael D. Coe, *The Maya,* Thames and Hudson, London, UK and New York, NY 1993.
- David Freidel, Linda Schele and Joy Parker, *Maya Cosmos, Three Thousand Years on the Shaman's Path,* Morrow and Co, New York, NY 1993.
- Sylvanus G. Morley, *The Ancient Maya,* Stanford University Press, Stanford, CA 1946.
- Linda Schele and Mary Ellen Miller, *The Blood of Kings, Dynasty and Ritual in Maya Art,* George Braziller, New York, NY 1986.
- Linda Schele and David Freidel, *A Forest of Kings, The Untold Story of the Ancient Maya,* William Morrow and Co, New York, NY 1990.

PRIMARY SOURCES

- Gordon Brotherston, *Book of the Fourth World, Reading the Native Americas through Their Literature,* Cambridge University Press, Cambridge 1992.
- Diego de Landa, *Yucatan before and after the Conquest,* Dover, New York, NY 1978.
- Bodil Liljefors, *The Hitch Hiker's Guide to the Maya Universe—An Exploration of the Books of Chilam Balam,* Lund University, Lund, Sweden, 1996.
- *Popol Vuh, The Mayan Book of the Dawn of Life,* Translated by Dennis Tedlock, Simon and Schuster, New York, NY 1985.
- Ralph Roys, *The Book of Chilam Balam of Chumayel,* University of Oklahoma Press, Oklahoma City, OK 1967.
- J. Eric S. Thompson, *A Commentary on the Dresden Codex,* American Philosophical Society, Philadelphia, PA 1972.

OTHER

- Robert Bauval and Adrian Gilbert, *The Orion Mystery, Unlocking the Secrets of the Pyramids,* Heinemann, London, UK, 1994.
- Robert Bly, *The Sibling Society,* Vintage Books, New York, NY 1997.
- Zecharia Sitchin, *The Twelfth Planet,* Skin and Day Publishers, New York, NY, 1976.
- Neale Donald Walsh, *Conversations with God: An Uncommon Dialogue,* Putnam, New York, NY, 1996

ABOUT THE AUTHOR

Carl Johan Calleman was born in Stockholm, Sweden at noon on May 15, 1950 (the exact midpoint of the month named from the Roman goddess Maia) on the day 5 Jaguar in the Classical Mayan tzolkin count. For the past seven years he has devoted himself full time to disseminating information about Mayan calendrics and has lectured on this topic in seven different countries and among other things appeared on Swedish, Finnish and Mexican television. He was one of the main speakers at the conference on the Mayan calendar organized by the Mexican chapter of the Indigenous Council of the Americas in Mérida, Yucatan during the spring equinox in 1998. He has published calendars and a book, *Maya-hypotesen* (1994), in Swedish.

He is also a scientist with a Ph.D. in Physical Biology from the University of Stockholm. In this capacity he has, among other things, been a Senior Researcher at the Department of Environmental Health at the University of Washington in Seattle. As a cancer expert he has lectured around the world, from MIT to the Chinese Academy of Preventive Medicine in Beijing, and he has worked as an expert for the World Health Organization. He currently teaches Environmental Technology at Dalarna University in Borlänge, Sweden.

His Internet address is *http://www.ioon.net/mayaonics*, which publishes information in English.

Information about meditations during the Venus passages is available in English, Spanish and Swedish at *http://hem.passagen.se/alkemi/gaia2012.htm*

A 100-page manuscript focused on the practical use of the Maya Calendar entitled *The Sacred Calendar of the Maya - A Path Towards Enlightenment* has been prepared for publication by the author.

ADDENDUM – Simplified Version of the Contents of this Book:

There are only Nine Heavens, Nine Qur'anic Heavens, the projection of each of which is repeated seven times in the Creation of each Underworld. The rest of Creation is a LIGHT show maintained by the illusion of time.